FAGIN'S CHILDREN

Fagin's Children

Criminal Children in Victorian England

Jeannie Duckworth

Hambledon and London

London and New York

Hambledon and London
102 Gloucester Avenue
London, NW1 8JHX

838 Broadway
New York
NY 10003–4812

First Published 2002

ISBN 1 85285 391 3

A description of this book is available from the
British Library and from the Library of Congress.

Typeset by Carnegie Publishing, Lancaster
Printed on acid-free paper and bound in
Great Britain by Cambridge University Press

Contents

Illustrations

Preface

This book is about criminal children in the nineteenth century. There have been other books about nineteenth-century prison life, vicious crimes and women in gaols, but none on the situation of children who were sentenced by law to the same penalties and punishments as adults. Crime and poverty were inseparably associated and most of the young who suffered gaol sentences were victims of poverty; wholly uncared for by family, church or state.

The first half of the nineteenth century witnessed far-ranging changes to the traditional social order, mainly in the form of agricultural and industrial revolutions, a new order bringing conflict and confusion to the long-established social pattern. A mass of humanity poured from the countryside into towns and cities, particularly London, without any prospect of employment or shelter. Children ran wild on the streets, surviving as best as they could, often by crime, and only the tough and quick-witted survived. Into this heinous morass, well-intentioned individuals poured charity money without any serious effect while the state did not interfere. The truth of the matter was that the enormous extent of the problem was not understood. Later a few social reformers, whose ideas on saving children from vice and a life of crime finally struck a responsive chord in the Victorian awareness, made an attempt to reform and educate young offenders rather than punish them.

Education, in fact, was the answer. Without the 1870 Education Act and its following amendments, Britain could not have competed in the world of advancing technology and trade the way in which it did. Along with 'reformatories', removing young children from the streets and putting them into schools in a well-organised manner was the main factor in reducing the juvenile crime rate as well as improving the country's work force.

It is a huge subject and impossible to do justice to within the limits of a single volume. I have endeavoured, however, to trace the important phases in the history of juvenile crime throughout the nineteenth century: from the early days, when children were shackled and thrown into gaol with hardened old lags, to the more enlightened times at the end of Victoria's reign, when prosperity brought with it a better idea of civilisation.

Juvenile crime is still with us, although society and the types of crime have altered significantly. Children under the age of sixteen years are still causing problems by offending against the law and cases are on the increase year by year. Perhaps we can learn a lesson from the past.

Vicious Childhood

'It would often be better if children had no parents at all.'
Anthony Ashley Cooper, Lord Shaftesbury[1]

At the beginning of the nineteenth century there were few towns in Britain where the inhabitants did not know one another. In small towns, and particularly in villages, the clergyman, the squire, the teacher and the parochial overseers all kept a kindly eye on the humbler classes and the Poor Law catered fairly well for those in need. People went to church or chapel for moral and spiritual help and social order was well defined, understood and accepted. All this was to change during the century, due to a massive rise in population combined with an agricultural and industrial revolution.

The first modern census in 1801 revealed a population of 10,500,000; by 1851 it was 21,000,000; and in 1901 it was 37,000,000. At the beginning of the century the majority of people lived in the country but, after the end of the Napoleonic Wars in 1815, there were a series of bad harvests resulting in high bread prices. Hunger and the risk of famine drove many people into towns to seek their living. The bread crisis was followed by rapid enclosure of land and mechanisation of farm machinery, reducing the need for manual labour. At the same time, industrialisation progressed steadily, creating a new order of labour which had no place for the old apprentice system. As the old order crumbled more and more of the rural unemployed were forced to move to urban environments.

In the decade between 1821 and 1831 Liverpool, Manchester, Birmingham and Leeds all had increases in population of 40 per cent. In London in the parish of St Matthew, Bethnal Green, the population rose from 45,676 in 1821 to 62,018 in 1831, and south of the river in the parish of Lambeth from 57,638 in 1821 to 87,856 in 1831.[2] The Poor Laws, which had evolved to meet the needs of a rural society, just could not cope with this new urban population. Under the old system rich and poor lived in close proximity and the better off had control and influence over their less fortunate neighbours, but when the masses moved to large towns they lived in obscurity away from any moral or helpful influence. The increasing population was predominantly a young one, facing an unfamiliar environment with no families to turn to, no employers and no clergymen to guide them. Although they had greater independence due to the severing of local ties and family and village authority, urban living presented obvious drawbacks. There were long periods of uncertainty and the inexperienced newcomers often suffered chronic underemployment and low wages, so the freedom was combined with considerable hardship and pressure of need. As a result, many evolved a way of life based on opportunity and crime. Migration to towns was also potentially dangerous because crime was rare in the countryside and the naive young migrants were exposed to all kinds of hitherto unknown bad examples. Despite the drawbacks, generation after generation flooded into the growing towns, where they found the streets were not paved with gold. In many cases they entered the ranks of criminals by necessity.

One of the biggest problems facing town authorities was knowing how to cope with this rapidly growing urban population. Cities were synonymous with dirt, disease, overcrowding and noise, which inevitably rendered them unhealthy places in which to live and in some districts there were more deaths than births. Epidemics occurred with great frequency but still the population continued to expand as more and more and yet more poured in from the countryside.

For the newcomers finding shelter was a nightmare, for every room, attic, any space at all was occupied several times over. Many lived in communities known as rookeries – no-go areas – where poverty was paramount. In London these areas were in Shoreditch, Bethnal Green, Whitechapel and Clerkenwell. It was not known how many thousands of people existed there but it was realised that they rarely had proper jobs and subsisted by crime, begging and prostitution. All big cities had such spots – Manchester had Deansgate; Salford, Gathorn Street; Liverpool, Waterloo Road; Nottingham, Marsh Street; Glasgow, Salt Market; Dublin, Liberty; and Edinburgh, Canongate. In Leeds the Domestic

Missionary Society carried out a survey (published in 1853) on the dwellings of the 'lower order of people'. They visited 658 houses and cellars containing 3457 people, out of these only 247 children had ever attended a school. In those 658 houses there were only sixty-two privies.[3]

Lord Shaftesbury, the Evangelical reformer, was determined to see the conditions in London's slums for himself. In 1846, in company with Dr Southwood Smith, he ventured into the dark, narrow alleys, where the walls were running with filthy slime and the pathways were open drains. He discovered unsanitary, dilapidated rookeries crammed with human beings. At one point he was unable to go beyond the entrance to an alley, so overpowering was the smell. Some courts had one leaky privy to serve the surrounding dwellings; others had no sanitary arrangements whatsoever. One thing struck him especially – the children, whom he described as a race of beings apparently unknown to the outside world: nondescript, unknown, uncared for, begging on street corners, squatting on doorsteps, wading in the gutters. Some had no home, some had no name. The sight aroused his curiosity as well as his pity.[4]

Another observer, the journalist Charles Knight, who entered St Giles's Rookery, London, in 1841 described it as:

> A dense mass of houses so olde that they only seem not to fall, through which narrow and tortuous lanes curve and wind. There is no privacy here, every apartment in the place is accessible from any other. Whoever ventures here finds streets thronged with loiterers of all ages. Walls the colour of bleached soot, doors falling off their hinges, door posts worm-eaten and where slivered panes of glass alternate with wisps of straw and lumps of bed ticken or brown paper, bespeak the last and frailest shelter that can be interposed between man and the elements.[5]

These rookeries were beyond the control of law and order. Fugitives could pass unnoticed among a desperate, outcast humanity who looked after each other in the intricacy of the warren to save themselves from the law.

The magistrate Gilbert Abbott A'Becket helped Charles Buller, President of the Poor Law Board, in an enquiry as to the state of dwellings of the poor. He reported:

> I found the dwellings very much overcrowded rendering it quite impossible that anything like morality or decency could be observed among the inmates

and leading, no doubt, to indiscriminate connection, bringing into existence
a class of unfortunate children likely to prove a fertile source of crime. The
worst cases were found in the common lodging houses where they take nightly
lodgers but it extends to houses inhabited by families occupying rooms by
the week and themselves taking in lodgers. My enquiries took me to Norfolk,
Suffolk, Essex and the town of Reading. In all large towns into which people
are driven from the agricultural parishes, in every case there seems to be a
most unwholesome accumulation of persons, morally and physically.[6]

A survey in Manchester in 1840 stressed the existence of a class of
juvenile delinquents concentrated in certain quarters of the city which
were congenial to criminals. Such areas were known to be the source
of both moral and physical contagion and crime. W. B. Neale traced the
careers of such children from their first steps in juvenile delinquency,
through street selling, which often served as a front for petty pilfering,
to pocket picking and eventually organised crime. Parents often encouraged this process, forcing their offspring to beg or steal. Lacking affection
and supervision, juveniles often displayed their early independence,
many became gamblers and drunkards at an early age and soon learnt
to live off the immoral earnings of young girls. But, thought Neale,
circumstances and parental irresponsibility rather than innate depravity
produced this outrageous behaviour, and of a hundred cases he examined, sixty were the offspring of dishonest and thirty of profligate
parents.[7]

Girls of this class posed a particular problem. Henry Mayhew con-
fronted it in 1862:

> Some have wondered why the daughters of the poorer classes principally
> serve to swell the number of our streetwalkers. Are poor girls naturally more
> unchaste than rich ones? Assuredly not. But they are simply worse guarded
> and therefore more liable to temptation. The daughters of even the middle
> classes are seldom or never trusted out of their mother's sight so that they
> have no opportunity for doing wrong. With poor girls it is different. Mothers
> have either to labour for their living or do the household duties themselves
> so that the girls are employed to run errands alone from the tenderest
> years and when she is strong enough to work she is put out into the
> world to toil for herself. Either the mother has to do slop work or go out
> charring or washing or harvesting or sit all day at a stall in the streets. If this
> mother is away from home all day the children are left to gambol in the

gutters. What reward can society look for from such a state of moral anarchy and destitution? [8]

Juveniles formed a large proportion of the criminal class in England in the first half of the nineteenth century. With the influx of the labouring classes into the towns, living conditions became totally inadequate and employment scarce, so that many children were forced into the streets, idle and destitute. They were left to bring themselves up with others as neglected as themselves. They did not choose to be criminals but grew up in a criminal environment and, learning by copying what they saw around them, soon inherited dishonesty like a disease. Up to the 1870s there were no schools available to them and honest work for the young was hard to come by. Few were prepared to employ illiterate, ragged youngsters, although some managed to live by such 'honest' work as sweatshop labour, street sweeping, holding horses or hawking cheap articles. However, vagrant children, who had no homes, nobody to look after them, nobody to care for them, nobody to give them a meal by day or shelter at night, who slept on steps, under arches or in markets, eventually found themselves committing offences against society. To boys and girls like these prison could be a blessing, offering them food and shelter.

Until the latter half of the nineteenth century, childhood was a brief and unimportant phase of life. Infant mortality rates were high and those who did survive were quickly introduced to the responsibilities of adult life. As children had neither rights nor independent status they were vulnerable to all forms of physical and economic exploitation and abuse. Intervention in family life was unknown. No separate legal code or court system existed for juveniles; and children over the age of seven were tried, imprisoned and transported on the same grounds as adults. Many of those involved in maintaining the law realised that young law breakers were never really children in heart and mind, their unchildlike behaviour being the result of the environment in which they lived and particularly of parents destitute of all sense of moral responsibility. Delinquency arose from too early an exposure to hardships and demands of life and many children were driven to crime and vagrancy by sheer necessity. Such young children could not be fully responsible for their misconduct; they were often 'more sinned against than sinning'.

Parents were held to blame for many young children being sentenced to a term of imprisonment. In 1847 Mr Rathbone, a Liverpool magistrate, recorded:

> A child was put in the dock – a child of whose beautiful appearance any mother might be proud. She was placed in the dock for begging on the streets. A policeman had traced her mother to one of those low lodging houses in which no fewer than fifty-one persons were found huddled together. He found her with another five children whom she was totally unable to support. What did she do? She sent those children into the streets to beg; to be punished if they did not bring home to her the means of subsistence. My fellow magistrate, Mr Rushton, said to me 'Good God! What shall I do with this child?' (who was only six or seven years old and whom the officers had to raise up in the dock that she might be seen), 'shall I return her to her savage mother?' The child said she did not wish to go home. 'What must I do? I have either to convict her to gaol or return her to an unfeeling and savage parent. I believe I must commit her to gaol for twenty-one days as the safest place for the child.' The girl was accordingly sent to gaol.[9]

It was indeed a dilemma for the magistrates who realised that they were powerless to save that little girl from her inevitable fate, and they must have felt some revulsion at having to imprison so small a girl who had done nothing but obey her mother. At the end of the three weeks imprisonment the girl would have learnt not to dread a place where she had been looked after more carefully than in her home, and, following the experience, she would not only have had no one to guide her but also no fear of the law to restrain her.

In the 1840s there was not much hope for children such as this. Many with equally wretched backgrounds were used by their vicious parents as a means of providing money. As in the case of the flower girl who was sent out into the streets by her father at the age of nine to sell flowers and bring him the proceeds. Frequently she was out till past midnight and associated with other 'flower girls' of a loose character. Her parents were probably well aware of the manner in which she got the money that she took to them each night. Her father would give her no supper if she did not bring home a 'good bit of money'; in fact they lived on what she earned. She was once arrested and sent to prison. The very night she came home from gaol her father sent her out into the streets again.[10]

The 1851 prison memorandum of the Rev. W. Osborn, chaplain of Bath Gaol, Somerset, gives another example of children used by their parents for dishonest purposes:

> This morning two little boys, Joseph and Henry Eades, twins, were discharged from this gaol. Their history is remarkable. Their father works as a labourer on the railway; their mother is dead but their father has married again. Joseph was first imprisoned aged ten for begging and given one month. On enquiry of the child it was evident that poverty was the immediate cause of the offence but the neglect of the parents the real cause. His account of himself is as follows:
>
>> Stepmother ties up wood; father brings it home; I sell it. He got it from the railroad; he brings it every night. I sometimes get sixpence for what he brings home at night. I have been taken up three or four times by the police and let go again. I ran away from home because father would beat me for being so long out selling the wood. My brother ran away because he could not sell his wood and stopped away three or four months. Now I live about the streets all day, get money by begging and go to lodgings at night. There are more than twelve boys and girls sleep there every night. Father and mother don't know I'm in gaol. When I go out I shall go begging again because father will beat me for being away so long. Father is kinder to me than mother – she serves me worse than he do!
>
> I visited this family and found the child's account correct. I offered to take the child into a refuge but there appeared no willingness on the part of the stepmother that I should do so. His brother, Henry, has exceeded him in the number of commitments. On 27 February 1849 he was committed for vagrancy and given four months separate confinement. Again for vagrancy in July 1850 and a third committal in company with his brother for felony on 24 December 1850 and punished by twenty-one days and a whipping – their crime being that of stealing wood from the railway.[11]

Those eleven-year-old twins, with their wild habits, bad characters and prison brands, which would have stamped them as unfit for any honest livelihood, soon discovered that they could maintain themselves by begging and occasional theft. To them this and living in cheap lodgings was far preferable to selling their father's loot and being constantly beaten and abused.

In every large town there were youngsters like these. Begging, like theft, was a matter of opportunity. Young children were sent out to pester people in public places; others were given flowers, pins, matches and other trifles to offer for money. The constables found it difficult to deal with this incessant child begging, for there was a grey area between genuine begging and law breaking, so generally they didn't bother to arrest youngsters for selling goods without a licence or for pestering people. They would have got no thanks for presenting them to magistrates who, as we have seen, were at a loss as to how to deal with them. Children could be hired by adults, for a few pence a day, to beg for them. There were master beggars just as there were master thieves.

A letter in *The Times* for 22 March 1862 recounted:

> On a bitter cold wet morning my attention was attracted to a little girl of seven or eight years of age crying bitterly. Her garments were miserably thin and her poor little feet had scarce any covering as she dragged herself along on the cold pavement. The poor little thing could only say, 'I am so cold' and that she had no parents alive. Of course I gave the child a trifle and begged a policeman to see what could be done for her; but he could do nothing. I am myself a father and am not ashamed to say I was unmanned by the sight.

On 24 March 1862, a letter in response noted:

> He did precisely the thing he ought not to have done. He gave her 'a trifle'. Did he see what she did with it? His uncommunicative policeman probably did and smiled grimly as he saw her run round the corner into the adjacent gin shop and give it into the hand of the blear-eyed hag who had hired her for the day and who, with a greater or lesser blasphemy in proportion to the amount of the contribution, drives her back into the cold to distil the tears of 'unmanned fathers' into gin.

This was a well-known form of begging known as a 'shallow-lay' – young girls and boys standing in the streets in cold weather with scanty clothing in order to excite the compassion of passers-by. The technique was a useful source of income to both adult criminals and youngsters. Another letter to *The Times* claimed:

> There is nothing unusual in children being employed to beg for adults. They hire children to accompany them because of the sympathy they attract. In 1839 the rate of hire for a child was threepence a day and the takings estimated at three or four shillings a day at least. A crippled child was worth sixpence and as much as four shillings a day had been paid for the hire of a deformed

child. A school of say half a dozen children was two shillings, and twopence extra per child was charged after midnight and garments were supplied at twopence a day.

Of course it was not only strangers who used children to beg for them. On 28 January 1848 another letter in *The Times* described how two girls of eleven and thirteen were sent out by their father to sing in the streets and how they carried with them their two-year-old brother and stuck pins in him to make him cry to increase the sympathy of passers-by.

There were thousands of children turned loose every day into the streets to forage for themselves by parents who were unable, or unwilling, to maintain them. These youngsters haunted the streets and lived by skill or luck; they had to be quick and cunning to survive. They had no education, religious or secular and were subjected to no restraints. They never heard words of advice or kindness, only the language of the masses which they picked up as they grew up, copying adults in shouting curses and using foul language. Ignorant and vicious parents brought up their children in ignorance and vice. In the first half of the nineteenth century there was great indifference by both parents and the community to the suffering and exploitation of children.

Street children had no idea of social behaviour. They owned nothing themselves and helped themselves without any sense of conscience to the goods of others. When they were convicted by magistrates they could not understand the justice of a sentence which punished them for having done something which was indispensable to their existence.

Such a child was Cheap John, described by Henry Mayhew in his investigation into social conditions in the 1850s, *London Labour and the London Poor*, as

One who was bred to the streets. At the age of five or six as a poor neglected wretch sent out each day with a roll of matches with strict 'injunctions' not to come home without selling them and to bring home a certain amount of money upon pain of receiving a sound thrashing, which threat was mostly put into execution whenever he failed to perform the imposed task. From a dreadful life he left home when he was eight with his nine pennyworth of matches and set off for London where he stopped in lodging houses paying twopence for the share of a third, quarter, fifth or even a sixth part of a bed according to the number of children who were in the lodging house on a

particular night. He survived and amazingly did not receive his first gaol
sentence till he was sixteen.[12]

John *was* lucky to escape conviction until he was sixteen. Others, who
like him had parents who neglected them, appeared in gaol more
regularly:

> Aged thirteen, his parents are living. His father is frequently intoxicated; and
> on these occasions the son usually left home and associated with bad char-
> acters who introduced him to houses of ill fame, they gambled and lost all
> their money. This boy had been for five years in the commission of crime
> and had been imprisoned for three separate offences. Sentence of death has
> twice been passed on him.

> Aged ten, was committed to prison having been sentenced to seven years for
> picking pockets. His mother is living but he does not know where she resides.

> Aged twelve, has a mother who encourages the vices of her son. She turns
> him out into the street every morning and he is beaten severely when he
> returns in the evening without some article of value.

> Aged eight, his mother is living but she is a very immoral character. This boy
> has been in the habit of stealing for two years. In Covent Garden there is a
> party of between thirty and forty boys who sleep under the sheds. These
> pitiable objects when they arise in the morning have no other means of
> procuring subsistence but by the commission of crime. This child is one of
> that number and has been brought up to several police offices on eighteen
> separate charges.[13]

The Select Committee on the Police of 1828 were told:

> There were last night sleeping under the green stalls in Covent Garden, boys
> who dare not go home without money, sent out by parents to beg or to steal;
> I believe this is the same in the Fleet market and other markets, urchins with
> no home to go to, or if they have, dare not go there without sixpence. It is
> not uncommon to see infants of five, six or seven with a few matches in their
> hands at midnight and on being questioned why they did not go home
> answered that their mothers will beat them or even if they took only twopence
> they would get no supper.[14]

After disclosures in the press about beggar boys sleeping rough in
Covent Garden a committee was formed to investigate the problem.
Their report attributed juvenile crime not merely to unemployment and

distress but to the collapse of family discipline under the impact of economic stress:

> Of late the supply of labour in the metropolis has been greater than the demand and the committee are of the opinion that the distress to which the poor have been exposed from this stress has in great measure produced that laxity of morals which has rendered a considerable number of parents regardless of the welfare of their children. The want of employment, the prevalence of improvident morals, the degrading tendencies of the Poor Law and the increased facilities for the consumption of spirituous liquors have doubtless contributed much to deteriorate the moral character and consequently to weaken the natural affections of the lower classes of society.[15]

The children of these disaffected lower classes suffered physical degradation as well as an unwholesome moral condition induced by the vices of their parents. Many were labouring under bodily injuries, malnutrition, scrofula, rickets, cutaneous disorders and the effects of syphilis. They looked pale, haggard and emaciated – they were old before they were young. In fact, few were capable of any real laborious occupation. Boys who were sent by refuges and ragged schools to be examined by the surgeon of one of Her Majesty's receiving ships at Portsmouth were often rejected as being physically disqualified for a sailor's life.

Quite early in the century, a few people were beginning to express concern over the extreme youthfulness of many convicted criminals as they realised that there had been an alarming increase in the number of offences committed by children. At first, knowledge of the problem was largely confined to a few law administrators, but a more precise insight into the extent and changing pattern of crime followed the introduction of Home Office Returns in 1805. Though at first they did not distinguish adults and juveniles, they did reveal a rapid rise in crime and this was attributed to an increase in juvenile offenders. The figures confirmed a massive rise in crime committed at a much earlier age than formerly and it was ascribed primarily to parental neglect. Young children who were put out into the streets to fend for themselves often had no idea that, say, taking food from a stall was wrong, they regarded it as more of a game to outrun the stallholder. If they were expected to thieve and steal then their only notion of duty was to thieve and steal; no one taught them right from wrong.

In his statement to a Select Committee on Gaols in 1835, W. A. Miles, secretary of the Prison Discipline Society, confirmed the problem of parental neglect:

> When parents are themselves dishonest, or when they spend their time in gin shops instead of purchasing bread for their offspring, what can be the result except crime, when a boy's stomach is ravenous for food. It is in the nature of things that a child can have no respect for parents where he is ill-fed and worse treated; would not any animal fly from an arm which is only upraised to beat, and never to reward or feed it. Hence arises the number of homeless urchins who prowl and sleep in the street in a worse condition than many dogs ... parents in so many cases utterly abandon or iniquitously train their children that they are unworthy of having any control over them. Many persons consider these juveniles to be parentless but this opinion is erroneous for, out of 600 cases of juveniles under seventeen, 58.66 per cent have fathers; 28.83 per cent have mothers and 12.51 per cent are orphans or have been abandoned. From which it appears that out of 100 cases the proportion is say, 87.5 who have parents living.[16]

Many children who ended up in gaols or houses of correction were the victims of vicious parents who had abused them, as in the case mentioned in the journal of the Rev. John Clay, chaplain of the Preston House of Correction, Lancashire, for 13 March 1852:

> The only juvenile committal during the week is that of a child aged ten named John Marshall but it is his fourth committal, his offence being 'sleeping out' and the history connected with him is one of a truly deplorable nature. Never, indeed has a case been presented to me showing more clearly the justice and necessity of visiting the sins of the children upon the parent, when those sins are manifestly the consequence of the parents' neglect and cruelty. This poor child is the younger brother of William Marshall aged eleven, who was discharged on 20 February from an eighteen months imprisonment for robbing a shop till in conjunction with another boy of fourteen whom it was necessary to sentence to transportation.

> The prison history of these two brothers is:

> *William Marshall*, aged eleven in 1852. Committed June 1849 (aged eight) sentenced to one month; November 1849 sentenced six months; August 1850 sentenced eighteen months.

> *John Marshall*, aged ten in 1852. Committed June 1849 (aged seven)

sentenced to one month; June 1850 sentenced fourteen days; December 1850 sentenced fourteen days; March 1852 sentenced seven days.

I have the domestic history of the children in William's own words: 'My father kept a jerry shop in Heatley Street. He was drunk very near every night, my mother died through my father beating her; my mother sauced him for going to other jerry shops to get drink when we had plenty of drink in our own house; and then he punched her all up and down the house and she was crying all day with him punching her and shouted many times while he was agates, "murder", she did not die at once, she was very badly for two or three weeks. It was not long before my father wed again and the woman's name was Aggy Stevenson. My father was a porter at the railway station, he came home drunk one Friday night and he took James and me saying he would take us to the canal and drown us. He told our stepmother to reach for our shoes, she said 'If you're going to drown them you may as well leave the shoes for John'. He took us and threw me in and I should have been drowned only for a boatman.

Our schoolmaster kindly made inquiries as would lead to a confirmation of this account, and the result is, that the poor child's statement is well founded. It appears that the father had kept a low beer house, the Black Cat, in Heatley Street and while there he buried his first wife; he afterwards came to Albion Street where he married his present wife, who already had a child of her own, so in a short time there were three sets of children living together. Several of the neighbours spoke of the cruelty to the boys, and how 'She locked them up in the house, tied them to bed posts and clammed them shamefully'. 'Once,' said a neighbour, 'my lad heard something knocking and looked around, it was one of the Marshall lads knocking at the skylight to get in. He had been tied up but got loose, he got out, naked, and came down the gable of one of the houses. Neighbours gave him some clothes. I filled his belly.'

This statement relates to the younger boy, John. Mr Castle, our school-master, found that it was a matter of notoriety in the neighbourhood that Marshall had taken two of his boys to drown them in the canal. Another woman who lived nearby said that the following morning she went to Marshall's house and 'saw a child's clothing lying soaking on the floor'. I have given the particulars somewhat more fully to show the pitiable circumstances which drive some children into crime and also to show the truthfulness of a narrative which would otherwise have been considered incredible.[17]

Cruelty to children by parents seems to have been widespread, particularly when step-parents were involved. Another case was reported by Gilbert Abbott A'Becket, a Southwark magistrate:

I had a case recently in which a woman having married for a second time had a son of eleven years, this child was brought before me charged by his stepfather, his own mother and his own elder sister, who all, I am sorry to say seemed extremely anxious that he should be sent for trial, for stealing a sum of money which they swore was in an open desk in an open room. They all ensured me that they knew the boy had been a thief for at least four years. There was a deficiency of legal evidence and I knew there would be no conviction and therefore I did not send the boy for trial. They were extremely annoyed at my not doing so ... I desired the boy to be taken home. The boy came to me at the Police Court last week completely wet to the skin having been, he told me, wandering about ever since. His stepfather would not take him in, he told me he tried to get a neighbour to intercede with the father; to no avail. I went to the house of that neighbour, a respectable person and found the boy to be correct in his statement. The boy is now in a workhouse, at my request, that he might not be wandering about in the streets.[18]

In his evidence before the Select Committee on Criminal and Destitute Juveniles in May 1852, Captain W. J. Williams, Inspector of Prisons, reported:

Juvenile criminals are invariably from the lower orders – parents are not always neglectful but they are placed in a certain condition of life in which it is impossible to have control over them. They have used every inducement and have even gone to monstrous cruelties at times to prevent their children getting out into the streets. The labourer who is out from six in the morning till six at night and the wife who has younger children to attend to cannot have control over children which others have. I have known them to chain them to bedsteads and practise the greatest cruelties in order to keep these boys in. I have also known considerable kindness. While in Liverpool the extraordinary kindness of the Irish is more shown in that town than anywhere else, from the numbers who congregate together and the number of destitute orphans there. There are a number of children who have lost their parents by fever or otherwise who are entirely protected by other women. The kindness of the Irish towards children is remarkable; they take these children into their houses and act the part of the mother to them.[19]

In 1839 the Governor of Parkhurst Gaol, which was then a prison for boys awaiting transportation, made a list of his boys together with remarks on why he thought they had entered crime. The causes were: bad company; not corrected by parents; stubborn temper; parents both drunkards; cruelly used by them; placed by mothers into a workhouse; sent out by mothers to beg and steal and forced into crime; ignorance; and low associates.[20]

There was another, purely financial, reason why children were thrown out of a family home and expected to support themselves. The moment a child was convicted of theft he ceased to be a burden on his parents, also, all expense was taken from the parish. If sentenced to prison, the county paid for him; if sentenced to transportation, the country paid.

By the middle of the last century it was estimated that there were 350,000 pauper children in parochial care. They, however, were by definition not neglected. It was the 100,000 street urchins estimated to be roaming around London who were the neglected ones.[21] The armies of neglected children have been attributed to the high birth-rate which made a large child surplus inevitable and, without parental attention and control, children such as these created a great problem for local authorities and the law.

Referring to the registers of the Westminster House of Correction in 1852, Mr Antrobus, a visiting justice, recorded:

> Sixty-five boys were totally destitute, 390 had one or both parents drunkards or had been imprisoned or transported. In another register 99 out of 175 had relatives who might be called jailbirds, ten had fathers in prison, nine had brothers transported, four had sisters in prison, eleven had cousins transported, three had uncles in prison, one had an uncle transported and an aunt in prison. Again, out of 192 young girls, forty-seven had neither father nor mother, three had a stepmother, two a stepfather, fifty-three had no father, fourteen had no mother, eleven had a father and a stepmother, seven a mother and a stepfather, four were not able to say whether their parents were alive or dead, twelve others had parents who had separated, two were illegitimate, three had parents who were insane and only one came from a respectable family.[22]

In the cities and centres of high population, bad and neglectful parents do appear to have been responsible for their children's criminality as the following short extract from the Liverpool Gaol Register of 4 February 1846 suggests:

Walton Gaol, Liverpool[23]

Age	No of times in custody	Comments
16	4	Father drunk and debauched, lived with the mother of this boy by whom he had several children, she was profligate and all her children turned out to be thieves.
16	3	Mother a notoriously bad woman, encourages her son to steal, harbours other lads and receives whatever plunder they bring.
14	4	Cannot find boy's parents, he has been allowed to run wild.
14	2	Parents notoriously bad, their children all bad and their house an iniquitous harbour for juveniles of both sexes.
13	2	Father cohabited with boy's mother for several years, a most abandoned woman by whom he had several children.
12	1	Parents both drunken and dissipated, allowed their children to go with any company.

In Bristol, the social reformer Mary Carpenter, related a case of parental neglect:

> The boy came out of the Bridewell prison and his father pleaded total inability to do anything for him. The boy is constantly in rags, though his father has a good trade. I have heard from the Church Readers of the district that the father lives in a common state of utmost immorality and that there is no possible chance for this boy but a life of the blackest crime. Such cases show that it is from the management or low moral condition of the parents, rather than poverty, that juvenile crime flows.[24]

Nevertheless, children over the age of seven, whatever their condition, were subject to the law of the land. What could the magistrates do but administer that law fairly. They were not all heartless, uncaring men and the sentencing of children did cause them problems. It obviously distressed the Recorder of Hull, Yorkshire, who was quoted in *The Times*, 24 January 1854:

> Let us ask ourselves what is the difference in the eye of God between us – all of us guilty before Him – and the poor wretch who may presently stand

at the Bar? One glaring difference is this. We have had virtuous and watchful parents training us from childhood by precept and example; all our wants cared for and our eyes fixed only on the sunny side of life. But here is one who has sucked in guilt and misery in his mother's milk! He has seen only starvation, drunkenness and brutality around him. He has been positively coerced into crime! Poor soul, when he would have done good, evil has been present with him. No man has cared for his soul; and the selfish world looked on in complacency while this poor creature was being hurried along from the cradle to the gallows, or if that world interfered at all it has been only to punish! I sit here as a judge, to administer the law of the land; and it is in my power to inflict such a one to hard labour or to condemn to many years penal servitude. Do you suppose it is agreeable to me to do this? And when I have so discharged my sad duty I ask you, are you yourselves as Christian men in your consciences satisfied and content that the 'law should take its course'? What course – when dismissed from gaol, possibly with a soured spirit what becomes of him? No fond parent or kind friend is waiting outside for the little outcast, to nourish the faintly repentant spirit; no one cries 'God bless him' and in desperation he returns to his old haunts, companions and crime. What is this but to thrust a patient just recovering from a deadly disease again into the fatal focus of contagion.

2

Fagin's Academy

'In our vast and wealthy city of London, there wander, destitute of proper guardianship, one hundred thousand boys and girls in fair training for the treadmill, the oakum shed and finally the convict's mark.'

James Greenwood [1]

In the preface to the 1841 edition of *Oliver Twist* Charles Dickens described the situation to which many homeless children were condemned:

The cold, wet, shelterless, midnight streets of London; the foul and frowsy dens, where vice is closely packed and lacks room to turn; the haunts of hunger and disease; the shabby rags that scarcely hold together – where are the attractions of these things?

Life for the street children was arduous and brutal and only the toughest survived. These youngsters could occupy a place in society anywhere between pauper and convict, and the authorities regarded them as a social nuisance. If there had been any proper work available, most of them would have been willing to do it, but, as there was not, by necessity, most turned to pilfering. Nothing, it seemed, would induce them to have anything to do with the Poor Law and its officers. Perhaps they had bitter memories of their early days in a workhouse; the cold building, frequent beatings and unrelenting hard work with only a bowl of gruel at the end of it, and therefore thought it better to eke out an existence by scavenging and stealing when the opportunity arose.

The irregular existence of criminal children veered between highs and lows; times of plenty and times of utter destitution. As many of them had no family or home to return to, they relied on lodging houses for shelter; or if their 'trade' had been unsuccessful, sheltered under arches, bridges or anywhere, sleeping on the pavement. They were often cold, wet and did not know where the next meal was coming from. When they were successful, however, they would eat and drink their fill and enjoy spending their temporary riches. At times like these, drunkenness was a problem, and not just in London. A letter was published in the *Cheltenham Journal* in 1844 regretting the inaction of the justices in closing inns with a bad reputation and referring to young girls scarcely arrived at the age of puberty, dragged before the bench to answer for drunkenness, swearing and disorderly conduct.[2]

The behaviour of the urchins received universal condemnation. Their uncontrolled existence embraced all the symptoms of social disorganisation and challenged the very foundations of ordered society. Exposure to crime-infested areas seemed to generate social misconduct and studies of the new prison records and enquiries among offenders confirmed the massive problem of juvenile delinquency. Poverty was put forward as the principal cause. There were a few youths in a position of earning a good living who ran away from their masters seeking adventure, or thinking they could do better for themselves in a city, but these were very few. The majority were victims of neglect, corruption and the prevailing attitudes of the time.

James Greenwood (1832–1929), whose brother Frederick was editor of the influential *Pall Mall Gazette*, worked for his brother and at his suggestion spent a night in the casual ward of a workhouse; this launched him on a career as an investigative journalist and he set out to make basic facts about social conditions accessible to a wider public. He became deeply concerned about neglected children, particularly juvenile criminals, and wrote:

> It is an accepted fact that daily, winter and summer, within the limits of our vast and wealthy city of London, there wander destitute of proper guardianship, food, clothing or employment 100,000 boys and girls in training for the treadmill, the oakum shed and the convict's mark. There are those born in the workhouse who are abandoned by the unnatural mother. There are the strays, discovered by the police on their beats, consigned to a workhouse and never owned. There is the offspring of the decamping weaver or shoemaker who goes on the tramp to better himself but not succeeding does not regard it as worth while to tramp home again to report his ill-luck. These and such

as these can ascribe their pauperism to neglect on somebody's part, others are neglected through sheer misfortune – when death snatches a father away or illness causes redundancy.[1]

Without parental or parish support and moral guidance these wild youngsters were seen as having no respect for their 'elders and betters' and, influenced by those around them, grew up into criminal habits. James Greenwood continued:

> They believe the clergy are all hypocrites; judges and magistrates are tyrants and honest people their bitterest enemies. Believing those things sincerely and believing nothing else, their hand is against every man and the more they are imprisoned the more is their dishonesty strengthened.
>
> Some are thieves from infancy, their parents are thieves in most cases; in others, the children are orphans, or have been forsaken by their parents and in such cases the children generally fall into the hands of the professional thief trainer. In every low criminal neighbourhood there are numbers of children who never knew their parents and who are fed and clothed by the old thieves and made to earn their wages by dishonest practices. Here then, is one great source of crime. These children are nurtured in it. They come under no good moral influence; and until the ragged schools were started they had no idea of honesty, not to mention morality and religion. Sharpened by hunger, intimidated by severe treatment and rendered adroit by vigilant training, this class of thieves is perhaps the most numerous, the most daring, the cleverest and the most difficult to reform. In a moral point of view, these savages are much worse off than the savages of the wilderness inasmuch as all the advantages of civilization are made to serve their criminal habits. The poor, helpless little children literally grow up into a criminal career and have no means of knowing that they are wrong; they cannot help themselves and have strong claims on the compassion of every lover of his species.[3]

There were a few ways in which a vagrant child could earn an honest living – such as coal scratching, crossing sweeping, dung gathering or mudlarking. On the banks of the Thames in London when the tide was out, small children could be seen scurrying about in the mud, picking up the occasional bottle, shoe, nail, coin – anything that could be sold. Scavenging in the filthy mud of the river, into which the waste from thousands of buildings and people passed, was the only life they knew. Clad in rags, their bodies caked in mud, these children would often wade up to their middle, making their way among the boats and barges.

One practice was to knock lumps of coal off barges into the mud which they would pick up later and sell to near destitute people, like themselves, for a few halfpence. It was an easy move from such an appalling life to crime and violence, as a child who had groped around in a sewer for a pitiful living could never be expected to respect life and property. The girls would inevitably end up as prostitutes when they were old enough; an easier occupation and more lucrative.

Another child labour market existed in which the jobs required not muscular strength but dexterity and lightness of touch, like pin-making and needlework, to which children were better fitted than adults. They were, of course, paid less, often being content with pence whereas adults would have required shillings. After working long hours in uncomfortable conditions they soon learned that their hard-earned wages did not increase with their years. As the 'hands' grew and ceased to be children their services would be dispensed with to make room for even smaller workers, eager to take on the jobs on terms which the older children had come to despise and who now had to find another way to earn a living – somehow.

One occupation, to which only small boys were recruited, could actually serve as an apprenticeship to burglary. In the days when every room in a house had a fireplace there was a great deal of chimney-sweeping to be done. Climbing boys were used – and sometimes misused – for this dirty and dangerous task. When the occupational hazards of the trade, including broken bones, respiratory disease and groin cancer, were brought to the public attention in 1840 the legal indenturing of child sweeps was forbidden. Masters then had to recruit their climbing boys from among those whom no one cared for – the neglected and destitute. The boys had to be slight and wiry, they also needed a great deal of agility to get up the tall, narrow chimneys. Sweeps whose thoughts turned to burglary had some important advantages over their fellow thieves. A climbing boy's training was a first-rate preparation for burglary, for sweeps entered every room in a house and could study their lay-outs and contents, in fact they often sold this information to other criminals. Child sweeps could also be hired out to burglars by their masters. Being small they could crawl through spaces inaccessible to adults. Charles Dickens was a major influence in bringing unsavoury facts to the attention of his readers. In *Oliver Twist*, Bill Sikes confides to Fagin:

I want a boy and he mustn't be a big one – if I'd only got that young boy of Ned the chimbley sweeper's. He kept him small on purpose and let him out by the job. But the father gets lagged and then the Juvenile Delinquent Society comes and takes the boy away from a trade where he's 'arning money, teaches him to read and write and makes a 'prentice of him. And so they go on, we shan't have half-a-dozen boys left in the whole trade in a year or two.[4]

The new agricultural reforms were also responsible for many social mishaps, as in the case in rural areas where farm labourers were no longer boarded and maintained throughout the year by their employers. The hardly surprising result was that local prisons filled up in the winter months. Young men who had worked in harvest gangs until the autumn and could find no other work were often compelled to steal poultry or became involved in a brawl in order to get themselves committed to a House of Correction. This phasing out of 'living in' made landowners anxious about maintaining control over the labourers who no longer lived under their supervision. Servant boys were not taken into the house to be kept in subjection as previously; many now lived out and in consequence they went about as they pleased instead of being kept in order – there was no longer a mutual attachment between employer and employed.

Mill owners in northern England would have nothing to do with the workers once they left the mill at the end of the day. The burden of relieving the distress of the unemployed and controlling the young was left to the parish and the prison. This relinquishment of responsibility was happening all over the country. The Chairman of the Warwickshire Quarter Sessions, John Eardley Wilmot, blamed juvenile crime in Birmingham on the erosion of supervision of the masters over their young workers:

> Formerly the apprentice was taken into the house of the master; he was considered one of the family and he was boarded, lodged and educated by the master who was answerable for his conduct; now the master has ten to twelve apprentices and perhaps never sees them. They work ... then they are allowed to go exactly where they please and we know at that time of night, with boys, it is exactly the worst time that they can be their own masters and the consequence is that they are all thieves.[5]

Birmingham had a high rate of juvenile crime despite the fact that most boys had jobs, but youngsters who had good, honest jobs often found themselves in a position where they were swayed into crime. The prevalent crime was stealing from their masters. Theft was fairly consistent whether they were in work or not, as the trade of the town made it easy to steal metal objects which could never be identified after they had been thrown into the furnaces which the receivers kept hot in readiness. In the rapidly growing town the large number of small workshops offered many opportunities for theft, as much of the material had to be carried through the streets to and from 'out-masters' working for the master manufacturers. The boys involved in this were often waylaid by receivers and tempted into theft; in fact some apprentices disposed of their master's metal goods on their way home from work.

Manchester too had a problem with juveniles stealing from their masters, as the Chief Constable, Captain Willis, reported in the *Morning Chronicle*, on 29 October 1849:

> There is a considerable floating criminal population in Manchester, people who are known to both work and steal. Much juvenile crime was committed as a side line by those who had honest jobs. Cotton and other materials were stolen from the mills – but the boys more often steal when out of work.

Liverpool was second only to London, in as much as its juvenile criminals were hardened professionals. As it was an entry port from Ireland and an exit port for America, there was a high proportion of people in transit and the docks were a scene of much crime. The *Morning Chronicle* of 27 May 1850 stated that:

> Cotton bales lie in immense heaps on the quays where, in defiance of the utmost vigilance of the police, swarms of children prowl around during the day and at night to abstract it by the handfuls and conceal it amid their rags until they can transfer it to a depraved mother or father, who watches in a dark alley or in the shed of a warehouse to receive it. Sacks of meal, corn, beans, rice and coffee – all equally tempting invite young thieves to learn their trade. Cotton picking is however the principal source of plunder for the juveniles of Liverpool.

In the early part of the century crime among the young was common and unchecked; pick-pocketing, for instance, was a highly organised industry. From Elizabethan times there had been concern that young children were being taught to be professional criminals. Schools for pick-pockets *did* exist and a child starting out as an opportunist thief, if well-trained, could rise to become a member of a gang of exclusive professional pick-pockets. It was a rewarding business, for the prevailing styles of nineteenth-century fashion aided such offenders: the handkerchief poking from the back pocket of a tailed coat was easy picking; and the enormous skirts of the ladies made it difficult for them to feel when their purses were being snatched. Young thieves worked in groups and mingled in crowds particularly at fairs, markets or the races.

This schooling of children, who had probably only known life in the workhouse or the gutter, was a welcome relief to them. For the first time in their lives they found themselves with enough food to eat, a roof over their heads, companions and a chance of not being constantly flogged. The character of Fagin, in *Oliver Twist*, was probably based on the famous Jewish fence, Isaac (Ikey) Solomon, whose methods of employing and training boy pickpockets were the standard practice and remained so for several decades.

In the novel Fagin lived in the Saffron Hill area of London which in the 1830s was renowned for harbouring thieves' dens, flash houses and, in particular, the stolen silk handkerchief trade. Between 1837 and 1839, when he wrote *Oliver Twist*, Dickens lived within half a mile of this area, at 48 Doughty Street. The 1841 preface suggests that characters in the book were based on what he had often seen 'in actual life around me' and that he had 'for years tracked it through many profligate and noisome ways'. He did not rely on the common repute of Saffron Hill – he knew the area well:

> A dirtier or more wretched place he had never seen. The street was very narrow and muddy, and the air was impregnated with filthy odours. There were a good many small shops; but the only stock in trade appeared to be heaps of children, who, even at that time of night, were crawling in and out at the doors, or screaming from the inside. The sole places that seemed to prosper amid the general blight of the place were the public-houses; and in them the lowest orders of Irish were wrangling with might and main. Covered ways and yards, which here and there diverged from the main street, disclosed little knots of houses, where drunken men and women were positively wallowing in filth; and from several of the doorways, great ill-looking fellows were cautiously emerging bound, to all appearance on no very well-disposed harmless errands.

He may also have observed a real life 'Fagin' and his young gangsters, to judge from the following description:

> The walls and ceiling of the room were perfectly black with age and dirt. There was a deal table before the fire; upon which were a candle, stuck in a ginger-beer bottle, two or three pewter pots, a loaf and butter, and a plate. In a frying-pan, which was on the fire, and which was secured to the mantelshelf by a string, some sausages were cooking; and standing over them, with a toasting-fork in his hand, was a very old shrivelled Jew, whose villainous-looking and repulsive face was obscured by a quantity of matted red hair. He was dressed in a greasy flannel gown with his throat bare; and seemed to be dividing his attention between the frying-pan and a clothes-horse, over which a great number of silk handkerchiefs were hanging. Several rough beds made of old sacks were huddled side by side on the floor. Seated round the table were four or five boys, none older than the Dodger, smoking long clay pipes and drinking spirits with the air of middle-aged men.[6]

Isaac (Ikey) Solomon, was married to Ann, the daughter of an Aldgate coachmaster named Moses Julian. She, along with their four children, was transported to Van Diemen's Land in 1828 for receiving stolen goods, where she was assigned as servant to a police officer. Ikey himself had been tried and sentenced for theft in 1827 but had escaped from the Black Maria on his way to Newgate. The authorities discovered all too late that the vehicle had been driven by his father-in-law. By a devious route he finally reached Hobart where he found his wife, bought some land and a house and started a business. Of course everyone in Hobart knew who he was, for it was then a small town and full of his former colleagues, but he felt quite safe there because there was no warrant for his arrest, so he believed that the law could not touch him. However, he did not reckon on George Arthur, the astute Lieutenant Governor of Van Diemen's Land, who through sheer persistence managed to get a warrant from the Colonial Office in London and in November 1829 Solomon was arrested and returned to London, where he was tried and sentenced to fourteen years transportation. By the end of 1831 he was back in Hobart. In 1835 he got his ticket of leave and was finally reunited with his family. The story did not have a happy ending, for apparently Solomon and his wife quarrelled incessantly and in 1840, when she got her pardon, they broke up. Ikey died ten years later – not a rich man, for his estate was worth only £70.[7]

Ikey was what was known in the underworld as a 'kidsman'. Managers of child thieves trained them in just the way Dickens describes in *Oliver Twist*. According to a report in the *Household Narrative* of 28 January 1851:

> In the winter of 1850/1 the deputy of a lodging house of Gray's Inn Lane appeared on a pick-pocketing charge at the Middlesex Sessions. A police officer gave evidence that he had managed to peep through a window into the lodging house where he saw the prisoner surrounded by a group of small boys. From a line stretched across the room a coat was hanging with a number of handkerchiefs tucked into the pockets. Each child in turn tried his skill in removing a hankie without moving the coat or shaking the line. Those who performed well received the congratulations of the prisoner but bunglers were punished with a kick. Others used tailors' dummies and there was one method in which clothes used for practice were sewn all over with little bells that tinkled at the slightest vibration.

There must have been many of these thief trainers in the city of London. Henry Mayhew wrote:

> Youngsters are taught to be expert thieves ... a coat is suspended from a wall with a bell attached to it and the boy attempts to take a handkerchief from the pocket without the bell ringing. Until he can do this with proficiency he is not considered well trained. Another method is for the trainer to walk up and down the room with a handkerchief in the tail of his coat and the ragged boys amuse themselves by abstracting it until they learn to do it in an adroit manner. We could point a finger to three of these execrable wretches who are well-known to train juvenile thieves. One of them a young man at Whitechapel, another a young woman at Clerkenwell and a third a middle-aged man residing about Lambeth Walk.[8]

It was not only in London that there were 'Fagins'. The *Manchester Guardian* of 28 May 1821 gives a report of a boy arrested for petty felony after being found in possession of several articles of stolen property. He offered to show the authorities where others were and took beadles to a cellar where they found a man aged about fifty, superintending three boys breaking up stolen metal and 'cooing' (disfiguring) a large brass cock in the fire, to make it look like old brass. All were arrested. The 'master' was sentenced to fourteen years transportation and two of the boys, who had previous convictions, received two years in gaol and the other six months.

It would appear that the two very small boys who were committed to the Coldbath Fields House of Correction, London, in September 1835, were already well into their training. The Governor reported:

> On the 3rd instant X aged seven years and his brother Y aged six years were committed to this prison, charged with having stolen money from the till of a tradesman. The younger prisoner had, it seems, been instructed in this species of robbery (which had been practised successfully for some time) by his brother. The latter absolutely denies that he himself had been tutored by anybody but it is a well-known fact that very little boys are purposely tutored by thieves to creep under counters and rob tills, it can scarcely be doubted that these children are in reality the instruments of older delinquents.[9]

There was as wide a range of criminal activities as there were criminal juveniles to commit them. Each one seemed to fit into a specialist niche, from the lone opportunist sneak thief to young professional gangsters.

There were the sneaks and common thieves who were not much in evidence during the daytime, but as the lamps were lit in the evening these motley children began to appear. They were generally from six to ten years of age and of very variable dress. Some had no jacket, hat or shoes; ragged trousers hung by maybe one brace; clothes too large for them; trouser legs rolled up and most of their attire torn and never mended. They were unwashed and squalid, with hair either in dishevelled locks or cropped close to the head. Groups of these ragged urchins could be seen standing at street corners or crouching in groups by the pavement. Sometimes they would run alongside omnibuses, cabs, hansoms – hoping the passengers would throw them a coin. Market stalls were very vulnerable: one boy would attract the stallholder's attention while another took an article and disappeared into the crowd.

Stealing from tills was done by the same class of boys, generally working in little gangs of two or three. One well-tried method was that, while the shopkeeper was busy, one of the boys would throw his cap into a shop and then creep in on his hands and knees as if to fetch it. Any passers-by would think this a boyish prank. Meanwhile the young rogue in the shop crawled round the counter to the till and rifled its contents. If he was caught before doing this he said 'Let me go, those boys outside who have just run away, threw my cap in here and I came to fetch it'. Another method was for the boys to cause a disturbance outside the shop; when the shopkeeper came out, one of them would nip in and raid the till.

Stealing from clothes lines occurred in the better parts of town where there were gardens or large yards where washing was hung out to dry. Boys would clamber over walls and steal whatever they could reach. Articles would be divided between the gang and they would all go off in different directions to avoid detection. They could easily dispose of articles of clothing by day or night.

Pick-pockets often began their trade as early as five years old, either taught by relatives, companions or by specialist trainers. Great numbers of these ragged opportunists would loiter around the streets wherever there were numbers of people. They stole anything which had a value and either took it to their 'minder' or disposed of it themselves. Two or three boys would work together, one boy, standing by the victim with the others close by on the look-out. A boy picked the pocket and immediately passed the article to a companion, who in turn passed it to a third, then they left in different directions. These little gangsters were able to extract contents from, or even to cut out, a pocket without people being aware. Sometimes they used girls as decoys. They were so well-trained that the victims often had no idea that they had been robbed until later. By the time they were about thirteen or fourteen they may have earned a little money and were able to dress in a more decent way, perhaps even wearing hats and shoes. Then they could ply their trade in more fashionable areas, like railway stations and race-courses. At this age they seldom committed their crimes in areas where they were known but prowled around different areas of the city, and sometimes even travelled to different parts of the country.

Suspicion would have been aroused if they had tried to sell all their loot themselves. Fagin's gang would have given it to their master who would have a well-tried method of disposal, goods passing through two or three people to avoid detection. Or the boys could take it to receiving houses, sometimes coffee houses, hairdressers or tailors who acted as middle-men. Lodging house keepers too, were often involved in passing stolen goods.[10]

Whatever a boy could contrive to steal he could almost immediately convert into money. There was at all hours of the day and night an open market ready to purchase any plunder. Anything and everything

had a value. One young thief said that his first steps in crime had been
to walk behind hay carts and pull out as much as he could before the
carter appeared; he sold his petty pilferings to donkeymen and coster-
mongers. Another boy stole fruit from Covent Garden until he had
collected quite a stock. He then went into low neighbourhoods where
he sold it on the streets.

Loot could also be taken to marine stores which bought anything with
a value and no questions asked, or to rag and bottle stores which
specialised in old metal, material and waste paper. The most popular
'receivers', of course, were pawnbrokers, who were quite prepared to
take pledges from children, again with no questions asked.

The Rev. John Clay, chaplain of the Preston House of Correction,
was very concerned about young children frequenting pawnshops:

> To illustrate how at an early age children are taught the way to the pawn-
> brokers I refer to incidences in 1842 and 1844. A child of seven was committed
> for 'illegally pawning' – a few days previously his mother had sent him to
> pledge part of his own clothing obtained just before from a charity. Two boys
> of ten and twelve pledged a watch they had stolen from a canal boat. Another
> child of eight was committed for pledging books which he had stolen from
> his stepfather.
>
> The most striking illustration of the familiarity of children with the pawn-
> shop shows how older children may avail themselves of the opportunities
> given by the visits of younger ones to such places for the purpose of robbing
> them. A child of eleven watched another child of nine enter into one of these
> places and upon her coming out with the money (11s.) snatched it from her
> and in a short time had spent nearly the whole. The young culprit was
> committed for fourteen days during which time she was kept apart from the
> other prisoners. Three weeks after her discharge she was again committed
> for an offence of exactly the same kind.[11]

But it was in the common lodging houses, to which boys and girls who
had gained a few pennies gravitated, that were to be found the principal
foils and receivers of stolen goods.

One of the most notable features of these places was that they often
swarmed with children of all ages. Many were the children of the adult
lodgers and others were kept by resident beggars and thief masters who
trained them and used them for their own ends. A great number of the
child lodgers, however, were responsible for themselves – the numerous

urchins living on the streets as best they could, dodging the workhouse and the House of Correction and keeping clear of authorities, who were often willing to avert their eyes from further charges on the parish rates.

John Clay presented extracts from a paper drawn up for him by a convict whose own experiences and practice in criminal life made him a useful witness on any matter relating to juvenile criminality. The following remarks relate to what he terms as 'low lodging houses':

> From infancy up to thirteen or fourteen years of age and older they lie together promiscuously – father, mother or oftener stepfather or stepmother – with lads and girls of all ages from infants to adolescents. This is done to save lodging money, for a bed is only sixpence no matter how many sleep on it. It may easily be guessed that such places are the very hotbeds of disease as they are of vice and crime of every shape and complexion. Should any unfortunate be taken ill he or she is turned out of the house or sent to the workhouse. Any number of beds can be forced into an apartment, I have seen them covering the floor betwixt others that are on bedsteads so as to render it impossible to move without treading on a man, woman or child. Age, sex, relationship, all crowd together and the conversation is brutal, obscene and unrestricted; and various practices are carried out irrespective of time, place or witnesses; cursing, fighting, smoking etc. and men and women dress and undress without the slightest attempt at privacy ...
>
> I have seen 'schools' of boys and girls in training as thieves, collected around a reader, listening to tales of murder and singing songs respecting burglars, convicts, highwaymen, etc. These songs acting on the minds of the ignorant, vicious and excited lads cause them to become more reckless and hardened ... The children are made use of by their parents until ill-usage or other causes drives them away. The youngsters are under no apprehension of want, they have been taught to extract a means of living, as it were, out of a stone.
>
> They do not suffer the fear experienced by lads who run away from a settled home; their only alarm is that they should be caught and taken back to brutality and slavery. These children are at home in the first lodging house they enter, slang is their mother tongue – oaths, blasphemies and indecencies their matins and vespers.
>
> In large towns the lads soon become expert thieves; pocket handkerchiefs, shops etc., they first practise it and should one of them prove more intelligent and acute than his congeners, he is acquired by those who are a step or two higher up the ladder as the making of a 'good tool'. After serving in prison a few times he becomes adept and joins a 'first-rate mob' as a 'finisher' and

in the course of a very short time he is finished at the hulks or similar establishment'.[12]

These institutions were basically 'dosshouses', where beds were let out by the night. There was no comfort, cleanliness or decency, not even any ventilation, for windows were to let light in and keep cold out. The focus of the house would be a main room where a fire blazed summer and winter. Inmates brought and cooked their own food. Benches and a table or two would be the only furniture in here and the sleeping rooms contained beds jammed as close together as possible and which were shared by up to six people. Others slept on the floor, thus saving a penny. A tap or pump in a back yard provided water, and a collection of buckets or just a hole over a cesspit served as sanitation.

Young lodgers, children and adolescents were herded together. 'There was very wicked carryings on,' said a girl who had experienced this, 'on a full night we lay a dozen girls and boys into one bed ... some at the foot some at the top – boys and girls all mixed. I cannot go into all the particulars but whatever could take place in words and acts between girls and boys did take place.'[13] Even this was better than what could happen when people of all ages were mixed as in some lodgings and particularly in workhouse casual wards, where all males were put together and where small boys had no chance of escaping the attentions of mature perverts.

W. B. Neale gave a good description of a common lodging house in Manchester in 1840:

Let the reader imagine himself in a damp cellar or dark, dirty garret, where there are from six to fourteen beds ranged side by side and closely adjoining one another; in each of these beds he will discover from two to four persons of either sex of all ages and characters, generally, however, hidden from his view by the mass of clothes taken from those in bed and now hanging on lines in various directions, and he will form some conception of a common lodging house. Let him imagine that the temperature of the room is at fever heat owing to the total absence of all means of ventilation and in consequence of so many persons breathing and being crowded together in so small a place; let him imagine himself assailed by a disgusting, faint, sickening effluvia, he might then conceive the effects produced on entering these crowded dormitories. Let him remember that the bed-linen is rarely changed – once in six months – and that in those beds, meanwhile have been located an ever changeful race of diseased and sick as well as convalescent persons, possibly infested with all manner of vermin. This is the reality of the horrible spectacle presented by not one but by many hundreds of common lodging houses in Manchester.

Owing to the filthy state of these houses juvenile offenders are generally found afflicted with scabies, itch and the tinea capitis or scald head and a variety of other infectious diseases and it is here too that they become familiarised with scenes of infamy offensive to every principle of morality; and become initiated into every species of criminality by the examples of the adults around them.[14]

These lodging houses were calculated to encourage immorality and crime among the young, who received their 'education' listening to the conversations around them. Boys boasted about their triumphs. When they had money they gambled and drank, just like the adults, and boys and girls of this class were promiscuous from an early age. Most of the boys over twelve, and some younger ones, lived with girls. The Select Committee on Criminal and Destitute Juveniles of 1852 was told that many young criminals lived with girl prostitutes and that they had been known to have venereal disease at the age of twelve.[15]

The behaviour and familiarity with the adult world and its pleasures among street children contradicted all middle-class standards of childhood, morality and propriety. Horrified investigators described such behaviour in terms of a savage animal-like existence and strong contrasts were drawn with an idealised, obedient middle-class child, sheltered by stringent, affectionate parental supervision. What they did not realise was the extent of the problem of neglect. There was no way of knowing the numbers of homeless children involved, for births were not registered until 1837 and for a long time after that the numbers were inconclusive. Illegitimate babies were often ignored or even destroyed at birth. If they did survive they were later sometimes abandoned in the streets to be discovered either by the police and sent to a workhouse, or by a 'Fagin' or, all too often, sold to a brothel.

Hordes of the homeless joined the army of professional thieves, young gangsters acquainting themselves with the intricate machinery necessary for carrying on a successful career in crime. They had to learn that, in order to succeed in a burglary, it was necessary to be in connection with 'putters up' who knew how to plan the robbery and had the

knowledge to execute it and to know the 'fences' who would receive
the stolen property; how essential it was for forgers to know how to
obtain the right materials for the job and 'smashers' to pass off the
money to the public; and how with pickpocketing it was necessary to
go out with 'swells' to cover the actual offence and who knew where to
take the stolen items. Crime was a business and criminals had to be
educated in their craft.

Common lodging houses served as schools where gang members could
instruct one another. A lad starting out could always find companions
in a like situation with whom to exchange experiences. To children like
these the world could be a cold, empty place, but in the lodging houses
they were always welcomed – particularly if they had a few pennies (and
if they didn't they would soon be advised on how to get some). They
were received on equal terms with others of their group. For the first
time in their lives they were listened to and the more crimes they could
quote, the better would be their reception.

Mayhew met a group of these young gangsters:

> A congregation of criminals – all boys, the hair almost of all the lads was cut
> very close to the head, showing their recent liberation from prison; indeed
> one may tell, by the comparative length of the crop the time that each boy
> had been out of gaol. Their behaviour was very noisy and disorderly, coarse
> ribald jokes were freely cracked, exciting general bursts of laughter. With
> respect to the age, the youngest boy present was six years old, he styled himself
> a 'cadger' and said his mother had sent him out to beg. There were seven of
> ten years, three of twelve, three of thirteen, ten of fourteen and twenty-six
> of fifteen. Some had chalked on their hats the figures which designated the
> sum of the several times they had been in gaol. Some had run away from
> their homes because of ill-treatment; some confessed to being ruined through
> their parents allowing them to run wild in the streets and be led astray by
> bad companions and others were taught thieving in lodging houses.
>
> ... the announcements in reply to questions as to the number of times that
> any of them had been in prison were received with great applause, which
> became more and more boisterous as the number of punishments increased.
> When it was announced that one ... had been in prison as many as twenty-
> nine times the clapping of hands lasted for several minutes and the whole of
> the boys rose to look at the distinguished individual.[16]

There was a 'pecking order' of seniority among the young thieves.

This was described by W. A. Miles of the Prison Discipline Society in
1839:

> I have observed that boys in Newgate who have been sentenced to death
> (although the boy as well as the judge and every person present knew that
> he would not be hung in pursuance of that sentence), conduct themselves as
> boys of a superior class to the transport lads. The boy under sentence of
> transportation for life is of greater consequence than the boy who is sentenced
> to seven years, while the lad whose sentence is a short imprisonment is not
> deemed worthy to associate or converse with them ... severity of punishment
> is by them converted into a scale of merit. Pickpockets and housebreakers,
> whatever their position in the scale of merit, looked down on mere shoplifters
> who in their turn were superior to sneak thieves, eg the 'pudding slammer'
> who stole food from those leaving cook shops, was said to be the lowest class
> of all thieves, but even he looked down on those boys who were in prison
> merely for begging. Thus some boys were forced to steal for the sake of their
> 'characters'.[17]

He also gives an insight into the earnings of these boys:

> Pickpockets have frequently told me that they never had less than thirty
> shillings or £2 a week. During their 'harvest', which is the summer season,
> they have on average £1 a day and one lad who is well-known in the West
> End abstracts purses with such extraordinary dexterity that he makes no less
> than £20 a week. The possession of such money induces habits such as
> gambling and all have their girls who are even more depraved than they are
> and who live extravagantly on the plunder.[18]

Not many enjoyed such a good life, even if they were members of a
first-class gang, and in the course of time they would find themselves
in gaol, on a hulk or a transport ship.

More representative is the Shropshire lad who ran away to London
to seek his fortune. At the age of nine he ran away from his family in
Shrewsbury and made his way to London. He had a little money in his
pocket and soon found a cheap lodging house – a perfect place for
making criminal acquaintances. When his money ran out he took refuge
with a gang of boys whose headquarters were in a wheel-less old prison
van abandoned under the arches of the Adelphi. A man called Larry
bought the silk handkerchiefs the boys stole, paying them 9d. a piece;
boys who did not bring Larry their 'wipes' were not allowed to sleep in
the van. The Shropshire lad soon became quite accomplished, in fact

he began to show such an ability that Larry invited two men to come and watch him, meaning, no doubt, to sell him. Before this happened, however, he was caught and sent for two months in the Westminster House of Correction. When he came out his life changed, for waiting with a cab near the gaol gates were the two men who had seen him at Larry's. They took him to a house where he was given a bath, clean new clothes, ample meals and a short spell of training. He was destined to become a 'tooker', a picker of ladies' pockets. He later learnt that he was brought in as a replacement for a lad who had been sentenced to transportation. When he was judged efficient enough to start work he was sent with three others to St Paul's churchyard, which was then a centre for good, rather expensive shops, and where the boys studied the ladies for a promising victim. On his first outing he stole a purse containing £2, which he duly passed to a second boy who passed it on to a third. This is how the gang worked and they would occasionally have a rendezvous to check their routine. The new protectors treated him well, giving him a fair share of the takings. After a few weeks he was again caught and sent to gaol for three months. The gang leaders managed to provide him with some luxuries while he was in there, including meat, tea and even cigars. On his release they were there to greet him and this mode of life carried on for three or four years. When he was thirteen he took a mistress, a girl of fifteen, who acted as his decoy. They lived together in a couple of rooms, wore smart clothes and were never without money. He abused her, however, and she ran away from him and soon after he served another six-month sentence. When he came out this time he quarrelled with his companions whom he thought had swindled him. Leaving the gang, he gradually changed to inferior hunting grounds, going down and down the social scale, constantly in and out of gaol.[19]

Boys like this became trapped in a vicious circle of crime and punishment from which there seemed to be no escape – except transportation or death – or in the case of George Thomas – both. Just before his execution in 1836 George Thomas, alias George Nutt, confessed to the chaplain of Hobart Gaol, Van Diemen's Land:

> When I was between eight and nine I used to sleep with my mother and when I wanted some money I put my hand in her pocket and stole it and I

was not discovered, so a short time afterwards I stole something else and
from then on I was always pilfering. My father died when I was about eleven
and soon after I ran away and went and stole two chickens. I sold them to
a man who lived in our neighbourhood and kept an old iron shop and used
to buy things from boys. From then on I was always stealing and in bad
company. When I was between twelve and thirteen I became acquainted with
bad women. I was introduced to them by my companions. When I was twelve
I went shoplifting in the Old Kent Road, we stole a pair of scales but I was
caught and taken into custody; and sent to Horsemonger Gaol. After my
release we stole things in Chelmsford and for that I spent twelve months in
the House of Correction. This time when I came out I got into burglary ...

He continued in this manner until he was eventually transported and hung.[20]

The decline into criminality was a common story. In their condem-
nations it was easy for the general public to forget that these gaolbirds
were only children, who from the age of seven had been responsible for
their own actions. Matthew Davenport Hill, the Recorder of Birmingham, was well aware of the problem when referring to a delinquent in
1855. Hill described the child:

The latter is a little stunted man already – he knows much of what is called
life – he can take care of his own immediate actions. He is self-reliant, he
has so long directed or misdirected his own actions and has so little trust in
those about him that he submits to no control and asks for no protection.
He has consequently much to unlearn – he has to be turned again into a
child.[21]

3

Crime and Punishment

'There is no indulgence more fatal to a boy than a series of light
punishments, this familiarised his mind to degradation and left him
in a path which would lead him step by step to the gravest crimes
and consequently to the heaviest inflictions known to the law.'

Matthew Davenport Hill [1]

On 7 August 1841, *Punch* published a 'literary recipe', describing 'How
to cook up a startling romance':

> Take a small boy, charity, factory, apprentice or otherwise, as occasion may
> serve – stew him well down in vice – garnish largely with oaths and flash
> songs – boil him in a cauldron of crime. Season equally with good and bad
> qualities – infuse petty larceny, benevolence and burglary; honour and house-
> breaking; amiability and arson – boil all gently. Stew down a bad mother –
> a gang of robbers, several pistols and a bloody knife. Serve up with a couple
> of murders – and season with a hanging match. N. B. Strongly recommended
> for weak stomachs.

It had long been believed that capital punishment was an essential
deterrent not only for murder but also for crimes of property. When
Charles Dickens witnessed a public hanging from a hired room over-
looking Newgate Gaol in London, he was appalled not so much by the
execution as by the wickedness of the spectacle. He wrote:

> I was, purposely, on the spot, from midnight of the night before; and was a
> near witness of the whole process of the building of the scaffold, the gathering
> of the crowd, the gradual swelling of the concourse with the coming-on of
> day, the hanging of the man, the cutting of the body down, the removal of
> it into the prison. From the moment of my arrival, when there were but a
> few score boys in the street, and those all young thieves, and all clustered
> together behind the barrier nearest to the drop-down, to the time when I

saw the body with its dangling head being carried on a wooden bier – I did not see one token in all the immense crowd, at the windows, in the streets, on the house-tops, anywhere, of any one emotion suitable to the occasion. No sorrow, no salutary terror, no abhorrence, no seriousness, nothing but ribaldry, debauchery, levity, drunkenness, and flaunting vice in fifty other shapes. I should have deemed it impossible that I could have ever felt a large assemblage of my fellow creatures to be so odious.[2]

For centuries public executions had been the scene of riotous spectacle, attracting the dregs of society as well as the curious, yet it was not until 1868 that executions were carried out in private within the prison walls and a further century before sentence to death by hanging was finally abolished. In previous centuries execution of the sentence of death had been commonplace but by the early nineteenth century it was realised that, as a deterrent, capital punishment did not work; for while men were publicly hanged for robbery, burglary and house-breaking, the incidence of these crimes continued to increase. As the century progressed the number condemned to hanging diminished considerably and the number of juveniles hanged in the first half of the period can be counted on one hand.

In 1800 when a boy of ten was sentenced to death the judge refused to respite the sentence, because of 'the infinite danger of it getting about that a child might commit such a crime with impunity', and many judges of the day still really believed that this was a danger. In 1801 a boy of thirteen was hanged for breaking into a house and stealing a spoon; two sisters aged eight and eleven were hanged at Lynn in 1808; in 1831 a boy of nine was hanged at Chelmsford for setting fire to a house and in 1833 another nine year old was sentenced to death at the Old Bailey for pushing a stick through a cracked shop window and taking twopennyworth of printer's colour.[3]

Juveniles continued to be sentenced to capital punishment until the middle of the century. Between 1801 and 1836 at the Old Bailey alone 103 children received capital sentences – all were commuted to imprisonment or transportation, this latter method of alternative punishment gaining in popularity as the population expanded and the gaols filled up. In the five years 1812 to 1817 780 males and 136 females aged under twenty-one were transported to Australia.[4]

Few legal distinctions were made between the offences, mode of trial or punishment of children and adults. However, up to the age of seven it was presumed that children were incapable of criminal intent (*doli incapax*) and could not be held responsible for breaking the law. Between seven and fourteen they were presumed innocent unless the prosecution could prove their ability to discern between good and evil (*doli capax*). In most cases the fact that the offence was committed suggested that the perpetrator possessed a guilty mind and therefore punishment was justified. One notable exception was that boys under fourteen were presumed by the law to be unable to commit a rape and therefore could not be found guilty of it; the law presumed them impotent as well as wanting in discretion. Children over fourteen were considered fully responsible for all their actions.

The term 'juvenile' was not always easily defined. Although registration of births was introduced in 1837, it was not until 1875 that it became compulsory. Prison officers and local officials usually had to rely on appearance or the criminal's own declaration of age to determine whether he or she qualified as a juvenile.

In 1887 the Rev. J. W. Horsley, chaplain of Clerkenwell Gaol, London, wrote in his *Jottings from Jail*:

> We take very little notice of names and ages in prison as for various reasons they are apt to alter with each prison entrance. Thus Frederick Lane, aged fifteen, who has just been sentenced to eighteen months imprisonment, was previously in custody as Alfred Miller aged fifteen, John Smith aged sixteen, John Collins aged sixteen, John Kate aged seventeen, John Kythe aged seventeen and John Keytes aged seventeen. In 1883 he is fifteen but in 1881 he was seventeen. But lads and lasses are usually over sixteen while there is a chance of being sent to a reformatory.[5]

Young criminals often claimed to be younger or older than they were and, of course, gave different names on different occasions. They made their choice in the light of the advantages and disadvantages in a particular town or prison of being classed as a juvenile. In some prisons juveniles had a better diet and were not sent to the treadmill. Other young convicts claimed to be completely illiterate in order to get into the prison school because good progress reports in learning earned them a good character. By changing their identities they would often avoid being sent to higher courts even after several convictions. This was especially true in London where there was a profusion of magistrates' courts which often passed sentence in ignorance of a prisoner's record in other districts. After the 1860s the identification of prisoners became easier as parish registers became available for checking names and birth dates. Later in the century photography was used for prison records.

One underlying cause of the increase in juvenile offenders was the fact that children were sent to prison for the most trivial of offences. If the object of imprisonment was to separate an offender from society in order to make him or her a better member of it, the imprisoning a child aged seven to fourteen for a few days was highly unlikely to accomplish this aim. After receiving the evidence of several Select Committees the government recognised this fact and in 1847 passed a Bill:

> for a more speedy trial and punishment of juvenile offenders and that persons not exceeding fifteen years may be summarily convicted by two magistrates and if the examining magistrate thought the offence too trifling to merit punishment they may dismiss the accused at once.[6]

The outcome was that each case was left for the individual magistrate to decide upon.

Mr Antrobus, one of the more understanding magistrates of the city of London, remarked in 1852:

> Send a child to prison for stealing an apple or orange or even for snatching some trifling article imprudently or culpably exposed for sale on the streets; or indeed for having a vagrant parent – the act is monstrous and can only tend to increase moral pestilence.

He cited a table on children committed to the Westminster House of Correction for various petty thefts during 1851/2 and by this showed that fifty-five children under fourteen were committed for stealing fruit or some article under the value of sixpence and forty-eight for stealing something of value between sixpence and one shilling.[7]

With decisions left to magistrates, there were bound to be irregularities in sentencing. There also tended to be one law for the rich and another for the poor. Lord Eldon's confession in the House of Lords in 1827 that as a boy he had been a great poacher was greeted with laughter. When two boys were accused of stealing fruit at Cambridge in 1824 it was asked 'What is the crime of a boy stealing a hatful of apples? This was committed daily by the most high-born youths of the country.' But it was said from the bench: 'Garden plunderers are of a different description and it is necessary to restrain this species of crime which, like Sabbath-breaking, may be considered a prelude to other and deeper transgressions.' The two boys referred to were described as 'old offenders' and sentenced to transportation. Another boy on a similar charge was sent to the House of Correction for a month and three more, though caught red-handed, were acquitted for 'the jury felt the execution of their duty productive of grievous cruelty'.[8]

Many children suffered from anomalies of justice at a time when society seemed oblivious to their plight and there others were incarcerated who deserved pity rather than punishment. The social reformer Mary Carpenter reported the case of children aged seven and eight in the Millbank Penitentiary, London, who did not know why they were there, and of another girl of eleven who was sentenced to a year's imprisonment for stealing a sovereign. The girl did not know the difference between a sovereign and a shilling.[9]

Another pitiful case was that of the youngest prisoner ever recorded at the Littledean House of Correction in the Forest of Dean; Peggy Freeman, aged only five, who was held there from 22 August to 4 October 1803 as a vagabond and was then transferred to the county gaol.[10] The poor child had probably been abandoned and was therefore completely destitute. As no local parish would take the responsibility of looking after her, the only place for her was in prison.

Vagrant children were encouraged to 'move' from parish to parish so as not to be a burden on a particular parish where they were not settled. In a letter to *The Times*, 28 March 1856, Thomas Lloyd Baker, who had been largely responsible for the reformatory movement wrote:

On a visit to Tothill Fields Prison, as good a prison as any under our present system, the governor, Mr Tracey, a man of excellent zeal, explained to me that certain placarded numbers fixed to a boy's arms meant the number of times they had been returned to the prison. Observing a boy of about eight years of age, who had pinned on his arm No. 6, I asked the little fellow for what fault he had been so often committed to prison? The answer was – 'For not moving on, Sir'. I looked surprised but Mr Tracey assured me that the boy had answered me with the perfect truth. He was in faith no ill-doer, only apt to be in the way of the police because like the boy in *Bleak House* he did not know where to go. Yet on either side of this harmless neglected one were little thieves of as arrant a dye as any organisation could proclaim. Now, what must the tendency of imprisonment be on such a boy as the poor little fellow who would (or could) not keep moving?

Charles Dickens's novel *Bleak House* had been published in 1853. Chapter 19 is actually called 'Moving On' in which the character of Jo, the ragged crossing-sweeper, is threatened with arrest because he will not move on:

> 'I'm always a-moving, Sir, I've always been a-moving and a-moving-on ever since I was born. Where can I possible move to, Sir?'

> 'He won't move,' says the constable, 'although he has been cautioned and therefore I am obliged to take him into custody'.[11]

The Vagrancy Act embraced a variety of offences, among which was gambling in the streets, but the great majority of those sent to prison under this Act were sent there for being found on the streets or in public places with intent to commit felony. Most other arrests were for petty theft, picking pockets and burglary. Magistrates did exercise discretion in individual cases and in country districts – for stealing an apple or some eggs say, a boy would be whipped and sent on his way – but in towns and cities those arrested on the streets were assumed to be vicious and to have well-conditioned associates, and this was taken into consideration when sentencing.

If these young criminals managed to avoid disease and the law they would grow up to be adult thieves and aim for higher stakes. Other boys were content to beg and steal small articles, either through lack of intelligence or because they did not want to get involved in serious crime. Those in this group were destined to become drifters, always in and out of prison for minor offences. The same was true of girls, the less intelligent being beggars and prostitutes while the brighter ones were primarily thieves using prostitution as a means of taking strangers unawares.

As they grew older and more experienced in their profession, the youngsters often moved out of their original areas where they had become known to the police and where they probably knew the inside of the local gaol all too well. London was still the favourite place in which to spend the winter, as it had the best opportunities and a good provision of lodging houses, refuges and workhouses, but in April and May the older boys and girls began to leave London heading for Bath or Brighton or other places with rich pickings. There were well-known circuits and the summer was known as 'harvest-time'. Fairs were a popular venue, where crowds of people would be milling around thinking only of enjoyment, and where the young thieves had excellent opportunities disappearing into the throng before the victims realised they had been robbed. The young thieves of Liverpool and Manchester frequently transferred their business from one town to another, as did those of Bristol and Bath. The motive behind this movement was to commit crimes in areas where their identities were not known. This movement around the country became a regular feature of their criminal life.

Dickens hints at this unstable lifestyle in the character of the convict, Abel Magwitch, describing his boyhood to Pip in *Great Expectations*:

> Tramping, begging, thieving, working sometimes when I could – though that warn't as often as you may think … a bit of a poacher, a bit of a labourer, a bit of a waggoner, a bit of a hawker, a bit of most things that don't pay and lead to trouble, then I got to be a man … I warn't locked up as often now as formerly but I wore out my good share of key-metal still.[12]

The Rev. John Clay, chaplain of the Preston House of Correction in June 1852, gives an idea of these travelling thieves in the days when Preston was still a relatively small town:

> In north Lancashire we have very few trained juvenile criminals who commit crimes as a means of support, they come to us now from Liverpool by railway; pickpockets and so forth … Liverpool, Manchester and Bolton have a large staff of trained thieves, any boy who shows an inclination towards thieving does not stay in a small town like Preston or Lancaster but goes to Liverpool or Manchester … There are very few trained thieves in Preston, Blackburn and Chorley.[13]

The coming of the railways opened up new opportunities for the criminal classes. By 1850 they could travel the length and breadth of the country, thus expanding their 'harvest ground'. Clever juveniles soon learned some original methods of subsistence like the one described by Matthew Davenport Hill, the Recorder of Birmingham, in 1852:

> We know that prison diet is given in different portions according to length of imprisonment and that a lad in prison for a month has less quantity of

food per diem than if he had been sentenced for twelve months. A curious illustration of this occurred at Birmingham some time ago. A lad had adopted the habit of getting into a railway carriage on the North Western line and travelling as far as he chose, when asked for the fare he said he had no money, upon which he was taken before a magistrate and summarily convicted and sentenced to many weeks' imprisonment. The moment he was out of gaol he got into another railway carriage and repeated the transgression. At last a railway inspector said, 'I believe this could go on forever; this is the course of life he has charted out for himself and has always had a sentence of six weeks or so, next time let him have a fortnight, when he should be put on a lower diet'. The hint was taken and the magistrate sentenced the lad to a fortnight's imprisonment upon which he burst out into a violent rage and said he had been much ill-treated, that he had always had six weeks before and that he had done the same thing and that he was entitled to six weeks. The diet allotted to imprisoning for a fortnight was not what he had bargained for and he could not put up with it. Some people in judicial posts do not realise that when administering punishment that when he lengthens the term in proportion to the magnitude of the offence he may be playing into the hands of the prisoner. Officially it is said that a long imprisonment exhausts the strength and demands a better supply of food than a short one.[14]

The extent to which these young criminals travelled is brought to light in a 'confession' of a boy awaiting trial in Gloucester Gaol in 1853. Fifteen-year-old James Butterworth, originally from Stockport, Cheshire, wrote down his history for the prison chaplain who promised to try and get him into a refuge rather than serve another gaol sentence. The account of his extensive wanderings is impressive and the fact that he was constantly meeting up with like-minded companions proves that he was not the only one taking advantage of a travelling existence.

In 1846 I was turned out from home by a bad stepfather to look for my own bread, I was about eight years of age. At first I tried singing on the streets but soon went to Ashton-under-Lyne where my brother worked in a bake-house. I decided to go to Manchester and got a job in a bakehouse myself. With my money I went to a singing-house where I met some singers who asked me to join them. I took £2 from my master's till and went to the singing-house where I found the others had left the night before. I went to Warrington and from there to Liverpool by railway but I could not find them so I went to Dublin by steamboat and stopped there till I'd spent my money. I had to beg to get money to go back to Liverpool. I went on the road again back to Ashton where I got 3s. off my brother and went to Huddersfield and from there to Barnsley and on to Sheffield. From there I went to Worksop and Nottingham and on to Loughborough and from there to Whitwick where I took a man's pocket and got 7s. 8d. Then I went to Longlane to sing there, I took 8s. from a pocket and went to Ashby, took lodgings and bought a pair of shoes. Soon after the police came and took me to a lock-up and I got a month in Leicester gaol. When I came out I went back to Stockport but my mother and father had gone. So I went to Manchester and then to Rotherham where I met a man at my lodgings who asked me to go with him to London. We went to Woolwich and from there to Chatham and Gravesend and then I went back to London and stopped there all that winter and the next summer but I never found no money. I went next to Doncaster and worked for a time on the Northern railway but I was soon on the road again. At Huddersfield I found a companion and we went to Leeds and from there to Goole where we were both locked-up. I got ten days, he got seven days. When I came out I went to Hull where I got two months for stealing some meat. After this I met up with two others and we went to York and from there to Ripon. At Masham we killed a goose and I was sent for trial where I waited for two months and ten days and got a month's sentence and a flogging; the other two got off. When I came out I broke into a house at Pately Bridge and stole 3s., two books, a pair of boots and a silk handkerchief. I then went on to Skipton where I found another mate and we went to Otley where we got locked-up for stealing some wool and lead and was sent for trial at Wakefield gaol. I got two months and he got six months. When I came out I went to north Wales where I found another mate and one Saturday night near Caernarvon we broke into a stable and took two fowls and a milk can. At a place called Llandeilo I broke into a house and took two shirts, a pair of stockings, a coat, a new jacket, a pair of knee-britches and a waist belt and went to Bala where I sold them. From there to Llangollen, Ellesmere, Whitchurch and on to Newcastle. I went to Congleton, Buxton, Derby, Lichfield, Birmingham, Coventry and at Market Harborough I stole a watch and two combs but I was caught, sent to a lock-up and sent to Northampton gaol. I was two months awaiting trial and got three months. When I came out I went to Warwick and got into bad company, I got locked-up for sleeping out and fourteen days in the Bridewell. I got out and went to Stratford-on-Avon and met another mate and we went to Shipston and Camden where I stole a pair of stockings for him, we got sent to a lock-up and now we are waiting for our trial in Gloucester gaol. The Chaplain told me if I would tell him the truth about my history he would try to get me into some institution.[15]

James Butterworth's story gives an excellent insight into the life of a destitute child constantly on the move, singing, begging and thieving to survive and perpetually in and out of gaol. His written history was found among the papers of a reformatory school near Gloucester, so it seems that the chaplain did get him into an institution to be trained for a better life. The manager of that reformatory, Thomas Lloyd Baker, was seriously concerned about the effects of imprisonment on young children. In a letter to the *Gloucester Journal*, 17 November 1860, he wrote:

> To anyone who not merely reads over the list of convictions with the exclamation 'Hardened little scamp, he deserves punishment', but who really thinks, 'what hardening effect these repeated imprisonments have on a boy's mind,' such histories as the following are terrible and saddening:

He gave the example of one of his reformatory boys, James Adams, who was aged eight in 1855 and whose criminal record was

25 June 1855	Stealing iron	3 months
1 December 1855	Assault	1 month
2 February 1856	Found in a loft	3 months
5 June 1856	Stealing a top	3 weeks, whipped
15 November 1856	Throwing stones	7 days
17 December 1856	Stealing a pipe	3 days, whipped
12 January 1857	Stealing iron	2 months
19 March 1857	Assault	7 days
25 May 1857	Stealing a till	3 months
24 November 1857	Stealing a handkerchief	3 months
24 February 1858	Stealing meat	14 days, whipped
29 May 1858	Trespassing	3 months
31 August 1858	Stealing fruit	14 days
16 September 1858	Stealing fruit	7 days

As a further example of the type of crimes committed by children who were sent to prison and the sentences they received, the arrest record of Thomas McNelly, aged thirteen in 1836, is another edifying tale. A London magistrate cited him as an example of the petty imprisonments handed out by the police courts at that time: [16]

15 April 1836	Wilful breaking of glass in St Saviour's church	7 days
30 April 1836	Sleeping in open air	Discharged
29 May 1836	Stealing coal	1 month
6 July 1836	Stealing brushes	3 months
17 November 1836	Stealing wood	Discharged
23 December 1836	Stealing carrots	14 days
31 January 1837	Stealing cheese	3 months
29 April 1837	Stealing a pair of drawers	1 month
2 August 1837	Stealing a handkerchief	Discharged
18 October 1837	Stealing pair of trousers	3 months
23 January 1838	Stealing 3 handkerchiefs	1 month
23 February 1838	Stealing some braces	Discharged

Boys like these were only petty thieves but they spent their time in prison, often while awaiting trial, in the company of professional criminals, flash London mobsmen, receivers and drunks. Around the middle of the century it was becoming apparent that repeated short sentences for offences such as stealing food had no real deterrent effect and placed children in the company of adults who would school them further in crime. As early as 1828 the Select Committee on Criminal Convictions reported:

> The present system of allowing imprisonments for young offenders, besides the expense and inconvenience attending it, greatly permits the growth of crime. The boy is committed to prison for trial; the degradation and the company he meets there prepares his mind for every vice; after a long delay he is sentenced to six months or one year's imprisonment, he herds with felons and comes out an accomplished thief, detesting the laws of the country and prepared with means to avoid them.[17]

Prior to 1847 if a boy was brought before a magistrate on a charge of theft, and it was decided to try him at petty sessions, the hearing had to be postponed until the petty sessions were held. Therefore the magistrate either had to commit the prisoner into custody in the meantime or take bail for his appearance at a future date, which would have been impossible for most juveniles. Therefore, as soon as he was committed

Age	Offence						Punishment	
	Simple larceny		Stealing from person		Other offences		10 years transportation	
	M	F	M	F	M	F	M	F
8	2		1					
9	8	1	1		1			
10	16							
11	29		1		1	1		
12	44	2	5		1			
13	49	4	10	2	1	1	1	
14	76	9	14		2			
15	46	11	12	1	2		2	
16	107	16	41	6	3	3	9	1
Total	377	43	84	11	11	4	12	1

to gaol, the evil sought to be avoided at once occurred. He had to remain for weeks perhaps months in prison without being subject to discipline; and, even if he was innocent, the whole machinery of indictment had to be applied to investigate the case before he could be punished for his crime.

Children were generally sentenced to the same retributive punishments as adults, graded by statute and judicial precedence according to the magnitude of the offence. Age by itself gave no right to special treatment and children were tried with the full publicity and formality of judge and jury or magistrate. Like adults, children were tried for lesser offences before magistrates and for more serious crimes before judges. A felony was a crime graver than a misdemeanour.

Children were also liable for all the main forms of punishment – execution, transportation, imprisonment and fines. They had no legal right to be tried differently until the 1847 Juvenile Offenders' Act made it possible to dismiss minor charges, after which individual magistrates were sometimes able to exercise a compassionate distinction. Depending on the case, they could dismiss the charge or, if the child was convicted of simple larceny, send them to gaol for up to three months with or without hard labour, or pay a fine not exceeding £5, or (if male) could have them privately whipped.

Punishment							
7 years transportation		6 to 9 months		1 to 6 months		up to 14 days	
M	F	M	F	M	F	M	F
1		1	1				
		3	5				
		4		6		4	
		15		8	1	2	
1		17	1	23		4	1
		24	3	25	2	3	
6		28	4	38	3	1	
3		23	5	28	4		2
9	3	60	6	39	10	1	3
20	3	176	20	172	20	15	6

A summary of a return showing the number and age of prisoners up to sixteen years, committed for trial at the Middlesex Sessions during the year 1846 is shown in the table above.

The value of the property stolen by these 530 juveniles was only £158; the cost of their prosecution £445; the cost of their maintenance in prison after conviction £964; hence the expense to the public, during one year, of these 530 children was £1410. To this must be added the expense of transportation of thirty-six of them, which Matthew Davenport Hill reckoned at not less than £82 each, the grand total coming to £3952.[18]

By the 1840s more and more magistrates were turning away from transportation as a means of punishment for juveniles unless they were very hardened, as implied by J. Shaw, a Dublin magistrate who tried on average 350 juveniles a year:

I generally give them, for the first offence, three months; for the second six months; and if it is a young boy I do not transport him but give him twelve months imprisonment for a third offence; sometimes, not often, I pass sentence of transportation upon a boy under fifteen if he is a hardened offender, and has been convicted frequently before. About a third of those tried have been convicted of former offences. The greater part are destitute and abandoned children, or the offspring of profligate parents, but many are the children of small tradesmen; I have sometimes dismissed these children on the promise of the parents to look after them.[19]

The idea of fining children for their misdemeanours was strangely haphazard, as in the case of the two children aged two and six years, who were brought before Edinburgh magistrates and charged with laying snares for the purpose of catching game in an adjoining field. The youngest child attended the learned justice carried in his mother's arms. The crime was proved and the evil doers of two and six were each fined £1 6s. 10d. including expenses, or failing payment, thirty days imprisonment.[20]

Mary Carpenter pointed out the anomalous situation regarding juveniles, fines and the law to the Select Committee on Criminal and Destitute Juveniles:

> In English Law children are considered incapable of guiding themselves, they are therefore entirely subjected to the guidance of their parents; they are not permitted to apprentice themselves, a child has not the right to dispose of his earnings, he has no power of willing property, he is considered incapable of guiding himself. The father is responsible for his maintenance, if he neglects to provide him with food the child can appeal to the parish who will punish the father for neglecting him. But the moment a child shows he is really capable of guiding himself by committing a crime, from that moment he is treated as a man. He is tried in public and the law is exercised towards him as if he were a man, while his father is from that moment, according to law, released from his obligation to maintain him. There are great inconsistencies in the law ... if a child is found guilty of a felony he is to be fined £5 and in default of paying he is to be imprisoned, now, how can a child possess £5 of his own when by the law all his earnings belong to his father![21]

A popular option of 'discerning' magistrates was corporal punishment. Whipping of male juveniles was carried out throughout the nineteenth century, being regarded as a useful alternative to imprisonment – and a lot cheaper. The levels of enforcement varied tremendously throughout the country as did the age of offenders, the number of strokes given and the instrument used. After sentencing, boys would be taken to the nearest gaol, whipped and sent on their way.

The gaol registers for Gloucester gaol contain the following records of corporal punishments for juveniles

JB, aged fourteen, stole 2s., 6 August 1858, twenty-four strokes birch rod.

TB and JM, aged twelve, stealing two fowls, 1 September 1859, twelve strokes each birch rod.

WS, aged eleven, stole a copper jug, 3 October 1860, twelve strokes birch rod.

GC, aged thirteen, stole two half crowns, 15 November 1860, twelve strokes birch rod.

In the Bristol House of Correction at the same time they used a cat o'nine tails and up to twenty-four lashes were given for similar offences.[22]

The Juvenile Offenders Act 1847 empowered courts of summary jurisdiction to order juvenile offenders under the age of fourteen to be whipped; in 1850 the age limit was raised to sixteen. The Victorian historian Luke Owen Pike witnessed a flogging with a cat o'nine tails and wrote:

> Few or none are present except the officials of the gaol or visiting justices; spectators are not admitted within the prison to see a fellow human being beaten when they have no better motive than mere curiosity. The prisoner is fastened to a 'triangle' or to an apparatus resembling stocks, so that he can move neither hand nor foot. His back is bared. The man who wields the cat shakes out its nine thongs, raises it aloft with both hands and deals the criminal the first blow on the shoulders. A red streak appears on the bared skin. Again the thongs are shaken out, again the hands raise and again the whips are brought down with full force and the streak grows redder and broader. A turnkey gives out the number as each stroke falls; and the silence is broken only by his voice, by the descent of each successive blow and by the cries and groans of the sufferer.
>
> Anyone who has witnessed such a scene may wonder to what good it is enacted. If the object of punishment is not vengeance but the prevention of breaches of the law, it seems useless, so far as example is concerned to flog a prisoner within the prison walls. The whole purpose of such a deterrent must lie in the vividness with which it can be presented to the imagination of persons who have a tendency to commit but who have not yet committed an offence for which flogging may be legally inflicted.[23]

The Rev. J. Field, chaplain of Reading Gaol did not believe in whipping as a punishment:

> I have never seen any reclaimed by corporal punishment, I believe it has a hardening effect, like in the case of W. W., now aged sixteen, his father and

mother absconded before he was a year old, leaving the prisoner in the care of an aged grandmother by whom he was brought up under no control. He was once whipped and has since become perfectly reckless.[24]

A victim of corporal punishment, a former inmate of the reformatory ship *Akbar* in Liverpool, reported on his punishment in later years:

I was sent to the *Akbar* at the age of fifteen for stealing and was quickly made aware of its tough discipline. One day I cheeked an officer badly and the captain, awarding me fifteen strokes of the birch, told the man known as the Punishment Corporal, 'See that you give this rascal a sound flogging'. All the boys paraded on the quarter deck where the flogging horse had been put out. I was stretched across it, with my legs and arms tied with canvas straps so I couldn't move and my pants were pulled down. Then the Corporal taking his time birched me on my bare buttocks, swishing me with all the vigour he could muster. I clenched my teeth and tried not to squeal but at the third stroke let out an ear-splitting yell. It was like nothing I had ever experienced, my weals burned and stung like fire and I howled unashamedly. When they released me from the horse, my bottom, cut and bleeding all over, was like a white-hot ball of fire and I stood in front of the ship's company, weeping and squirming with pain and humiliation. After a few weeks my scars disappeared and I was none the worse for being flogged. A caning outside the trousers, though unpleasant, didn't worry us too much, but a birching on bare skin was something we greatly feared – it really hurt.[25]

The boy was made an example of before his associates and his story confirms that flogging *was* a brutal punishment for youngsters – but over the years it was never a viable deterrent. Even so, the corporal punishment of juvenile offenders was not abolished until 1948.

If, after being given a 'light' sentence of a fine or a whipping, a child did reoffend he could be pretty sure of receiving a gaol sentence and in the first part of the century this would have proved an unpleasant experience. Prison was regarded primarily as an instrument of punishment rather than of reform, or as a place to hold criminals awaiting trial or the execution of their sentences. Prisons were places of detention where offenders of all types were huddled together indiscriminately. Prior to 1820 young boys were confined to the same cells as hardened prisoners. A boy of nine could have found himself locked up at night with thieves, murderers, depraved people of all sorts – and no doubt these children were abused. This evil situation was realised by the authorities and after about 1820 boys under sixteen were kept apart, given their own wards and looked after by warders.

A select committee of 1818 found free association between prisoners common in most gaols. Newgate, where children of the 'tenderest age' were confined in cells with older prisoners, was the most notorious.[26] Similarly in Bristol, Thomas Folwell Buxton, a prison reformer, stated that boys were allowed to intermingle with men and without distinction of age, wore heavy irons and, even at the better disciplined prisons of Gloucester and Salford, boys were treated as adults and subjected to the rigours of the treadmill.[27]

In 1834 national criminal returns were made and for the first time information on the age and education of offenders was provided. When the returns were studied it was realised that, despite growing industrial prosperity, crime was apparently increasing out of all proportion to the rise in population and this increase was greatest among the young.

The statistics for 1837 in respect of the age of juvenile offenders were:

Gaol Commitments, 1837

Age	Male	Female
7	—	1
8	11	1
9	22	1
10	50	15
11	70	12
12	150	25
13	295	31
14	453	65
15	480	87
16	734	151
Total	1962	334

From these figures it can be seen that there were nearly six times as many boys as girls in gaol. Of the 358 aged twelve and under, one was sentenced to death; thirty-seven were transported; 231 received gaol sentences; nine were whipped only; three fined and seventy-seven acquitted. In addition to gaol sentences of those aged twelve years and under, thirty-two were sentenced to be whipped once and twelve twice; of those aged eleven years, fifteen were to be whipped once, two twice and one thrice; of those aged ten years, twelve were to be whipped once, one twice; of those aged nine years, five were to be whipped once and one twice and one aged eight years once. Two children of nine years and one of eleven were sentenced to ten years transportation; and one of eight years, two of nine, eight of ten, four of eleven and nineteen of twelve years were sentenced to seven years transportation. The child of twelve who was capitally convicted for robbery had his sentence commuted to one month's imprisonment.[28] Ten years later in March 1847 the governor of Tothill Fields House of Correction, London reported:

> 600 convicts, one third of them are under the age of sixteen. Of these ten are under eight and thirty-six between eight and ten. Another third of the whole being females and one poor child had been committed at the age of six, an object of wretchedness and misery.[29]

The tremendous upsurge in juvenile crime continued as the century progressed and was at its peak when Henry Mayhew did his research in the late 1850s. His despondent comments sum up a dismal situation which society in general was at last beginning to notice.

> Statistically the melancholy and degrading conclusion is that there are altogether between 11,000 and 12,000 juvenile criminals annually passing through the prisons of England and Wales and that between 3000 and 4000 of that number appear in the gaols of London, and we must admit that there are as many young thieves and vagrants outside the walls of the prisons as within them, making an army of boy and girl criminals – a prodigious number.
>
> What fate eventually befalls these graduates in crime? How many died and rest unrecorded among the gravestoneless mounds of prison burial grounds? [30]

4

Prison Life

'Never mind, Charley,' said Fagin, soothingly, 'they'll all know what a clever fellow he was; he'll not disgrace his old pals and teacher. Think how young he is too! What a distinction to be lagged at his time of life!'

Charles Dickens, *Oliver Twist*, on the arrest of the Artful Dodger [1]

Jack Dawkins, the Artful Dodger, would soon have found that it was not such an honour to be sent to Newgate as Fagin had suggested to Charley. His life there would have been uncomfortable and restricted, although by 1838, when *Oliver Twist* was published, improvements had been made and boys under sixteen were kept apart from other male prisoners and a school had been opened for them in which they were taught by a fellow convict.

Charles Dickens visited Newgate Gaol as a prison visitor in the autumn of 1835; it was the first criminal prison he ever visited. He was shown around the special section, consisting of a yard and two wards, which had just been set apart for boys and commented:

In a tolerably sized room in which there were some writing materials and some copy books was the schoolmaster with a couple of his pupils; the remainder having been fetched from an adjoining apartment, the whole were drawn up in line for our inspection. There were fourteen of them in all, some with shoes some without; some in pinafores with jackets, others in jackets without pinafores and one in scarce anything at all. The whole number had been committed for trial on charges of pocket-picking; and fourteen such terrible little faces were never beheld. There was not a redeeming feature among them – not a glance of honesty – not a wink expressive of anything but the gallows and the hulks. As to anything like shame or contrition, that was entirely out of the question. They were evidently all gratified at being thought worth the trouble of looking at, but we never looked upon a more despicable sight because we never saw fourteen such hopeless creatures of neglect before.[2]

While in Newgate, Dickens also inspected the female ward and was particularly moved by the spectacle of young girl prisoners. His description of one girl receiving a visit from her mother and a second girl visiting her mother, shows his compassion and understanding of a heinous situation, as evidenced in his comments on the second girl, who was not then a prisoner but was obviously likely to become one; or a street walker or some kind of delinquent:

> The girl belonged to a class – unhappily but too extensive – the very existence of which should make men's hearts bleed. Barely past her childhood it required but a glance to discover that she was one of those children born and bred in neglect and vice who had never known what childhood is; who have never been taught to love or court a parent's smile or even to dread a parent's frown. A thousand nameless endearments of childhood; its gaiety, innocence, are alike unknown to them. They have entered at once upon the realities and miseries of life and to their better nature it is almost hopeless to appeal. Talk to THEM of parental solicitude, the happy days of childhood and the merry games of infancy! Tell them of hunger and the streets, beggary, stripes, the gin shop and the pawnbroker's and they will understand you.[3]

As well as Newgate, Dickens visited Coldbath Fields House of Correction in Clerkenwell, which was at the time the most vicious part of London with the highest murder rate and the densest criminality. He also visited the Westminster House of Correction in Tothill Fields. He befriended the governors of these establishments, Captain George Laval Chesterton (governor of Coldbath Fields from 1829 to 1854) and Lieutenant Frederick Tracey RN (governor of the Westminster gaol from 1834 to 1855). He claimed to 'know the prisons of London well' and to have 'visited the largest of them more times than I could count'.[4] In his prison perambulations he also went to the children's prison at Parkhurst on the Isle of Wight which was exclusively for juveniles awaiting transportation. These prison visits must have provided him with a wealth of material for his novels. They also gave him a rare insight into the conditions and affairs of the criminal classes, of which the middle-class reading public of the time would have had very little knowledge.

The only people who would have known about crime and punishment were those who were involved in it – the legal classes and the lower classes. It is difficult to determine the public attitude towards criminal children before the nineteenth century. The unruly apprentices of Elizabethan times were sent to houses of correction but until the late eighteenth century ages were rarely mentioned in records or prison calendars; many people did not know their own age. John Howard, the prison reformer, drew attention to the indiscriminate mingling of men, women and children in the gaols of the eighteenth century. He was also shocked to discover that gaolers were not salaried officers but depended on fees from prisoners. It is, therefore, highly likely that as children would have been unable to pay these fees, they would not have been sent to gaol. In those unenlightened times young children would have been whipped and sent on their way for their misdemeanours, or perhaps, as a deterrent, made to witness a prisoner being 'publicly burnt on the hand'. Branding, as a form of punishment, was still practised in the late eighteenth century. The first evidence of ages being given in the Calendar of all the Prisoners in his Majesty's Gaol of Newgate in the city of Bristol for Felony and other criminal Matters, April 6 1793, indicates that, of twenty-six inmates, three were aged fifteen, fourteen and twelve.[5]

Punishment by imprisonment and its associated maltreatment was intended to prevent future violations of law, but as the crime rate continued to soar, some argued that punishment should be intensified; ideas of how this should be achieved included such extremes as hanging prisoners in chains, whipping to death, castration and branding. However, it was decided that, as the ultimate sentence of death by hanging had failed to prevent a rise in crime, anything of a lesser severity was not worthy of consideration.

The best deterrent seemed to be to make prison life as unpleasant as possible, as the Rev. Sydney Smith advised in his report to the Prison Discipline Society:

A gaol should be a place of punishment from which men recoil with horror – a place of real suffering, painful to the memory, terrible to the imagination. We would banish all the looms of Preston gaols and substitute nothing but the treadmill or capstan or some species of labour where the labourer could not see the results of his toil – where it is monotonous, irksome and dull as possible – pulling or pushing instead of reading and writing – and no rewards. Deprivation of diet is an important part of punishment as thieves are usually gluttonous and sensual and there is nothing they feel more bitterly in confinement than a long course of water-gruel and flour puddings. There should be no tea or sugar, nothing but beating hemp, pulling oakum and pounding bricks – no work but what is tedious. Mrs Fry is an amiable, excellent woman, but hers is not the method to stop crimes. In prison there must be a great deal of solitude; coarse food; a dress of shame; hard, incessant, eternal labour; the unrelenting exclusion of happiness and comfort. Men, women, boys and girls should all leave gaol unimpaired in health but heartily wearied of their residence there, and taught by sad experience to consider it the greatest misfortune of their lives to return there.[6]

Imprisonment was meant to be a bad experience but it appears that the most harmful time for a juvenile was the period he spent in gaol just after he had been arrested, while he was awaiting trial. In a speech in the House of Commons, Sir Thomas Folwell Buxton, a prison reformer, described such a prisoner's lot:

The prisoner after his commitment is made out is handcuffed to perhaps a dozen wretched prisoners in a similar situation and marched through the streets, sometimes a considerable distance. The moment he enters prison irons are hammered on him; then he is cast into the midst of a compound of all that is disgusting and depraved. At night he is locked up in a narrow cell with perhaps half-a-dozen of the worst thieves in London, or as many vagrants, whose rags are alive and in actual motion with vermin. He may find himself in a bed and in bodily contact between a robber or a murderer or between a man with a foul disease on one side and one with an infectious disease on the other. This was while he might be awaiting trial, if he was acquitted he would then be dismissed from the gaol.[7]

Although boys were kept separate from adults once they had been tried and sentenced, during that period awaiting trial they were often incarcerated with older suspects and without the discipline and control offered by warders. In 1835 the governor of Newgate, William Wadham Cope, was called as a witness to a Select Committee on Gaols and quoted the case of a fifteen-year-old boy, committed for stealing two pairs of boots, who had spent a week before his trial in the notorious 'Chapel Yard' in the company of thirty other prisoners; some tried, some untried, in custody for various offences – housebreaking, highway robbery, theft,

passing bad money and more. He had to sleep in a room with twenty
of them, some sleeping on the floor on mats as there were not enough
bedsteads. When examined, the boy had told the governor that the
conduct and language of the prisoners he was obliged to associate with
was most depraved and shocking. His pockets were frequently picked
as they robbed one another. There was gambling all day long; and the
boys boasted about their former robberies, told obscene stories and sang
vile songs. They even kept back part of their bread rations to sell to
other prisoners for gambling money and the guards occasionally brought
in ale to sell.[8]

Another example of confining the innocent and the guilty together
before trial comes from a *Report of the Inspector of Prisons, 1836*, and
concerns the gaol in Giltspur Street, London, which also served as a
House of Correction and a Watch House:

> To this place are often committed boys before they have been taken to a
> magistrate; others remanded for examination; others for trial; others con-
> victed by sentences of the Central Court; others summarily convicted and
> others apprehended at all hours of the day and night for being disorderly in
> the streets. The prison is, in a great measure, also an asylum for the houseless;
> and its wards and yards exhibit at all times a most disgusting accumulation
> of crime and destitution. The contracted space and crowded state of the
> Giltspur Street Compter render any approach to separation quite impractic-
> able. The number of boys who are committed to this prison for being found
> abroad at night, or for other acts of vagrancy, is very considerable. As it is
> not possible to confine them apart from others, they are constantly placed
> in contact with notorious and hardened thieves. On a late visit we found
> several cases of this description; one, a sailor boy, who, having been ship-
> wrecked, had been committed to the prison as a place of refuge, until a vessel
> could be provided for him. This boy was in a ward with twelve men, some
> of whom had been remanded on charges of felony, embezzlement and
> misdemeanours. And yet, objectionable as was this association for a boy
> simply destitute and who had not been charged with any crime, there was
> no other part of the prison in which he could have been placed, with less
> danger to his morals. In the Vagrant Yard were several lads, in the closest
> intercourse with others who were notorious offenders.[9]

It was not just in the London gaols that conditions like this existed.
In the north east at Newcastle-on-Tyne, an eleven-year-old boy was

sentenced to two years imprisonment for larceny at the expiration of which he was to be transported for life as it was his second offence. During the month he spent at Newcastle gaol awaiting trial he was put with tried and untried prisoners who were herded together in a yard. They had no work and no attempt was made to keep silence as there was no officer responsible for them. The boy was subjected to swearing and bad talk which was made worse by the month's confinement together. He learnt the histories of what the others had done and how they had done it – a thorough instruction in crime. Religion was laughed at, and as in London, the prisoners spent their time gambling for money and food.[10]

Another example of the conditions young prisoners were subjected to was given by the Rev. J. T. Becher, an early advocate of Friendly Societies, who described the Southwell House of Correction, Nottinghamshire:

> When a prisoner arrives at the gate his commitment is inspected and he was consigned to the ward appropriate to offenders of his denomination without undergoing any previous investigation to ascertain his cleanliness or health; by which omission vermin and the itch were not infrequently communicated to the whole of his miserable associates. If he was convicted of felony or misdemeanour or even charged with these offences, he was fettered and confined in the felons' ward; a turnkey secured him in the dungeon at night and released him in the morning ... without moral instruction, without laborious industry, pinched with hunger and generally half naked, he dragged about his chains in all the squalid wretchedness of abject penury until the day of the trial arrived or the term of his sentence expired; when emaciated by the baneful atmosphere of the dungeon and unhabituated to the exercises of any employment by which a livelihood might be acquired, he was turned loose upon the public to practise all his former crimes with the additional ones derived from the lessons of his abandoned companions ... Those who had committed inferior offences such as trifling assaults, non payment of penalties, misbehaviour in service or apprenticeship, or acts of vagrancy avoided the miseries of the dungeon; but were necessitated to use the same apartment for every purpose; 18 ft square, of this space the bedsteads occupied more than a quarter, three sometimes four in one bedstead, or lying on straw on the floor, without any bedclothes except what charity had accidentally supplied. Night pots, cooking utensils, plates, basins, food cooked and raw, coal, various articles of dress and diet all promiscuously jumbled together, dirty and clean in this small room; where even the prisoners

complained that vermin and filth were to be accounted among the most afflictive severities attending their sentences.[11]

When a boy was committed to prison he was in for a pretty rough time. First or second offences usually carried a one to three weeks sentence. During the first week, however, the prisoners were given only bread and water as sustenance; in the second and consecutive weeks the diet improved but they had to do hard labour – if they were big enough this could mean a turn on the treadmill. The more severe sentence of penal servitude meant imprisonment for three years or longer with compulsory labour.

A little better than prisons were houses of correction, where first offenders, women and minor offenders were usually sent. They had a slightly less harsh regime, although hard labour was available for those serving more than one week, but they did make an attempt to improve inmates by religious and secular education. Sometimes these institutions were known as 'bridewells' after the original Bridewell Hospital which was converted from a hospital for the poor by Edward VI into a place of confinement and penitential amendment for unruly London apprentices and disorderly persons, as well as sturdy beggars and vagrants. After this, houses of correction in various parts of the country began to be called 'bridewells', a name coming in the course of time to be used as a general term for a place of amendment. It was understood to be a place of safe custody, punishment and reformation to which criminals were committed when sentenced to imprisonment for terms varying from seven days to two years, the idea being to check early criminality of minor offenders requiring a short term in a local lock-up.

During the first quarter of the century the system of sentencing was fairly haphazard, often depending on where the accused lived and what gaols were available locally, rather than on the nature and seriousness of the crime. In 1824 Robert Peel introduced a measure aimed at standardising penal treatment. He recommended that each county should have one gaol and at least one house of correction.[12] Prior to this every class of criminal from pickpocket to highwayman or murderer was sent to the local common gaol or lock-up, whether convicted or under conviction. Houses of correction were then used for vagrants and simple thieves. The Act of 1824 introduced a system of classification for all prisoners; separating those convicted and awaiting conviction. For instance in London:

Prisons for Offenders after Conviction

A. Convicted prisons, for transports and penal servitudes – Pentonville, Millbank, Brixton Female Prison, Hulks
B. Correctional prisons for persons serving short terms: Holloway House of Correction, Coldbath Fields House of Correction, Tothill Fields for boys and females, Wandsworth House of Correction.

Prisons for Offenders before Conviction but after Committal by a Magistrate

Clerkenwell House of Correction, Newgate, Horsemonger Lane. Lock-ups previous to committal in police cells.

Houses of correction were generally divided into the following sections: A reception unit, no labour ward, hard labour ward and female ward.

An account of the Littledean House of Correction in the Forest of Dean describes the accommodation in the 1840s. The reception unit had one cell, one bath, one fumigating room and health checking cells, called lazaretto cells, for new arrivals. The no labour ward had five common cells, five separate cells, one punishment cell, one wardsman's room, one yard and one water closet. The hard labour ward had eleven common cells, ten separate cells, two yards, two water closets, one exercise shed and one treadwheel (boys under fourteen were exempt from this). The female ward had five common cells, four separate cells, one yard, one water closet, one wash house, one laundry and drying room. The rest of the accommodation consisted of two lodge-keeper's rooms, four keepers' rooms, two storerooms, one prisoners' clothes room, one infirmary for men and one for women, a chapel, a chaplain's room, schoolroom, committee room and a water reservoir.[13]

In the Westminster House of Correction at Tothill Fields, which was for males under seventeen and females, the boys' section had ninety-three separate cells, which were 8 ft long by 6 ft wide and 9 ft high, and a large dormitory which could cater for eighty. In the separate cells the only ventilation was a hole in the wall. There was no water or light or anything for summoning the warder. There was no form of heating. The windows were louvred and unglazed but they could be closed at night. The furniture consisted of an iron bed, a straw mattress, one blanket in summer, three in winter, a small stool and a zinc pan. When the institution was visited by a prison inspector, Frederick Hill, on 7 July 1856, he found 271 inmates under seventeen. By that time eighty-seven slept in the dormitory, 177 in the ninety-three separate cells and seven in the reception cells.

The rising incidence of crime and a growing distrust and fear of the underclasses were seen as threatening to an increasingly urbanised Britain. This resulted in the 1840s in the creation of a spate of modern penitentiaries. Solitary confinement developed as the favoured method of punishment. It was seen as the best way of preventing contamination, particularly of the young and, despite the great expense which the system involved, these new gaols were constructed to accommodate a separate and silent regime. Pentonville, which was built in 1842, had 500 separate cells. The carefully thought-out plan involved separate sleeping and employment in single cells, interspersed with daily chapel, time on the treadwheel and exercise in silent association. This was tempered by occasional visits from the chaplain, surgeon and visiting justices. Under the separate system, prisoners occupied single cells night and day. They were given pious books to read, if they could, or handicrafts to execute – but more often just left to meditate on their sins. Food was pushed into the cells through hatches so designed that the warder could see the prisoner without being seen by him. In some gaols prisoners wore masks or caps with low peaks so that nothing could be conveyed by their features and they would have difficulty in identifying each other. The separate system proved very expensive to run.

The silent system was the slightly better regime. Under this, communication by word, gesture or sign was prohibited. Prisoners were allowed to work together under very strict supervision. Permitting work in silent association made it possible to introduce a much greater variety of work, by which it was hoped to make the prisoners pay for their own keep and from which it was reasonably expected that better results could be obtained than from the treadwheel or crank. The obvious drawback was that prisoners could never be prevented from trying to communicate with each other, so the system required an extensive supervisory staff and more punishment for breaching the rule of silence. Ideally they should have slept in separate cells but the numbers involved rendered this impossible and warders had to be with them night and day to watch for any infringement of the rules.

The separate system proved particularly unsuitable for children, endangering their health and providing no outlet for their restless growing bodies and minds. Prison inspectors Frederick Hill and John Williams discovered that offences within the separate systems were more frequent among children than adults and concluded, 'So marked is the distinction in the feeling and habit of manhood and youth that it is impractical to engraft any beneficial plan for the lengthened confinement of boys upon a system adapted to adults'.[14] They thought that prison confinement starved them of the very spirit of childhood. At the ages of thirteen and fourteen, they believed that youths were in an unstable state of body and mind and that they did not have the power of reflection and contemplation of adults – but they did have intensive feelings. 'The youthful mind is so elastic, the desire to play and the inclination for trivials are such that bringing boys like this under a strict system which is assigned to grown-ups, is a perfectly unnatural state for a boy.'[15]

When Wakefield Gaol, Yorkshire, adopted the separate system they soon dropped it in respect of juvenile offenders. It was found that when boys were first put in separate confinement they seemed to suffer from debility and contraction of the joints; the authorities even detected 'feeble mindedness'. So the plan was dropped and instead of picking oakum in isolation the boys were sent out to work in the garden. The chaplain at Wakefield, the Rev. Whitworth Russell reported:

> In the case of very young children, separation is not productive of good effects. There is an elasticity about childhood which it is essential to maintain. An adult, having his character and habits already confirmed and stored, has resources upon which he can fall back but a child has no such resources.[16]

A child in prison was placed in a condition quite discordant with his nature; he was not allowed to raise his voice or use his natural energy. It was the common experience of prison officials that juveniles were by far the most difficult prisoners to deal with. They could be impudent, disobedient and intractable, but most of all they were vulnerable.

On entering a prison for the first time youngsters would discover a place of perfect order and silence. On reception at Pentonville a new prisoner was inspected by the medical officer, lectured about the rules and punishments by the guards, preached at by the chaplain, then stripped naked and made to stand before an officer in a state of nudity while every part of his body was examined. In the days when identification was difficult, physical descriptions of newly arrived prisoners were taken for the prison records. Convicts were measured and their bodily marks recorded, colour of hair, complexion, tattoos, moles, birthmarks and, in the case of girls, length of foot. After handing in their clothes and possessions, prisoners were given a bath; it may have been the first bath many of the youngsters had ever had.

The bathroom at Horsemonger Lane Gaol, London, was a room of about 18 ft by 18 ft with an iron grating over hot air pipes for the purpose of ventilation. There were two baths 5 ft long by 2 ft wide and 2 ft deep supplied with hot and cold water. Boys were measured for height and weight and given appropriate prison clothing, including shoes. On the walls of this room were an assortment of leg irons and cuffs and a machine for fumigating clothes to destroy vermin. After the bath a convict barber would cut off the hair as close to the head as the scissors would allow. Onto their allocated clothing would be attached their prison number; prisoners were hereafter referred to by this number. By the time they left the reception unit boys were left in little doubt that they were in a place of punishment and repression.

The original Tothill Fields Prison was a 'bridewell' built in 1618. It was demolished in 1836 and a new building was erected on the site; the institution eventually became known as the Westminster House of Correction. In 1850 its intake was restricted to females and males under seventeen, thus separating completely young prisoners from the hardened older ones. In 1855 there was a daily average of 270 juvenile inmates. There were thirty-one warders to look after them, a governor, two chaplains and a surgeon. The prison operated the silent system.

A gun summoned warders to their duty in the early morning and cell doors were unlocked at 6.30 am, when the prisoners passed out with their uncovered slop buckets and water cans to empty the former and fill the latter (the water tank and place for emptying slops were together). Cells had then to be cleaned, stone floors scrubbed and cells made ready for inspection. The boys washed their hands and faces every morning and had a warm bath once a month. After washing they went straight to the work room.

Timetable for the Boys' Prison, 1855 [17]

7.00 am	–	Work
8.30	–	Breakfast
9.15	–	Chapel
10.15	–	Exercise, work and school (in detachments)
2.00 pm	–	Dinner
3.00	–	Exercise and work
5.00	–	Work given in
5.30	–	Supper
6.00	–	Lock up for the night
6.15	–	Warders go off duty

They had a slightly different routine at the Holloway House of Correction, where more emphasis seems to have been placed on schoolwork: [18]

5.45 am	–	Rise, slops, wash
6.00	–	Work
7.20	–	Breakfast, clean cell
8.10	–	Chapel
9.00	–	Exercise, work, school
12.45 pm	–	Dinner, prepare school lessons
2.00	–	Work, school
5.45	–	Supper, work in cell
8.00	–	Sweep cell, wash, prepare lessons
8.45	–	Sling hammock, bed

Religious education was a major part of the prison reform system and in the houses of correction it was closely linked with basic secular education. The small classes involved meant that any boy or girl willing to take advantage of the system could make real progress; particularly if they were serving a long sentence. The illustrations of the Tothill Fields, Westminster, girls' and boys' schoolrooms give an excellent indication of the educational methods used at the time. Girls were only taught reading and writing on slates but boys wrote on paper with quill pens sat at desks with inkwells. The roman numeral board and the domino-like counting boards indicate that boys were also taught simple arithmetic. It is ironic that up to the 1870s the only schools in Britain provided by the state for children were in gaols.

Work was intended to be punitive hard labour and nineteenth-century prisoners spent much of their time picking oakum – the pulling to pieces of old tarry ropes for use in caulking the planks of wooden ships or for re-use as new ropes. The job had the merit of being easily learned and easily controlled. There was also a steady demand for the end product. A warder served out oakum, called 'junk' by the boys, for the day's labour. Each bunch was weighed and placed in a basket. Boys aged sixteen had 2 lb to work, under sixteens had 1.5 lbs and the under nines had 1 lb. Some of the young ones who had been in prison many times became experts at 'fiddling away' at the dirty, unravelled yarn, better than their older comrades. They worked at the oakum for five hours a day and in that time they were expected to finish the amount given to them. Silence prevailed as all around the room warders, perched on high stools, had their eyes fixed on the young urchins ready to put a stop to any attempt at communication. At Tothill they even had their dinner served in the oakum room. Other boys were employed in making and mending prison clothing and shoes. Over the years, as wood gave way to iron in the construction of ships, and sail gave way to steam, oakum products were no longer needed and sewing became an alternative labour – the making of sacks out of hard, stiff canvas.

Other forms of 'hard labour' were not so constructive and took the form of punishment rather than work. The most notorious device was the treadwheel (sometimes called the treadmill), which was a big, iron frame of steps around a revolving cylinder. Prisoners, both male and female in the early century, trudged up the steps in their own separate compartments on the wheel for up to six hours a day. It was like climbing a mountain for nothing. In 1843 the Prison Inspectors' General Survey expressed an opinion that treadmill labour was prejudicial to health for certain categories of prisoner and that in future it would be an improper punishment for females and boys under fourteen years of age.[19] There was no mention of boys not working other forms of hard labour, which up to 1865 included the crank, capstan and stone crushing. The crank was a wheel with a counting device fitted into a box of gravel which the prisoner had to turn by handle for a given number of rotations; it was another useless activity which did nothing but move gravel in a box.

A special type of crank was developed at Leicester Gaol which made the operation more difficult. The gaolers devised a system whereby no convict could eat or drink until he had completed a given number of revolutions of the crank – 1800 before breakfast, 4500 by dinner and 5400 before supper. It was this form of hard labour, which was given to juveniles as well as adults, which led to one of the most scandalous cases of legalised cruelty recorded, resulting in the suicide of a fifteen-year-old boy. Rumours of this event reached the general public and a royal commission was set up to investigate the matter.

At Birmingham Gaol hard labour consisted of 10,000 revolutions of the crank before 6 pm. When this was not carried out the prisoner was kept in the crank cell until late at night and, if the work was still not done, he was deprived of his supper, receiving no food until 8 am the next morning, when he was given bread and water. To meet the numerous cases of failure to complete the demands, a special punish-ment jacket was introduced. The prisoner, was 'muffled' into this straitjacket, having his arms tied together behind him and a leather stock fastened tightly round his neck. He was then strapped to the wall of his cell in a standing position. Strapped in this manner to the wall, prisoners, chiefly boys, were kept for periods of four to six hours and in some instances a whole day, for non-performance of crank labour. If they fainted or passed out during that time a bucket of cold water was thrown over them. The straitjacket was used without discrimination of age. One of the victims, Lloyd Thomas, aged only ten, told the Commission that he was kept in the jacket and collar, but not strapped to the wall, for three consecutive days.

Fifteen-year-old Edward Andrews was one who resisted this cruel regime. After two months of refusing to work the crank and suffering the associated punishments, he hanged himself in his cell on 17 April 1853. The prison schoolmaster was the last person to see him alive. He reported to the commission:

> Andrews had the straitjacket on Sunday morning for two hours. It made shrivelled marks on his arms and body. A bucket of water was placed by him

in case of exhaustion. He stood there, cold, red, bare feet and soaked in water. The ground was covered with water. He looked very deathly and reeled with weakness when liberated.

The Royal Commission's ultimate judgement was: 'With respect to the case of Edward Andrews, we are of the opinion that by the order and with the knowledge of the governor he was punished illegally and cruelly and was driven thereby to the commission of suicide.' The essence of the report was that the boy's death was unfortunate but not a matter for criminal prosecution.[20] The use of the crank continued as a form of hard labour until 1898.

The case of another boy who probably died as a result of punishment is to be found in the report of the Prison Inspectors on Millbank gaol in June 1846:

24 November 1845. James Richmond, aged ten years, was received from Edinburgh and remained under the regular discipline of the prison until removed to the infirmary on 5 May 1846 where he died on 22 May. The Male Defaulter Book will inform your Honourable House of the number of days this boy was confined to a dungeon on 1 lb of bread and two pints of water per diem. There was no bed allowed him during this punishment having only boards to lay on during the night with one rug and one blanket to cover him and also the number of days this boy was sentenced to bread and water diet while under punishment in his cell.

Governor's reply 'This boy had been reported and punished twelve times previously for various offences, complaints being constantly made against him by the chaplain, schoolmasters and in short by all the officers who had anything to do with him and for which he was repeatedly admonished. Punishments were light having only once had bread and water for three days before being placed in a dark cell. Five weeks elapsed after his last punishment before he was taken ill.

Chaplain's statement 'James Richmond was an exceedingly bad boy, both in respect of conduct and disposition, that such a boy should frequently incur punishment cannot be a matter of surprise.

Chaplain's journal, 22 May. The boy, James Richmond, died in the infirmary this afternoon; the unhappy boy retained the same obduracy of temper under sickness as he had habitually evinced since his coming to the prison. Rev. J. Penny, Chaplain.

Extracts from the prison misconduct book show James Richmond's offences and punishments:

1 December 1845, for marking his dinner tin and having urine in his cell pint – bread and water for two days.

20 December 1845, for only picking one coir in three days – bread and water for two days.

24 December 1845, for impertinence at school – bread and water one day.

25 December 1845, for having a very dirty cell and making water in his coir – bread and water for two days.

20 January 1846, for breaking handle of his cell pint – bread and water for two days.

26 January 1846, for having his cell and pewter dirty – bread and water for two days.

5 February 1846, for having a dirty cell and wantonly breaking his signal – bread and water for three days.

10 March 1846, for breaking his signal stock and concealing it in his bed – bread and water for two days.

13 March 1846, for disorderly conduct at school – bread and water for two days.

24 March 1846, for having his cell and pewter dirty – bread and water for two days.

26 March 1846, for rubbing the whitewash off his cell wall and when spoke to by the officer said 'you are a big b ... r' – dark cell on bread and water three days.[21]

If children did misbehave while serving a sentence, they could expect to receive some form of punishment. Flogging does not seem to have been much used once a child was actually in gaol. A few bad cases were forced to wear leg irons or handcuffs for a time, but a more common treatment was putting them in solitary cells for a few days or, even worse, in dark cells. These were specially designed punishment cells, very small, no furniture and totally without light. To be alone and in complete darkness must have been very frightening to a small child.

On her visit to Liverpool Borough Gaol on 8 August 1850, Mary Carpenter was taken to see the punishment cells and witnessed two small boys:

crying bitterly in dark cells; one, the officer said, was usually unruly and hardened and the other was being punished for beating another child as they went up stairs! Solitary confinement and a bread and water diet are generally found sufficient punishment; flogging is resorted to very rarely for insubordination. Handcuffs and irons have not been used for many years here except on going to trial.[22]

The following table shows the total numbers of punishments for juveniles in all the prisons of England and Wales for 1853:

Juvenile Prisoners[23]

Punishments		Totals
Handcuffs and irons		
males	5	
females	1	6
Whipping		
males	58	58
Dark cells		
males	1610	
females	101	1711
Solitary cells		
males	1146	
females	104	1250
Stoppage of diet		
males	11,616	
females	647	12,263
Other punishments		
males	336	
females	43	379
Total		
males	14,771	
females	896	15,667

The item 'Other punishments' would have included special treatments like that given to Edward Andrews. The most popular method of dealing with refractory children seems to have been stoppage of food rations.

Prison diet formed part of the overall punishment. To spend a week in prison was meant to ensure hardship. The food was extremely meagre; only what was believed to be the minimum necessary for health was given. In most cases this consisted of bread and water in limited quantities, for it was thought that a more liberal diet would encourage wrongdoers to commit crimes which would ensure a longer sentence.

This first week deterrent principle was described in a letter dated 6 December 1856 from Thomas Lloyd Baker to James Francillon, Chairman of the Gloucestershire Quarter Sessions:

> one week for first offences may appear at first to be too slight a punishment to deter others from risking it. But in a week's imprisonment the diet is unwholesomely low and the boy lives daily with a conviction that it is a very bad place. His associates will usually take their opinion from the experience of those who have been there. A week's imprisonment does not allow a boy to become habituated to it but makes him feel and tell his friends that a week in gaol 'half killed him' and he verily believes that a month would have quite done it! So the deterrent principle is brought strongly into action in the case of one week's imprisonment.[24]

In Newgate, prisoners without hard labour received only bread and gruel during their first week, after which potatoes were introduced. Those serving more than twenty-one days had soup and meat, vegetable soup (mainly peas) and the worst sort of meat. They also had cocoa – but not as we know it. It was made with solid flake cocoa flavoured with milk and molasses; the result was an oily liquid which contained so much oil that it floated on the surface. No knives were allowed, of course, and only a wooden spoon; the tough meat had to be torn apart with the teeth. Washing up was done in the cell bucket in cold water. Not surprisingly outbreaks of scurvy and various forms of digestive infections sometimes occurred.[25]

At Horsemonger Lane Gaol, the diet in 1860 was as follows: [26]

Boys Under Fourteen and Females

Class 1 – Convicts sentenced to any term not exceeding seven days

Breakfast	–	oatmeal gruel, 1 pint
Dinner	–	bread, 1 lb
Supper	–	oatmeal gruel, 1 pint

Class 2 – Convicts sentenced to a term between seven to twenty-one days

Breakfast	–	oatmeal gruel, 1 pint, bread 6 oz
Dinner	–	bread 6 oz
Supper	–	bread, 6 oz, oatmeal gruel, 1 pint

(Prisoners employed at hard labour to have an additional 1 pint soup per week)

Class 3 – Convicts not employed on hard labour for terms exceeding twenty-one days
Daily

Breakfast and supper	–	oatmeal gruel, 1 pint, bread 6 oz

Dinner

Sunday and Thursday	–	soup, 1 pint, bread 6 oz
Tuesday and Saturday	–	meat, 3 oz, bread, 6 oz, half a pound of potatoes
Monday, Wednesday and Friday	–	bread, 6 oz, potatoes 1 lb

Prison diets varied, of course, throughout the country; inmates could be lucky or unlucky. At the Somerset House of Correction at Shepton Mallet in 1833 each prisoner had daily 1 lb bread, 1 lb potatoes, 6 oz beef without bone and 1.5 pints oatmeal gruel; and when working on the treadmill also 1½ pints soup or gruel when leaving work. On the other hand, in the Cornwall County Gaol at Bodmin the daily ration for the first month of imprisonment was only 1½ lb bread with water and after that period a portion of gruel was added. At Beverley Common Gaol in Yorkshire they had the usual gruel and bread during the week, but on Sundays for dinner they had 'one quart of stew made of heads and bones with half a pound of potatoes.' [27]

Even the hard labour and poor food proved no deterrent to the ever-increasing number of juveniles incarcerated in the country's gaols. In the Coldbath Fields House of Correction in 1835 there were thirty-three aged eight, fifteen aged nine, twenty-two aged ten, thirteen aged eleven, two aged twelve, five aged thirteen and twelve aged fourteen. In Tothill at the same time there were twenty-three boys and fourteen girls aged between nine and sixteen – by March 1847 the number had risen to 200 boy convicts in that gaol. At the time of the prison inspection in 1835 in the Hereford Gaol, out of a total of fifty-six prisoners there were sixteen males and fourteen females under seventeen. Falmouth

Gaol, Cornwall, seemed to have a particular problem with juveniles: out of eighty-four male prisoners, thirty were under seventeen and all of the eleven female prisoners were juveniles.[28]

The fact that there were many more children aged twelve years and under than over that age in Coldbath Fields in 1837 is not surprising. The Criminal Tables of 1837 show that 358 youngsters of that age group were prosecuted in that year, most for the offence of larceny as the following table indicates:

Juveniles Aged Twelve Years and Under[29]

Offences	
Manslaughter	1
Assault	1
Burglary	1
Housebreaking	5
Curtilage breaking	3
Robbery	2
Horse stealing	3
Larceny, to the value of £5 in a dwelling house	2
Larceny, from the person	20
Larceny, by servants	13
Larceny, simple	276
Stealing fixtures	10
Embezzlement	2
Receiving stolen goods	7
Frauds and attempts to defraud	7
Arson, capital	1
Using counterfeit coin	2
Riot	1
Misdemeanour, administering poison to harass and annoy	1
Total	358

The numbers continued to climb ever upwards over the decades until by 1853 the number of juvenile offenders in prison reached just over 16,000; 11.1 per cent of the total prison population. Large towns and fashionable resorts were instrumental in some counties having a high crime rate: Somerset had Bath; Warwickshire included Birmingham; Gloucestershire had Cheltenham; and Sussex had Brighton. But by far the largest contributor to the gaol population was the metropolis of London. The juvenile prison at Tothill Fields, Westminster, went from strength to strength as an ever-widening range of criminal activities helped to put more youngsters behind bars. Many of the inmates were boys serving second, third or fourth terms, some even more. When they visited this gaol in 1855 Henry Mayhew and John Binney were struck by the numbers of recommittals and also the triviality of some of the offences:

In the oakum room 150 boys seated on low forms, some dressed in prison blue, marking they were imprisoned for misdemeanours and not sentenced to hard labour, these were summary boys, i.e. they had been committed by magistrates rather than after a trial. Others had yellow collars to the waistcoats of their grey suits, this was to mark them as sessions prisoners, or those who had been tried and found guilty. All the boys wore striped tri-colour woollen night caps which were arranged by tucking down the peak into an ordinary day cap. All boys wore on their left arm a large figure 1 or 2 in yellow cloth denoting the class of prisoners to which they belonged, the third class being unmarked were those sentenced to fourteen days or less. The second class were imprisoned for three months, whilst the first class had more than three months. Boys had red marks to indicate the number of times they had previously been committed, others had badges showing they were imprisoned for two years and others a yellow ring to denote that their sentence was penal servitude.

We found boys of seven years of age branded with a felon's badge, boys not even in their teens, clad in prison dress for the offence of throwing stones or unlawfully knocking on doors. An eight year old had stolen six plums from an orchard and was given fourteen days and a flogging!

Those who were in for misdemeanours were questioned by the prison visitors in the presence of a warder. 'What are you in for?' 'Heaving stones.' 'Heaving a stone through a street lamp.' 'Three times before', said the warder. 'Heaving clay.' 'This one has been in fourteen times, mostly for cadging'. 'Heaving stones.' 'Stealing a bell from a garden.' 'Heaving stones.' 'Four times before.'

In ten cases there was only one of a malicious and two of a criminal character; whilst the majority were imprisoned for such offences as all boys commit and for which imprisonment among thieves is surely the worst possible remedy. Further, there is a considerable number who are confined for offences that not even the sternest-minded can rank as crime and for which committal to a felon's prison can but be regarded by every righteous mind, not only as an infamy to the magistrate concerned but even as a scandal to the nation. To this class of offences belong the spinning of tops, the breaking of windows, heaving stones, sleeping in Kensington Gardens, getting over walls and such like misdemeanours for which many lads were suffering their first imprisonment.

We next enquired as to what a boy intended to do when he gained his liberty. 'Do?' And the boy answered without the least fear, even though the warder stood at his side, 'Why when I gets out of here I shall go thieving again – I 'aint got no other way of getting a living'.[30]

Boys and girls were well cared for during their time in gaol. They had a roof over their heads; food provided; they were cleansed and given clothing and shoes; a surgeon tended them when they were ill; a chaplain cared for their spiritual condition, and a schoolteacher taught them to read and write. None of this would they have when they were discharged. They were taken care of for a short time and then thrown out into the cold, hard world once more. On discharge parents, friends or guardians were always informed of the day of release, but very few ever turned up. When the gate was opened, the youngsters once more liberated, wretched, friendless, usually went off together in a gang, back to their lodgings and the only friends and advisers they could find who were the old, experienced inmates of such places.

There was a tendency to see confinement as a boon rather than a punishment, especially to the multitudes of juveniles who had begun to prefer prison to the workhouse or their own miserable homes. One young delinquent was reported as giving this explanation for having smashed a window of the Chelsea workhouse: 'Because, please, they give us 4 lb of oakum to pick in the workhouse in the day and it scrubs our fingers and we can't do it, in the prison we only gets 2 lb and far better vittles.'[31]

The 'comforts' of the gaol and the prison clothing and footwear, which were far better than their own, seemed objects of desire to some desperate youngsters. William Miles of the Prison Discipline Society recalled the following case:

A poor, ragged sweep of about sixteen years of age, without shoes or stockings and his red legs cracked with the cold, was brought to prison for some trifling offence. The warm bath into which he was put much delighted him, but nothing could exceed his astonishment on being told to put on shoes and stockings. 'Am I to wear them? and this? and this too?' he said, as each article of dress was given to him. His joy was complete when they took him to his cell; he turned down the bed-clothes with great delight, and, half-doubting his good fortune, hesitatingly asked if he was really to sleep in the bed! On the following morning, the governor, who had observed the lad's surprise, asked him what he thought of the situation? 'Think of it, master! Why I'm damned if ever I do another stroke of work!' The boy kept his word and was ultimately transported.[32]

5

The Hulks

'Of all the places of confinement that British history records, the hulks were apparently the most brutalising, the most demoralising and the most horrible.'

Sydney and Beatrice Webb [1]

The simple utterance of the word 'hulk' conjures up an image of degradation and viciousness which, particularly to those familiar with the Dickensian portrayal in *Great Expectations*, suggests, the Essex marshes; the clanking irons of chained men working on a mudbank; the high density of guards and fierce dogs alert to any sign of attempted escape; and offshore the rotting hulks of old warships swaying and lurching to the rhythm of the waves and tides. And so it was. The prisoners involved in this system of confinement were those regarded as criminals of the worst type and would have been serving sentences of transportation.

From the time of Elizabeth I enforced exile or transportation was the sentence next in severity to death. Convicted men and women were packed off to America and the West Indies as a convenient way of getting rid of them, and there was always a demand for labour on the plantations. The system continued until the outbreak of the American War of Independence, after which the transportation of convicts to Britain's transatlantic possessions became an impossibility. However, the law seemed to ignore this impediment to proceedings and continued to sentence wrong-doers to transportation, despite the fact that no destination was provided. Until the potential of Australia was realised, the gaols became impossibly overcrowded.

The idea of converting the hulks of old warships, past seaworthiness, into prisons, was first put into effect in 1776 and the prisoners involved were put to 'hard labour' at home in the necessary job of cleaning and banking the River Thames and other navigable rivers. Moored in the Thames estuary and other large harbours these temporary prisons soon became a regular part of the penal system. They were intended for prisoners awaiting transportation, or those unfit to go; but many of those so sentenced never proceeded any further. When Australia was opened up as a transport destination, due to the immense administration difficulties fleets could only be organised about once a year, so prisoners had to wait, sometimes for years, for a suitable ship, if they went at all. Their time on the hulk depended on the ships available and conditions in the colony, as well as on their own health and character.

Because of their unique nature, life on board these floating prisons was quite different from the landbound institutions Any of the convicts who had experienced the strict discipline of such gaols as Millbank before being sent to the hulks were instantly brought into contact with offenders who had not undergone any reformatory discipline whatever. The restrictive conditions on board made total supervision difficult and all the care taken at the other gaols to prevent men talking together and associating with one another was thrown aside, since the first freedom granted to a new convict was given when he reached the hulks and found himself in a crowded 'mess' where he would probably meet old companions in crime. The authorities declared that in these messes only rational conversation was permitted, but it was clear that forty to fifty men could not be crammed into one side of a ship's deck and swing elbow to elbow in hammocks at night without finding ample opportunity for free conversation.

Among those on board these hulks were many juveniles, who were subject to the same penalties, workload and discipline as their elders. As early as 1814 the Inspector of Hulk Establishments reported to the Home Secretary that there was one boy of eleven on board the *Laurel* at Portsmouth, two aged twelve on the *Retribution*, and one aged thirteen, four aged fourteen, four aged fifteen and nine aged sixteen on the *Portland*. The numbers rapidly increased, for between 1 April and 30 June 1827 there were 129 on the *Justitia* at Woolwich, 205 on the *Yorke* at Portsmouth and 238 on the *Euryalus* at Chatham, all aged sixteen and under.[2]

Some of the vessels used were very ancient. One, the *Discovery* had been in Captain Cook's fleet in 1776, so was at least fifty-two years old when it was used as a gaol. But it seemed that any old hulk was acceptable provided it could float. Vessels like the *Discovery* were unstable, overcrowded, damp, vermin-ridden, smelly and insanitary.

Just as the prison reformers were seeking ways to separate men from boys in the mainland prisons, so similar efforts were being made with regard to the hulks. In 1818 the chaplain of the hulk *Retribution*, the Rev. Thomas Price, suggested:

I have heard it mentioned that it is in contemplation to erect Penitentiaries for juvenile depredators; but I am of the opinion that it would be far better, and certainly would bear no proportion of expense, if a frigate were fitted up for their reception, instead of them being scattered as they are now through the different hulks and gaols ... In a ship of this kind, with proper overlookers – and everything would depend upon the choice of such persons – many of these poor children might be reclaimed. By being kept from all intercourse with adult prisoners they would in a few years outgrow the recollection of their former haunts; then according to their general behaviour and improvement, let them be recommended to the Royal Mercy.

Let it be remembered that they are at present but *children* and so situated as to claim our sympathetic concern; by thus doing all we can for them, we are but following the direction of the wise man who declared that if we train up a child in the way he should go, when he is old he will not depart from it.[3]

Price's agitation for a special hulk for boys caught the attention of the Superintendent of Hulks, John Capper, and in 1823 the hulk of the *Bellerophon* at Sheerness was set aside specifically for juvenile use. The *Bellerophon* was the ship in which Napoleon had been brought to England after Waterloo and had already been used as a hulk for nine years. It did not survive long as a juvenile depot, for after two years, in 1825, she was broken up and the boys were transferred to the much smaller frigate, *Euryalus*, which was moored at Chatham. The first chaplain to be appointed was the Rev. Thomas Price.

Price's recommendation that to be successful the juvenile hulk needed proper managers went unheeded. The first overseer, John Steadman, proved to have no special interest in the job. As a result conditions on board were chaotic. 383 boys were packed into the ship, making it impossible to attempt any form of classification. The overcrowding,

poor diet and insanitary conditions led to outbreaks of scurvy and
ophthalmia. Large numbers of boys in a limited space also proved
impossible to control, so much so that in the early days several mutinies
took place. Price insisted that a plan of separation and classification
must be adopted, but his counsel was again rejected; in fact the overseer
must have regarded him as something of a nuisance for after only a
short term he was transferred back to the *Retribution* at Sheerness,
whence he had come, and his place was taken by the Rev. Henry Dawes.
Classification of prisoners never materialised on the *Euryalus* and boys
continued to be herded together in appalling conditions; at one time
there were 400 on board and all the disadvantages of the adult prisons
were reproduced in the dark cells of the lower decks.

Dawes proved to be a bigoted and insensitive chaplain, not one to
criticise the captain or the situation on board, turning a blind eye to
the living conditions of the boys. He made his only concern their
religious education. He gave prolonged blessings before and after each
meal, made the boys learn long passages from the Bible and, at his
services, made sure his sermons lasted from between fifty minutes to
one hour. His lack of sensitivity to the incarceration of children in a
prison hulk is shown in his comment:

> It must be gratifying to a humane mind to know that unfortunate youths
> who are imprisoned in this ship are enjoying the blessing of a good religious
> education ... I would truly say I take a pride in my business; with respect to
> my success therein, verity compels me to say I am indebted to the steady,
> active and prompt cooperation from my captain.[4]

The boys *had* to behave well when they attended his services, with so
many guards around to make sure they did and knowing that the penalty
for misbehaviour was eighteen lashes of the cat even for minor offences
like whispering. For more serious offences the cane was administered
with no limit to the number of strokes.

Unlike their adult counterparts, the prisoners on the *Euryalus* did
not work outside the ship; in fact they never left the vessel from the
time they arrived till the day they were either transported or freed –
except to be taken to the hospital ship. Nor were they allowed any
visitors, so during the time of their confinement on board the only
people they came into contact with were their fellow inmates, their

strict, unapproachable guards and their maniacal chaplain. As their contribution to 'hard labour' most of them were taught tailoring by an older convict, and they were set to work in making clothing for the whole Convict Establishment. As with mainland gaols, the silent system was practised, even during their exercise period. After their midday meal they were escorted up on deck into the open air where they walked round and round the deck – no games were allowed. This one hour of walking round the deck in silence was the only exercise and fresh air they had during the day.

All children need some form of mental and physical stimulus but on the hulk *Euryalus*, under such a hard system of rigid discipline, crushing monotony and obdurate religiosity, this was not forthcoming. As a result the more spirited lads turned their attention to bullying their colleagues. It appears that bullying was incessant and organised; directed and encouraged by a group of boys who were known as the 'Nobs'.

Thomas Dexter, who as a youth had himself been a prisoner on the *Dolphin* and *Cumberland* hulks, was, in 1830, appointed assistant on the hospital ship *Wye*, moored at Chatham. He treated boys from the *Euryalus* and occasionally, as his work demanded, went on board. From this and his own experiences Dexter had a first-hand knowledge of what went on among the young inmates of the hulks. On 15 May 1835 he gave evidence to the Select Committee on Gaols and Houses of Correction:

> It is said that frequently judges sentence a boy out of mercy to the hulks – but if it were a child of mine I would rather see him dead at my feet than see him sent to that place. Many die in the hospital without any feelings of penitence.
>
> The oldest boy I have treated from the hulk was seventeen, the youngest six years seven months. I believe he was sentenced for robbery at Birmingham and the judge asked his mother if she would take him home again provided a lenient sentence was passed and she refused to do it; he was consequently sentenced to transportation that he might be taken care of. The boy died shortly after he came to the hospital and he was so young that he had hardly any religious or moral impression on his mind.
>
> Mr Hope, surgeon of the juvenile hulk *Euryalus*, was a religious man and very devoted to duty, the boys' behaviour in hospital was much more correct than on their ship. I had the opportunity of seeing their conduct on the

Euryalus and I should say that from their imprisonment there they must come out of it much worse than they went in. They did not so much dread the imprisonment but dreaded the ill-treatment of one boy to another. There are what they call 'Nobs', perhaps little boys that were no higher than a table top. I have seen them myself take a broomstick and strike a boy over the arm and almost break his arm and the other dare not say a word to him. The 'Nobs' had such an ascendancy and were so liked by the majority of boys that anybody that dared to say a word against them was sure to be pitched upon by all hands; I have known it when three or four have been obliged to be locked in a cell by themselves in order to shelter there from murder – those they would call 'Noseys', that is, those whom they considered had been to the officers to tell them anything that was going on.

There was sometimes up to forty or fifty boys in the hospital. I have known boys take an old copper button and apply it very hot to the skin and then apply soap and rum to a sore occasioned by the very hot button and wrap it up for two or three days and then show the wound to the doctor and then come to the hospital in a state piteous to behold; it would look like a sore, sometimes the settling of these cases gave more trouble than any others. I have known cases in which they have broken their arms to get into hospital; they hold their arms on a form and let the edge of the table drop on it, they would get other boys to do it for them. The excuse was that they had tumbled down a ladder. I have had patients come into the hospital who have declared that they have not tasted meat for three weeks, they had been obliged to give their portions to the 'Nobs' and had fed themselves on gruel and parings of potatoes and they have committed these acts to get into hospital in order to have a regular diet.[5]

Another witness before that Committee was Samuel Ogilby, a ten-year-old boy from the *Euryalus* who had been on the ship for twenty months. He had been sent from Newgate aged about eight, after being arrested for housebreaking by being pushed through a window by his brother, aged ten at the time, to open the door. They stole clothing and hinges. Samuel could not remember which house it was or where. This was not his first offence, as he had committed several others before he was eight. When asked if he would rather be sent to Botany Bay or stay in the hulk he opted for the former. However, he would have a further four years to serve on the hulk as at the time boys were not transported until they were fourteen or fifteen.

On 31 May 1835 there were 258 boys on board the *Euryalus*, the

1. The bright lights of the pub. Drink offered one of the few escapes from misery for both men and women, but often left children at risk.

2. The rookery, St Giles, in the early nineteenth century.

3. Children asleep in the street. Engraving by Gustave Doré.

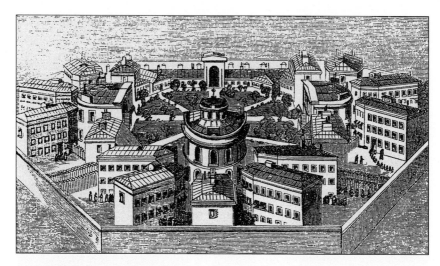

4. Tothill Fields Prison.

5. Boys exercising at Tothill Fields Prison.

6. Girls' school at Tothill Fields Prison.

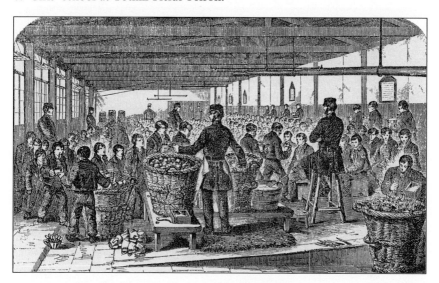

7. Dinner in the oakum room at Tothill Fields Prison.

8. The whip.   9. The whipping-post.

10. Cell with prisoner at 'Crank-Labour', Surrey House of Correction.

11. HMS *Discovery* as a hulk at Deptford, 1828.

12. HMS *York*, as a hulk at Portsmouth, 1828.

13. Mary Carpenter, the prison reformer. (*City of Bristol Museum and Art Gallery*)

youngest aged eight and the oldest sixteen. One boy, George Fraser, aged twelve, had already spent four and a half years on the ship. Of the twenty boys who had been on the ship for over two years, eight were aged twelve or under.[6] Perhaps these long-serving youngsters were the 'Nobs' and perhaps, in a short time, Samuel Ogilby would join their number. Such first-hand evidence as these witnesses provided, gives a much sounder idea of life on the juvenile hulk than the standard reports of the chaplain or overseer, who tended to gloss over the facts.

There were, of course, many more juveniles sentenced to transportation than could be catered for on the one hulk which was set aside for the purpose of detaining them. The *Yorke* at Portsmouth and the *Justitia* at Woolwich also held large numbers of juveniles. In fact, several aged under seventeen were present on every government prison hulk. They had to fit in as best as they could with the adult offenders.

The length of time boys spent aboard the hulks between conviction and transportation varied considerably. For instance Thomas Arnold, a thirteen-year-old labourer, was convicted on 3 March 1835 and on 18 June was put on a transport ship. He arrived at Hobart, Van Diemen's Lane, 102 days later. Thomas Patterson, aged thirteen, who was convicted of housebreaking and sentenced to transportation for life on 18 June 1816, was not so lucky. He spent four years on a hulk before being transported to New South Wales.[7] Boys under thirteen were not generally considered as transportees and had to endure conditions on the hulks or gaols until they reached a suitable age.

In Ireland there was no segregation of boys and adults on the two vessels used there as prison hulks. These were the *Essex* stationed at Kingstown (Dun Laoghaire) and the *Surprise* at Cork. During the time these hulks were in operation two boys under ten, 118 between ten and fourteen, and 292 between fourteen and sixteen served time on board. Life for the boys on the Irish hulks was even worse than on the English establishment, for as well as there being no segregation or classification of age or criminality, no work was provided to occupy their time. Prisoners had to wear leg-irons at all times and were subjected to such punishments as time in a black hole, stocks, neck yokes and reduced diet.[8] Little wonder they came out physically and morally stunted.

If conditions on the Irish hulks were bad, there was one destination which was far worse. Far away from the attentions of central authority the prison hulks stationed at Bermuda in the West Indies were the most notorious of all. There were four old warships used as offshore prisons in the 1830s – the *Antelope, Coromandel, Dromedary* and *Weymouth*. They were used for prisoners whose crimes were considered as serious, such as manslaughter, desertion and political offences. A few thirteen to sixteen year olds could always be found among the numbers.

In 1848 the Governor of Bermuda, Captain Charles Eliott, wrote to the Colonial Secretary, Earl Grey:

> I have the honour to transmit a list of sixty-eight prisoners under nineteen years of age ... I hope your Lordship will accede to my earnest wish for them to be removed as speedily as possibly from a mode of punishment attended with serious risks and consequences not to be thought of without shame and grief ... Poor and scanty food and the hard things of their infancy have for the most part left these lads with a low stature and more childish appearance than their age alone would explain ... Though it will shock HM Government to perceive that twelve of them are under sixteen years of age and that one, aged thirteen, has been sentenced to fifteen years transportation for sheep stealing! Sharp private whipping and a brief season of separate confinement on short diet and hard work would surely be a more appropriate punishment for these boys than transportation to the hulks. The reflection of their condition on release from such association is appalling both for themselves and society.[9]

The hulk establishment in Bermuda carried on until 1862, five years after their abolition in Britain.

By their very nature the hulks were unhealthy places. In the cramped conditions, diseases such as tuberculosis, scrofula, lung disorders, diarrhoea and scurvy were common. As washing and laundry facilities were minimal, human fleas proliferated and the poor diet of bread made from sour flour and no fresh vegetables was responsible for the diarrhoea and scurvy.

The daily regime on board the *Euryalus* was described in the Report of the Select Committee on Police in the Metropolis in 1828: [10]

5.30 am	All hands called.
5.45	Muster on deck, breakfast; then one of the three decks is washed, which is done every morning alternately.

6.45	Each prisoner brings his hammock, stows it away on deck and proceeds with his labour – making clothing for the Convict Establishment.
12 noon	Dinners are served by the officers and the prisoners are locked up in their wards to eat it, supervised by guards. After dinner they are allowed one hour in the open air – but they might play no kind of game. They walk round and round on the deck.
1.20 pm	Return to work.
5.45	Finish work.
6.30	School.
7.30	Prayers in chapel; then all prisoners mustered and locked in their wards for the night.

There is no mention of the boys being given any supper or any food after the midday meal, although each ward had a kettle of tea provided. If this was the case, no wonder the 'Nobs' commandeered the food from their less hardy shipmates.

Some young boys suffered this monotonous and monstrous regime for up to five years without ever leaving the ship. The experience must have left them, in James Greenwood's words, 'against every man'. The best they could hope for was to be chosen for transportation. Occasionally 'drafts' of boys were sent from the hulks when there was space for them on the transport ships. The most ever sent at one time from the *Euryalus* was on 13 November 1838, when 168 boys were despatched to Van Diemen's Land on board the *Pyramus*.[11] The hulk would not have remained half-empty for long; there were always plenty of candidates waiting to fill the available spaces.

In the end the juvenile hulk experiment proved to be a complete failure. This was confirmed by the Inspector of the Hulk Establishments, J. J. Capper, who admitted to the Select Committee on the Police that the results were not encouraging. When asked what had been the conduct of boys after release, he concluded: 'I am sorry to have to say it has been very indifferent for eight out of ten that had been liberated returned to their old careers.'[12] After hearing the evidence, the Select Committee recommended the abandonment of the use of hulks for boys and suggested instead the use of unoccupied barracks or forts near to the ports from which those sentenced to transportation would eventually sail.[13] This recommendation was ignored and the system carried on as usual and was still in operation twenty-seven years later.

The *Euryalus* continued functioning as a juvenile prison hulk at Chatham for another sixteen years to be scrapped in 1844 and the *Yorke*, which also catered for convicted boys, was kept going as a hulk at Portsmouth until 1852, when it was given back to the Admiralty to be broken up.[14] As late as 1854 it was estimated that 150 juvenile prisoners had passed through the hulks at Woolwich in that year.[15]

The failure of the hulk system in general eventually led to a spate of new prison building. Millbank was constructed at great expense on the principles of the separate system catering solely for those sentenced to transportation. This was shortly followed by Pentonville. The authorities knew that something had to be done for the boys on board the notorious juvenile hulks. Ideas were suggested, considered and then rejected. A new initiative was desperately needed.

6

Parkhurst: The Children's Prison

'We do try to give encouragement to deserving boys, our own good
nature permits us to give them as much as we can, but our real
difficulty is with respect to the bad boys, to control the hardened
and vicious and thieving lads with whom we have to deal.'

Captain Donatus O'Brien, Director of Convict Prisons [1]

The crucial initiative eventually came from the Select Committee on
Gaols, which sat in 1835, and decided that a separate prison for juveniles
should be established. Their recommendation soon gained parliamentary approval and in 1836 another committee was set up to report on
the proposed juvenile prison.

Dartmoor was first considered, but the expense of conversion proved
to be too great. Portchester Castle, which had been used for the confinement of French prisoners-of-war, was next looked at but the building
was too small and the church, which was part of the establishment, was
used regularly by local inhabitants – a good enough reason for making
the site unsuitable. Waltham Abbey and Enfield Lock were next considered, both being government-owned, but they would have needed
enclosing completely by a high brick wall and Enfield Lock was subject
to flooding, so both were dismissed.

On 18 July 1836 the committee looked at Parkhurst, part of the Albany
Barracks, on the Isle of Wight. The buildings concerned then stood in
the centre of fifty acres of land owned by the Crown. The site was
considered:

exceedingly healthy and remote enough from other buildings and having
adequate water connection for the conveyance of convict boys to the prison
and for their removal to the colonies when their period of confinement was
expired.

The buildings had previously been used as a hospital for the barracks and as an asylum for invalid children from the military school at Chelsea. This proposition was accepted and work went ahead converting the old hospital buildings into a juvenile prison to house 280 convicts. The architect selected was George Thomas Bullar, who in August 1836 estimated the conversion sum at £15,390. This amount, however, proved to be an underestimate for on 28 December 1836 the Inspectors of Prisons wrote to the Home Secretary, Lord John Russell, suggesting the sum be increased to £18,000 to allow for adapting the present buildings into a suitable prison.[2]

The Parkhurst Act was passed in 1838 by statute 1 and 2 Victoria, c 82 for establishing, for the first time in England, a separate prison for young offenders.

> 3. It shall be lawful for one of Her Majesty's principal Secretaries of State to direct the removal to Parkhurst Prison of any young offender, male or female, under Sentence or Order of Transportation and those under Sentence of Imprisonment, having been examined by an experienced Surgeon or Apothecary so appear to be free from any putrid or infectious distemper to be removed from the Gaol, Prison or place in which such offender shall be confined.

> 4. Every offender sent there shall continue there until they be transported or shall be entitled to their liberty or unless the Secretary of State shall direct the removal of such offenders to the Gaol from which they have been brought.

> 5. The Secretary of State can at any time order any offender to be removed from Parkhurst Prison as incorrigible and in every such case the offender so removed shall be liable to be transported or confined under the original sentence to the full extent of the terms specified in the original sentence.

Section 8 made it lawful for corporal punishment to be practised and Section 12 gave prisoners who attempted to escape an extra term of imprisonment when recaptured.

Although the idea of a separate prison for juveniles had been discussed and debated for many years, the resolution on which the first prison was based was rather vague about how the system should be run. For instance, in the original Act male and female offenders are mentioned, but when the prison opened only boys were admitted. The Act also refers to those 'under sentence of imprisonment', but only those sentenced to transportation eventually came. It appears that the early organisation of Parkhurst was left, more or less, to its first managers to approach the problems on their own as best as they could. Success or failure would depend on the sympathy and experience of those who held office.

On 26 December 1838, 102 boys arrived at Parkhurst; forty-nine from the *Yorke* hulk at Portsmouth and fifty-three from Millbank Gaol. On 10 January 1839 another two boys were sent from the *Yorke*. On 11 March twelve boys arrived from the *Euryalus* and another nineteen from the same hulk on the 20 May. Eleven more came from the *Yorke* on 1 August.[3] These 146 boys were the first inmates to serve their sentences in the new prison and they knew that they would stay there until their term was served or they were sent to New South Wales or Van Diemen's Land (Tasmania).

The first governor was Captain Robert Woollcombe, who reported in 1838 that the initial discipline consisted of deprivation of liberty; wearing an iron on the leg; a strongly marked prison dress; a diet reduced to its minimum; the imposition of silence on all occasions; and an uninterrupted surveillance by officers. Almost immediately attempts were made to modify and improve this draconian system. In February 1839 the Home Office instructed the governor that leg irons should be removed for good conduct and in September 1840 they were abolished altogether. In the governor's Annual Report for 1844 it is noted that: 'The previous diet had not been considered sufficiently nourishing to sustain the vigour of growing boys and that a new diet had been introduced in November 1843 and an improvement in the boys' health and energy had been recorded.'

To help towards the provision of fresh meat and milk for the ever-growing number of inmates, in 1839 Governor Woollcombe received the large sum of £500 from the government 'for the use of the farm'. On 2 March, four cows, eleven pigs, straw, oats, a cart and milk apparatus were purchased; on 1 May, four oxen and a sow pig were added to the livestock and on 11 July, £2 8s. 0d. was paid out for sowing ten acres of grass.[4]

As might have been expected, the first inmates of the new prison were sent from the hulks and these would have been the younger boys who still had a few years to serve. Those nearing the end of their term would have been kept on the *Euryalus* and the *Yorke*, being considered by that time too incorrigible or contaminated to benefit from a new system of training. The hulk boys, however, were only a small portion of the large number of children sentenced to transportation. The majority would have been kept in local gaols and in the 1830s and 1840s the greater number would have spent time in or passed through Millbank on their way to the transport ships.

Millbank Gaol, which stood on the banks of the Thames, on the site of the present Tate Britain Gallery, was built in the 1820s as a receptacle for:

> such convicts under sentence or order to transportation as the Secretary of State may direct to be removed there; they are to continue there until transported according to the law, or conditionally pardoned, or until they become entitled to their freedom ... thus appropriating this extensive penal institution as a depot for the reception of all convicts under sentence or order to Transportation in Great Britain in lieu of their being sent directly to the hulks. If the convict is young he is to be sent as soon as possible to Parkhurst provided he is a fit subject.[5]

Not all youngsters were automatically sent to Parkhurst; there was selection – they were not all considered 'fit subjects'. In the case of a very hardened offender, where there was a probability of his doing mischief to the new regime, it was up to the governor to decide whether or not to accept him. He would not, for instance, have accepted the 'Nobs' from the *Euryalus*. Another reason for refusal would have been the age and general demeanour of the boys.

The governor of Millbank told Henry Mayhew:

> When a convict is of extremely tender years we try to get him removed to a refuge – Her Majesty's conditional pardon being granted on his being received there. We consider prisoners of tender years – up to thirteen. Like one child we have of nine years of age who has been twelve times in prison.[6]

The problem of age and stature is also brought to light in the evidence of Captain W. J. Williams, Government Inspector of Prisons:

> When I was inspector of Millbank prison my attention was drawn to many of these boys who were really so diminutive and of an age which seemed to render them quite unfit for transportation at all, or of even being sent to Parkhurst; I therefore recommended that they be sent to the Philosophical

Society's refuge under conditional pardons. They were sent and the great majority turned out remarkably well.

There are a great number of small boys who ought never to be sent to prison at all but who are subjects for the Union Workhouse. I recall at Liverpool a recommendation I made several years ago was productive of good effect, which was, whenever there was a boy of this description who had no parent or relation, he should invariably be sent to the nearest workhouse. The parents of some of these children have lost sight of them for years ... Corporal punishment can never relieve us from the scourge of juvenile delinquency. On most boys it has no effect at all because they are slaves of a certain condition ... They can do nothing but come in and out of prison. After a certain time they get an uneasy feeling that they must be transported.[7]

An explanation as to why no young girls were sent to Parkhurst comes from the governor of Millbank:

There have not been many young girls at Millbank, very few girls of tender age have been received at the penitentiary. I cannot say what would be done with very young girls, I should have to refer for orders. There are two of fifteen here but they are the youngest.

Up to the 1850s boys sent to Parkhurst were under the serious sentence of transportation and would certainly have already experienced several terms in prison. A selection from the return of the number of previous imprisonments of boys admitted in 1852 shows:

Joseph Reid, aged eleven, 7 April 1851 at Liverpool, felony, seven years transportation, seven times.
Jonathan Moyses, aged eleven, 8 April 1851 at Ely, horse stealing, ten years transportation, seven times.
Robert Tasker, aged thirteen, 6 May 1851 at Perth, thieving, seven years transportation, three times.
Michael Quillan, aged thirteen, 19 May 1851 at Knutsford, stealing an ass, seven years transportation, five times.
John Toohey, aged thirteen, 20 May 1851 at Clerkenwell, picking pockets, seven years transportation, four times.
Thomas Adams, aged fourteen, 7 July 1851 at Nottingham, stealing a silver watch, seven years transportation, six times.[8]

Seven years was the normal sentence for youngsters. A few more serious cases had ten years and very rarely, for such offences as manslaughter, a fourteen-year sentence would be given. There were no juvenile 'lifers' at Parkhurst.

In name and in fact Parkhurst was a prison, established by the government for the reception of boys sentenced to transportation. Great expectations of the benefits were entertained by some benevolent and kind-hearted judges, who, when children were brought before them accused of felony and housebreaking, sentenced them nominally to transportation in the hope that they would soon be granted a conditional pardon or sent to Parkhurst. Others thought the discipline of Parkhurst would be good for a destitute boy in preparing him for a colonial life. Some used the sentence in order to give a boy a long and settled stay in an orderly system rather than allow him to be constantly in and out of gaol. Generally, boys were not sent out to Australia before they reached the age of fourteen, so many had only two or three years left on their sentence and, as young labourers were in great demand in the colony, it was highly likely that a boy would receive a conditional pardon on arrival allowing him an element of freedom he would never have had at home.

There were always more criminal children sentenced to transportation than there were places at Parkhurst, so many of them would by necessity have been sent out direct from Millbank. In 1844 Captain Groves, governor of Millbank reported; 'I received thirty-one transports under twelve years of age; seventy-five from twelve to fourteen; and 233 from fourteen to seventeen making a total of 339.' The following year he received thirty-four under twelve; eighty-two from twelve to fourteen; and 296 from fourteen to seventeen. In two years a total of 751 children were awaiting transportation.[9]

At one time the prison inspectors seem to have imposed an age limit on prospective entrants, as suggested by Sergeant Adams, Chairman of the Middlesex Quarter Sessions:

At the August Sessions I tried Thomas Miller, aged eight years, for stealing boxes and sentenced him to be imprisoned for one month and once whipped. At the January Sessions he was tried again for robbing a till. I sentenced him to seven years transportation for the purpose of sending him to Parkhurst but the prison inspectors thought him too young and too diminutive and his sentence was commuted to three months imprisonment. On 14 March 1846 he was again convicted of larceny, and as he had been in custody eight or nine times, he was again sentenced to transportation and again rejected by the prison inspectors, his sentence this time being commuted to imprisonment for two years. He was discharged on 13 May 1848 and in July 1848 was convicted again and sentenced to fourteen days imprisonment. On the 4th of this month I again sentenced him to be whipped and imprisoned for two days. He is now only twelve years of age so he will continue his career for another two years before he will be qualified for Parkhurst.[10]

In the Bill establishing Parkhurst periodical reports by visitors to the prison were required. The first Report, dated July 1839, gives an insight into the very early days when Robert Woollcombe was assisted by the chaplain, the Rev. Thomas England:

Prison duties are performed by half-past-seven, every bed is made up, dormitories cleaned and ventilated and made ready for inspection, prisoners and cells are inspected. Prisoners then march to breakfast at 8 o'clock. From 8.30 to 9 there is a religious service and Bible reading. From 9 to 9.45 an exercise period and then work commences. There are thirty-three tailors, twenty shoemakers and two carpenters. 12 to 12.45 more exercise. 1 o'clock dinner. 1.30 back to their trades. 6 o'clock occupations cease and prisoners have supper. 6 to 7.30 school period or exercises. 7.30 another religious service. 8 o'clock the watchman comes on duty and prisoners are locked up for the night. One has fifteen years transportation; twelve have ten years and eighty have seven years.[11]

In 1843 a new governor was appointed. He was Captain George Hall, who had previously been in the Civil Service involved in convict management in Van Diemen's Land. Unlike his predecessor, he was very knowledgeable about transportation and its application. One of the first changes he made was to divide the prison into five wards:

A general ward
A junior ward for boys under thirteen
A probationary ward
A refractory ward
An infirmary ward

Captain Donatus O'Brien, Director of Convict Prisons at this time, was well acquainted with Parkhurst and its problems. He was sympathetic to the idea of a probationary period:

We do try to give encouragement to deserving boys. Our own good nature permits us to give them as much as we can but our real difficulty is with respect to bad boys, to control the hardened and vicious and thieving lads with whom we have to deal. We bear in mind the character of these boys, they are exceedingly youthful, they are utterly reckless, many of them appear incorrigible, they have been in prison over and over again, therefore we place them in separate confinement giving them time and opportunity for reflection, where they may be able better to receive moral and religious instruction.[1]

On arrival at the prison all boys were put in the Probationary Ward where they were confined to a separate cell for a period of four months. They were placed under the special instruction of an officer and the chaplain and during this time their capabilities, character and habits were noted. Originally prisoners were forbidden to speak at any time but this rule was relaxed and at certain periods of the day, called 'recesses', when the boys came out of school, they were allowed to converse in the yard in the presence of the master, 'provided there was no boisterous merriment or unseemly conduct'. At all other times the silent system prevailed. In this ward boys were taught to read, spell, write and calculate. When not in school they were occupied in picking oakum under the surveillance of officers. After four months, on the recommendation of the chaplain, prisoners were removed to the Junior or General Ward according to their age.

In the Junior Ward they attended school for two and a half days a week and the rest of the time were employed in industrial labour. School routine in 1845 consisted of the ward being divided into two divisions with one attending classes on Monday, Wednesday and Friday and the other on Tuesday, Thursday and Saturday. There was a strong emphasis on religious teaching – Bible reading, analysing and memorising psalms and the catechism: but they also had secular lessons including – 'useful knowledge lessons', geography and the principles and practice of music. One day a week they had 'principles of arithmetic', including mental and Pestalozzian problems. In these sessions various sums were chalked up on the blackboard for the whole class. Reading and writing meant copying from Mulhauser's cards, dictation, spelling, reading, etymology, the meaning of words and secular reading, which included Chambers' *Introduction to the Sciences and Rudiments of Knowledge*. Their scriptural reading involved various books on religious principles and Ostervald's *Abridged Scripture History*.[12]

For their industrial work, about thirty boys were employed exclusively in the tailors' shop, twelve others helped with pumping the prison water supply and the remainder were engaged in agricultural labour. They were also instructed in knitting, which they worked at in wet weather. All boys had to take their turn in daily prison duties. A few boys were sent to Australia from this ward but generally they moved up to the General Ward when they reached the age of thirteen and if their behaviour warranted it.

In the General Ward boys were offered a wider range of employment. There was shoemaking, brickmaking, blacksmithing, gardening, painting, cooking and laundry work. In wet weather they did their knitting and made all the stockings worn in the prison. By 1850 there were eighty acres of farmland to attend to, so the majority in this ward would have been engaged in the fields and in looking after animals – just the sort of employment they would find when they were sent to Australia. To monitor this outside work a large number of guards were engaged to keep a watch on the lads and make sure there were no escapes. The guards were sometimes over-vigilant and would report any boy for the slightest breach of discipline and for not working to full capacity.[13]

The Rev. Joseph Spear, who was chaplain and superintendent of the Junior Ward from 1847, reported:

The Junior Ward consists generally of those aged twelve and under, we do sometimes have those as young as nine but very seldom. It is difficult sometimes to know the age of boys, we are obliged to judge by their appearance more than by their own representation for we cannot always depend on their statements.

At 7 o'clock in the morning we have a service which takes half-an-hour. During the morning I investigate all reports of misconduct brought before me by the principal warder. Sometimes I feel it necessary to see the warder who reported the boy in order that I may enquire fully into the case as I am always very anxious that no boy shall be punished without deserving it.

I visit the infirmary and read prayers and a chapter from the Bible while visiting the sick. I go round and visit the schools whilst the schoolmaster is giving instruction and am frequently in the yard whilst the boys are there.

On Sundays I take a Bible class of twenty boys. I have them entirely to myself. I go through the prison in that way. The boys read to me and I examine them on the scriptures. I speak to them in a familiar way. During the day I go out amongst the boys whilst they labour in the fields or at their trade. Sometimes an officer reports that a boy is not working diligently, I say a few words to the boy and encourage him to work better; that generally has a good effect. Each week I visit the boys in the Probationary Ward preparing them for life in the Junior Ward. I advise the governor when a boy is fit to come out of the Probationary Ward and a few times I have had to recommend that a boy stays there for a few extra months. At present there are twenty-five boys in the Probationary Ward and 200 in the Junior.[14]

In the Refractory Ward the boys being punished were subject to strict penal discipline. Each individual was in separate confinement and his diet was below that of the other classes. His only exercise was taken in silence marching round and round in an enclosed yard in the presence of officers. He wore a yellow suit in place of the ordinary prison dress. This class sat apart from the other prisoners in chapel. By this discipline it was hoped that the recalcitrant prisoners would be induced to exercise constant self-control for a considerable period. It was estimated that out of 300 boys about 6 per cent would be transferred quarterly to the Refractory Ward and accommodation was provided for about that number. This was the only ward in which corporal punishment was practised – forty boys were whipped during 1841. There was no corporal or shackled punishment in any of the other wards.

The Infirmary Ward was attended by a surgeon who reported each year to the prison inspectors. In 1841 Surgeon Benjamin Browning treated 418 boys during the year. The diseases he treated were – cynanche (severe sore throat), rheumatism, catarrh, diarrhoea, cutaneous and scalp afflictions, boils, abscesses and chilblains. Various cases of cephalagia (headache), ophthalmia, dyspepsia, colic and accidental wounds were also treated. All cases were recorded in a folio book. He blamed breakfasts of oatmeal gruel for the numerous cases of eruptions of the skin.[15]

In 1848 a small addition of bread was added to the usual allowance of breakfast gruel and soup was added to the dinner in another effort to improve the diet. By 1851 gruel was dispensed with altogether for breakfast; instead they had bread and cocoa with molasses. On three days of the week dinner consisted of a pint of 'very substantial' soup and the other four days 3½ oz boiled beef and broth with potatoes and bread. However, for supper every day they had – one pint of oatmeal gruel. The menu was the same every day except Sunday. Captain O'Brien explained:

> We have one special indulgence which may appear trivial – anybody who has had anything to do with juveniles will know that you cannot get at them in any way so effectually as through their stomachs – and taking that into consideration we have added to the Sunday dinner a plum pudding. Boys who have committed any trivial offence are deprived of their pudding, they are marched out and paraded up and down the yard while those who have conducted themselves properly are eating their pudding. It may appear to many people absurd that it should be so but practically it has had greater effect upon their conduct than almost all else.[16]

In 1851 there were twenty-four officers employed to watch over the prisoners; on average one to about eighteen boys. Warders could not punish boys but could report them for misconduct and recommend a meal of bread and water. They were obviously not popular with the inmates and there were instances of officers being attacked, particularly while supervising prisoners working in the fields. The worst of these attacks took place in March 1851 when an assistant warder, who was described as being mild and inoffensive, was very severely wounded by two heavy blows on the head struck by two different boys. The prisoners concerned were whipped, placed in solitary confinement and sentenced to wear leg irons. They had two months in solitary on a reduced diet and wore irons, even while sleeping, for the whole two months. 'Irons' in this case consisted of a ring round each ankle and a light chain connecting the two and another chain which could be attached to the waistband of the trousers or a chain cable. This punishment was ordered by the Director of Convict Prisons and was only used for atrocious cases.[17]

Parkhurst Prison was surrounded by walls but the farm was not. Boys who worked at trades were always within the walls, but for those who worked on the land there was always the temptation to escape. Over the years many tried to run away from the farm, as many as thirty-four in 1849, but none ever successfully got away from the island; they were all brought back, usually within hours of their bid for freedom. The best attempt was on the evening of 11 November 1847 when three boys contrived to escape by means of a plank which had negligently been left outside the saw-pit after dusk. The prisoners were apprehended and brought back the following morning, having in the meantime stolen some articles from a house in Cowes to aid their escape from the island; for this offence they were committed to the County Gaol at Winchester for trial at the ensuing Assizes. In 1849 five boys tried to set fire to their dormitory in an effort to escape, but the other boys, who were probably frightened by the incident, quickly summoned the watchmen and the matter was soon in hand.

There were some boys in the Refractory Ward who, in spite of solitary confinement, bread and water, extra drill and whipping, proved too tough to handle. These 'incorrigibles' were either transported as convicts or returned as ordinary prisoners, and, according to Section 5, would therefore forfeit their term of servitude at Parkhurst and serve the full term in a penal colony. The worst of the incorrigibles described in the Prison Register was John Gavin, aged thirteen, sentenced for larceny, who was described as a bad character and fractious. He was transported in June 1842 to Western Australia, where two years later he was executed for murder.

In the time they spent at Parkhurst before being shipped out to Australia the boys who did behave themselves and conformed to the system had a good opportunity to improve themselves. They received an excellent education, far better than anything that would have been available to them on the outside at that time, and they were trained either at a trade or in agricultural labour, both of which would put them in a good position for employment in the growing colony; they also received religious and moral instruction on a daily basis.

Governor Hall even went to great pains to get his charges confirmed before they were sent out, but this proved more difficult than he anticipated. In a letter of 31 October 1844 to the prison visitors he mentions:

> the matter of bringing before the Bishop for confirmation, annually, such of the prisoners as may be desirous and after careful examination, qualified, to receive that rite. We have already ascertained that scarcely an individual among them has been confirmed, in fact that would naturally be inferred from their past history and present situation. While in here, however, they are brought under the influence of a remedial system, the design of this instruction is to effect, if possible, amendment of the will and affections as the only sure means of producing amended conduct.

The visitors' reply was not very encouraging:

The confirmation of boys is one involving considerable difficulty. The penal condition of the boys and their habits of restraint and obedience – the inducements which they have to please and to deceive their superior officers – the distinction which the rite would confer and the hope which would be generally entertained that it would recommend them to the favour of their officers – are objections which induce us to think that it would not be expedient to administer the rite – at least in the manner proposed. We are also of the opinion that on the commission of an act of gross misconduct by a boy who had received confirmation – an occurrence by no means unlikely to happen – a bad effect, in a religious sense, would be produced on the minds of the prisoners at large.

Three years later, on learning that the Bishop of Winchester was to visit the Isle of Wight for the purpose of holding confirmations, George Hall tried again. He asked the bishop to consecrate a prison burial ground and while he was there to administer the rite of confirmation to prisoners whom the chaplain thought fully prepared to receive it. This time the visitors and the bishop agreed, and, on 21 October 1847, 187 boys were confirmed. Rev. H. Smith, chaplain of the General Ward, commented that, 'Had it not been that a short time previously a draft of 125 senior boys had left for Australia there would have been at least 100 more'.[18]

Only the prisoners who were regarded as incorrigible and irreclaimable were transported as convicts to penal settlements. The majority from Parkhurst were sent to parts of Australia where they were given a conditional pardon on arrival, making them free settlers so long as they stayed in the colony, or given a 'ticket of leave' which meant they could be immediately employed under certain conditions, or they could have been legally apprenticed – all under local supervision. In 1842/3 a scheme was tried whereby the most deserving boys were helped to emigrate to New Zealand, where they were apprenticed, but it was obviously not a success for none were sent after 1843. After this date boys who were recommended to be sent abroad were mainly sent to Port Philip or Western Australia where they would have been apprenticed on arrival. For instance, on the 20 August 1844, eighteen boys from Parkhurst were sent to Western Australia including:

Terence McGrath, who had come from the Westminster House of Correction, aged twelve, on 12 May 1841, charged with larceny. Described as a tailor and good tempered.

William Chifney, who had come from Newgate, aged thirteen, on 20 September 1841, charged with larceny. Described as an errand boy.

Charles Pengelly, who had come from Plymouth, aged twelve, on 25 October 1841, charged with larceny. Described as an active and clever boy.

Edmund Brewer, who had come from Exeter, aged thirteen, on 5 April 1841. Described as a labourer with good behaviour.

William Sparks, who had come from Maidstone, aged twelve, on 15 March 1841. Described as a labourer.[19]

The method of a boy's disposal was organised from Parkhurst. Prisoners remained at the gaol for two or three years until the governor decided that their conduct was good enough for him to recommend them to the Secretary of State for a 'ticket of leave'. On that recommendation the Home Department communicated with the Colonial Office and instructions were sent to the governor of a colony to furnish those named with 'tickets of leave' on their arrival. The boys were embarked on the next available transport ship and sent out. The Colonial Secretaries received notice from the colonies when it was desirable that so many prisoners were sent out. Ships carried between two hundred and three hundred transportees and the governor was informed by the Director of Convict Prisons that there was room on a certain ship for so many prisoners from Parkhurst.[20]

The boys so transported were immediately taken into employment by settlers who had probably taken other such boys and been satisfied with them. This was the great incentive at Parkhurst: inmates were made aware that if they did well and followed the rules they would have a good recommendation. They also realised that being so far away they would be exposed to less temptation than they would be if released at home and so removed from their former associations would have an opportunity of a new start in life. The boys regarded it as emigration.

The Rev. Joseph Spear was well aware of this desirability of getting to Australia:

Boys regard the colonial life for which they are destined more as a reward than a punishment. I have known boys prefer going abroad than returning home … if the choice were given to boys at Parkhurst to go home I am sure very few would prefer it.[21]

This admission that boys were reluctant to return home confirms the poor family life most of them had experienced. By the time they were approaching their final year before transportation there would have been little communication between them and their family or associates. There is no evidence in the records of any family visiting at Parkhurst. Apart from its isolated position, which made travel difficult, the directors discouraged any correspondence between family and friends.

> Under Rule 242 no prisoner shall be allowed to send or receive any letter during his confinement; but this general rule shall not preclude the committee of visitors from allowing a prisoner in special cases to be informed of the contents of a letter sent to him, or in special cases to answer a letter – the answer being approved by the committee.[22]

The prison authorities supposed that correspondence kept up between prisoners and their friends tended strongly to destroy in the minds of both parties the salutary effects of imprisonment, and they really believed that since communication by letter had been restricted the prison had attained a special penal character not found in similar institutions.

Younger inmates worked a seven-hour day, mainly indoors. Almost half their time was spent in classrooms, a fact which Captain Hall believed contributed in no small measure to the restlessness of the boys in his care, who had never been accustomed to so sedentary and confined an existence. In their report for 1849 the Prison Visitors expressed dissatisfaction with general progress and suggested a number of changes which would greatly alter the approach to the management of the prison.

Lieutenant Colonel Joshua Jebb, RE, Surveyor General of Prisons and Chairman of the Directors of Convict Prisons, who was also one of the visitors for the management of Parkhurst since its first opening, wrote to Sir George Grey in 1849:

> Parkhurst was arranged at a time when there was a class of older boys at Millbank and an institution at Point Puer in Van Diemen's Land to which all who misconducted themselves were immediately sent. Both these means of carrying out a period of discipline being now abandoned, some boys will be detained at Parkhurst for longer periods and the standard age will be raised.

In order to meet these changes and render Parkhurst a useful auxiliary in the present plan of convict management, I conceive some changes are now called for: First, the introduction of more labour and industrial training into the system. Secondly, that some incentives to industry and good conduct should be placed before the boys. Thirdly, that badges for good conduct, industry and attainment in school should be awarded and that there should be a classification based upon the badges obtained, to which certain small privileges should be accredited.

I am of the opinion that there is more school instruction and far less labour than is necessary or useful. When a boy has attained a certain point in school which has insured him an amount of information suitable to his situation in life and such as will facilitate his future progress, instruction should give place to labour and industrial training.

My experience is that when attainments in the ordinary branches of education are pushed beyond the point which gives boys facilities in reading, writing and arithmetic, the further cultivation of their minds in higher branches may make them under value the humble employments which are the only ones open to them on arrival in the colonies. Such as they become discontented and do not give that satisfaction to their masters that they might otherwise do. In such cases the school instruction which has been imparted at great cost becomes a bar to their success instead of promoting it.

There is a great want of inducement to industry. With regard to the classification and privileges attaching to it, I have found this principle of a gradation of punishment to work so well in the military prisons that I have no doubt it would prove a powerful incentive to good conduct.[23]

Jebb's propositions were adopted and from November 1849 much more time was devoted to industrial employment. Prisoners were 'classified' into smaller groups under an officer who had direct and continuous superintendence of the same boys and, as a stimulus to employment, they wore badges on their arms indicative of their good conduct. The boys who were 'badged' also received a small payment which they received at the end of their term or when they arrived in a colony. The system seemed to work satisfactorily, as there was a great diminution in the number of punishments and a marked improvement in general conduct. A boy had to be in the establishment for eight months before the money started accumulating, so four months after leaving the Probationary Ward he would be entitled to 2d. a week in the Junior Ward or 3d. in the General Ward. If his conduct continued to be exemplary after another six months he would receive 4d. or 6d. Those who were not well-behaved received nothing. It was from the 'badged' group that boys were selected for 'tickets of leave' or sent out 'on licence'.[24]

As for the extra labour, according to the yearly report dated 10 January 1853, there were about 500 inmates, 928 jackets, sixty-two waistcoats, 927 pairs of trousers, 1088 shirts, 188 flannel waistcoats, 206 pairs of drawers were made, 1939 pairs of socks were knitted, 261 pairs of boots were made and many more mended. The operation of the brickyard consisted of making 140,000 bricks for building purposes, 1260 large drain tiles, 6100 pantiles, 83,500 large and small field drain tiles, 4100 drainpipes and 1200 ridge tiles. The washing, baking and cooking was all done by prisoners. 12½ acres of land had been drained, four acres trenched, seventy yards of large tile drain laid, eighty-eight yards of new road made, 180 yards of old hedge grubbed up, 330 yards of road dug up, 1000 yards of new brook cut on the watercourse from the forest, three large cesspools for liquid manure dug, one large pond for liquid manure dug and two large heaps of clay and rubbish carted from the prison to the old clay pit. Boys were also employed in the farm yard attending to about ninety-five pigs and eight or nine cows. This work was done all the year round, on a meagre diet, by children aged between nine and sixteen.

An idea as to how the boys were employed day by day is given in the following Table, showing their work distribution for a week in February 1853.

Daily Distribution of Prisoners Confined at Parkhurst Prison
Week Ending 19 February 1853 [25]

		Mon	Tues	Wed	Thur	Fri	Sat
Prison duty	Cleaning	39	11	10	11	11	10
	Attending sick	1	1	1	1	1	1
	Pumping	22	22	22	22	22	22
Sick	Infirmary	25	30	29	30	31	32
	In cells	9	21	18	23	22	15
Productive employment	Bakers	3	3	3	4	3	3
	Painters	3	3	3	3	3	3

		Mon	Tues	Wed	Thur	Fri	Sat
Productive employment *continued*	Tailors	58	60	63	60	60	62
	Shoemakers	24	23	26	26	28	29
	Carpenters	7	7	8	5	6	8
	Sawyers	1	1	1	1	3	2
	Brickmakers	10	20	20	18	18	18
	Bricklayers	2	7	7	8	8	9
	Smiths	2	3	2	1	1	4
	Labourers	36	118	125	125	141	137
	Knitting	24	45	49	43	23	20
	Washing	10	10	9	8	6	11
	Cooks	9	10	8	10	10	8
	Gardeners	6	8	7	6	9	8
Instruction		238	136	129	142	141	140
Confined		19	9	8	1	1	6
Total numbers of prisoners		548	548	548	548	548	548

In 1845, ninety-four boys were removed from the gaol. Twelve were sent to Western Australia with conditional pardons; thirty-two to Van Diemen's Land with 'tickets of leave'; forty-two to Van Diemen's Land juvenile penitentiary at Point Puer; two received Her Majesty's pardon; one went to a refuge for the destitute; two transferred to Winchester Gaol; and four died.[26]

Three years later in the report of 1847/8 it appears that more boys than ever before were entrusted with liberty, for of the 396 removed from Parkhurst, 371 received conditional pardons and sixteen free or absolute pardons. Of the 396 who were discharged in 1847, on the 1 January, eighty-nine received conditional pardons and went out to Port Philip (Melbourne) on the *Thomas Arbuthnot*; on 25 May, eighty-four went on the *Joseph Soames* and on 17 September, 125 went on the *Marion* in similar circumstances. On 27 November, fifty-one went on the *Orient* to Western Australia to be apprenticed. Twenty-one were pardoned and removed to a refuge; sixteen went to a refuge for the destitute; four were removed to other prisons and five died.[27]

After that juveniles from Parkhurst were sent out in transport ships at the following times and to the following destinations:

21 July 1848	Van Diemen's Land
26 September 1848	Western Australia
19 October 1848	Western Australia
18 April 1849	Port Philip
9 July 1849	Western Australia
3 August 1849	Van Diemen's Land
1 April 1850	Van Diemen's Land
30 April 1850	Van Diemen's Land
26 June 1850	Van Diemen's Land
28 December 1850	Western Australia
23 January 1851	Van Diemen's Land
13 March 1851	Western Australia
15 December 1851	Van Diemen's Land
2 March 1852	Van Diemen's Land
13 October 1852	Van Diemen's Land
5 November 1852	Western Australia

Transportation as a means of punishment finally came to an end in 1852. No boys were sent to Port Philip after 1849. The last one to be sent to Van Diemen's Land was John Robertjohn, aged fifteen, who had been sentenced to ten years at Exeter in 1848 and spent four years at Parkhurst before being sent there in October 1852. The last boy to go to Western Australia was John Hearn, aged sixteen, who had been sentenced to ten years at Clerkenwell in 1849 and left Parkhurst in the last ship on 5 November 1852.[28]

After transportation ceased, the establishment carried on as a juvenile prison where boys stayed on to serve their time or were sent to other prisons if they had not done so by the time they were seventeen. Dartmoor, Portsmouth and Portland prisons were the most common destinations.

Up to 1851 courts were still handing out sentences of transportation, but from 1852 this became a sentence of penal servitude which consisted of a fixed period of cellular isolation combined with a prescribed task of isolated labour and deprivation of all privileges, followed by a period of associated labour and opportunities for progressive stages of improvement of conditions and earning remission of the original sentence. If he conformed to the system, after a considered time, a prisoner would be given a conditional discharge known as being out 'on licence', whereby he could work and earn a living under police supervision for a prescribed period. This replaced the old 'ticket of leave' system. If there was any irregularity in the behaviour of a boy out 'on licence' the licence would be revoked and the prisoner taken back into custody.

There was one big disadvantage to this system: employers, workmates and neighbours knew when a boy had been a convict, and they also knew the terms of his licence. Captain George Hall reports:

> Several of the licensed boys have been exposed to much inconvenience in consequence of the fact that they are liberated convicts being known in their neighbourhood. One who was and still is working hard at his trade as a sawyer and supporting himself creditably on the wages of a labourer writes that he is looked upon with distrust and if anything is lost in the village the constable comes to his cottage to enquire if he has got it. Another young man in domestic service, behaving well and having the goodwill and confidence of his master there was made miserable by being told that he was known to have been a convict and that he could not remain in the locality and gave up an excellent place and good wages in service because the neighbours were uncharitable and unfeeling. I mention these facts to show some of the difficulties to which those who are anxious to do well are exposed.[29]

Prison sentences for children became shorter in the 1850s as the establishment of reformatories began to take effect. For simple larceny this generally became one year to eighteen months and for more serious offences like housebreaking two to three years. Most boys were released at the expiration of their sentences or were sent out 'on licence' after about one year. Gradually younger boys were transferred to reformatories or refuges. Thomas Scammell, aged eleven, from Lymington, Hampshire, was committed for three housebreaking offences in February 1854 and then was transferred to a refuge in January 1855. Older boys were passed on into the mainstream prison system, like John Clarage, aged fifteen, from London who was committed for a series of housebreaking offences in 1853 and sentenced to ten years, he was sent to Portsmouth Gaol in 1857.[30]

From January 1856 Parkhurst started taking boys from other gaols besides Millbank. They were sent from all over the country to the juvenile prison, which by this time was sending boys on to reformatories and doing reformatory work itself. According to the prison register the last boy admitted was Frank Wilkins, aged sixteen, from Manchester, sentenced to one year for stealing lead, who entered Parkhurst on 16 December 1863. He was transferred back to Manchester Gaol on 13 April 1864 to serve the rest of his time because the boys' section of Parkhurst prison was finally closed on that date and the remaining seventy-eight inmates were escorted to Dartmoor Prison by Captain George Hall, who was by then retired, but who as governor had worked devotedly to better those committed to his charge.

7

Transported Beyond the Seas

'Thomas King, an errand boy, aged sixteen, was sentenced to be transported for seven years with several others for picking pockets. On being told his fate he said "Thank you, your Lordship, we are much obliged to you".'

The Times, 17 September 1832

For eighty years after the First Fleet dropped anchor in Botany Bay the transportation of convicted prisoners from Britain helped the development of the new colony by providing an essential labour force. The availability of land plus organised convict labour made both commercial enterprise and private settlement an attractive proposition. There were, however, other more strategic factors underlying the initial exploitation of the new continent. At the time the British Empire was still expanding. In order to continue this expansion into the vast areas of Asia and the Pacific, the Royal Navy needed ports, materials, provisions, ships and a convenient supply of ready labour; thus the colonisation of Australia became a crucial component in the overall political plan.

The convicts who were involved in this distant undertaking would have had no idea of these underlying strategies. As far as they were concerned, their removal to such an isolated part of the world was intended to be a severe punishment. In an effort to control the rampant crime rate, the British government elected to transport its felons 'out of sight and out of mind' to the new colony on the other side of the world from which few would ever return.

> Of those precious souls for who nobody care;
> It seems a large cargo the country can spare;
> To ship off a gross or two do not delay:
> They cannot too soon go to Botany Bay.[1]

At the time it seemed a convenient solution to the problem of dealing with the superfluous prison population. During the eighty-year period of convict transport around 160,000 men, women and children were shipped in bondage to Australia, although, due to gaps in the records, the exact number will never be known.[2]

An Act of 1779 enabled the courts to transport convicts 'to any place beyond the seas',[3] and at the beginning of the nineteenth century the place turned out to be Australia. To qualify for transportation a man, woman or child must have been convicted by due process of law. In passing sentence on a shop boy, convicted of stealing two shillings from his master in 1810, the Recorder of the Old Bailey said:

> Samuel Oliver, you have been tried by a jury of your country and found guilty of one of the worst descriptions of theft. You ungratefully betrayed the trust reposed in you by your employer who paid you to be faithful to him. It is greatly to be lamented that so mean an offence should bring you this shameful situation; yours is a crime which the courts are determined never to treat with lenity. It is so harsh a violation of confidence and of every bond of civil society that, whenever it is proved, it cannot be punished with too much severity. The sentence therefore of the court is, that you be transported beyond the seas for the term of seven years.[4]

That judge would probably have had no idea of what he was sentencing young Samuel to, for early in the century people would have had only vague notions of what conditions were like in far off New South Wales – let alone where it was. He would have faced a very long, uncomfortable sea journey and perhaps experienced storm or even shipwreck; he would have been exposed to infectious diseases, parasites, seasickness and often famine. On arrival he would have had to cope with vice-ridden older prisoners and a severe regime. The boy might have suffered, perished or even prospered; the judge seemed not to care so long as he got rid of him. Later, in 1843, Sir James Graham of the Colonial Office left the boys who were sentenced to transportation in Parkhurst in little doubt as to their fate:

> Every boy who enters Parkhurst is doomed to be transported and this part of the sentence passed on him is immutable. He must bid a long farewell to the hopes of visiting his native home, of seeing parents, or of rejoining his companions. These are the hopes and pleasures which his crimes have

forfeited. He is being sent to a place where every hardship and degradation awaits him and where his sufferings will be severe.[5]

When the available statistics are analysed it appears that most of the juvenile transportees came from urban areas, particularly from the city of London, where there existed a class of persistent young criminals, living from hand to mouth and drawn into crime by their environment. Other cities, too, had their problems and in an effort to solve them sentenced their young felons to transportation. The Inspector of Irish Prisons reported that 'many boys aged between thirteen and sixteen were transported from Dublin and Cork',[6] and an Inspector of Worcester Gaol commented on the incorrigible nature of Birmingham boys who were ill-behaved and recommitted many times until they were inevitably transported. In 1828 the Chairman of the Warwickshire Quarter Sessions said: '90 per cent of the prisoners tried were from Birmingham and half of these were boys'.[7]

In Dublin boys brought to trial for a second time were transported; in London it did not seem to matter how severe or trivial the offence as the regularity of appearance that got them transported; in Warwickshire a second offence was enough; in Yorkshire it was the third time young felons came forward; and at Leeds and Manchester one magistrate transported them for housebreaking even if it was their first offence.

Theft was considered a serious crime and in order to discourage it heavy sentences were handed out. Children were transported for stealing almost anything. In 1840, eleven-year-old Edwin Rose was sentenced to be transported for seven years for stealing two loaves from a baker in Cheltenham. He had been committed twice before, once for stealing two haddocks and once for stealing bread; as a result this young larcenist, whose only crime was stealing food, was packed off to Australia.[8]

George Welch, aged eleven, was sent in 1839 for stealing sugar; Charles Kenney, fourteen, from Dublin got seven years for stealing shoes; Frederick Slough, eleven, for stealing three spoons; and Sylvester Carthy, aged ten, was sent to New South Wales in 1837 for stealing money, along with another seven ten-year-olds, two aged nine and one child of eight years.[9] But, probably the very youngest transportee was the child an old warder at Millbank remembered and mentioned to Henry Mayhew 'a little boy about six years, sentenced to transportation; and the sentence carried out into effect too, though the poor child couldn't speak plain'.[10]

Very few young girls were transported. A sample selecting every twentieth unit from a total of 150,000 showed that only five females between the ages 10–14 appeared. The male equivalent aged between 10–14 was seventy-six and between 15–19 was 1,117.[11] These figures are confirmed by statistics from the counties. For instance, between 1815 and 1835 the Gloucestershire courts sentenced seventy-five juveniles under sixteen to transportation of whom only four were female.[12] The total number of female convicts sent to Australia was 24,960, about 15 per cent of the total number of prisoners. The estimated average age was twenty-seven years, one year older than the average for men, which suggests that generally they were not shipped out under fifteen. References to individual ages of those conveyed on transport ships are sadly lacking.

With few exceptions, the convicts on the transport ships came from the lowest social class and many of the children would have been orphaned or abandoned, destitute and used to looking after themselves from an early age, a scenario described by the transportee Abel Magwitch in Dickens's *Great Expectations*:

> In gaol, out of gaol, in gaol out of gaol. There you have got it that is my life pretty much down to such times as I got shipped off ... I've been carted here and carted there, put out of this town and put out of that town and stuck in stocks and whipped and worried and drove. I've no notion where I was born than you have – if so much. I first became aware of myself down in Essex a-thieving turnips for a living. So far as I could find there warn't a soul that see young Abel Magwitch with as little on him as in him but wot caught fright at him and either drove him off or took him up ... This is the way it was, that when I was a ragged little creetur as much to be pitied as ever I see, I got the name of being hardened. 'This is a terrible hardened one' they says to the prison visitors, picking out me, 'may be said to live in gaols, this boy.' Then they looked at me and I looked at them and they measured my head, some of 'em – they had better a-measured my stomach – and others give me tracts what I couldn't understand. They always went on asking me about the Devil. But what the devil was I to do? I must put something in my stomach, musn't I?[13]

Magwitch seems to have been portrayed as a travelling boy, but most of the children who were 'shipped off' had never been more than a couple of miles from their place of birth; had never seen the sea and had no idea about the place they were going when they were clapped in irons and thrust into transport ships.

As soon as possible after being sentenced to transportation prisoners were removed from their local gaol, put into open carts, fettered together with others to prevent escape, and taken either to a hulk, Millbank or a gaol in the port of departure to await embarkation. For various reasons some never went, serving out their time in these places. Those who did filed onto the ship still wearing fetters, even though they were very closely guarded. The irons were removed only when the ship was in open water.

The journey usually took between four and five months. After clearing the English Channel the ships went down to Tenerife to take on water and supplies, then via the Cape Verde Islands over to Rio de Janeiro for more supplies, then across to Cape Town for final supplies before the long trip across the Great Southern Ocean to Sydney or Hobart. Between 1787 and 1868 the Crown financed 825 shiploads of prisoners at an average loading of 200 per ship. After initial difficulties, the system of transportation became efficient and by nineteenth-century standards quite safe. Very few ships were lost and the average death rate from illness on board was just 1 per cent at the height of the system in the 1830s.[14]

Some journeys, of course, were more hazardous than others. The *Neva* in 1835 hit a reef off King Island in the Bass Strait with a loss of 225 souls. On the *Norfolk* on which young Edmund Crockett, aged fifteen, found himself in July 1834, all the passengers suffered from ill health and eventually had to be transferred to another ship, the *Lady Kennaway*, only to find there was disease on that ship too. Seventeen had died and eighteen were too ill to continue the journey and they had to return to Cork. Another two were to die on the journey, but eventually Edmund Crockett landed at Hobart on 13 February 1835 after a fraught journey of seven months at sea.[15]

On board ship the prisoners were very well guarded and spent much of the time locked in specially constructed cells on the various decks in each of which 6 ft square, wooden berths were shared by four inmates. The captain of the vessel had little to do with the convicts, the officer responsible for them being the surgeon-superintendent, who was responsible for the preservation of discipline on board, being armed with a sort of power as Justice of Peace. He kept a daily log, in duplicate, and was bound to give a copy of this and to make a report on the voyage to the Governor of Sydney on arrival. The duller the surgeon's notes, the more successful was the journey. His log contained details of daily life aboard ship – cleansing, scraping, sprinkling chloride of lime, tending the sick, lancing abscesses, fumigating clothes and blankets, dispensing advice, purging, bleeding and occasionally burying the dead.

In his evidence to the Select Committee on Transportation in 1837, surgeon Thomas Galloway reported on some of the boy convicts he had escorted to New South Wales:

> There was a portion of the ship entirely reserved for boys. There was a school on board and a schoolmaster who was a convict. There were seventy or seventy-two boys on board aged from twelve to sixteen, some of them a very bad character. It was a big disadvantage having so many together and produced a bad moral effect on those who were least contaminated. I do not think there were any that could be made worse while on board ship and some that came on board with very bad characters appeared at first to improve, but I have known them simulate that effect on purpose to get indulgences. On one ship I took out, when punishment was very frequent, many of them appeared to be reformed, but after my return to the colony next time I heard that twelve or fourteen of them had been hung, some for murder, and forty or fifty of those I had carried out were on the roads in chain gangs.[16]

Juveniles always presented a problem. Up to 1815 men, women and children were transported together, but after this, as in the hulks and gaols on shore, an attempt was made at segregation, although on some ships boys were shipped with men until 1833. On most vessels a separate area was made available for youngsters to sleep, but they still mingled with older prisoners on deck. The average number of under seventeens on each convict ship was forty-three. The few girls involved were kept in the women's quarters. It was not until the late 1830s that the experiment of sending out juvenile offenders in separate ships was tried but, of course, this could only apply to boys.

The 296 ton *Frances Charlotte*, which had been built in Chittagong in 1817 and classed AE1 (not quite A1) was used to transport 150 convict boys to Van Diemen's Land. It turned out to be a very successful voyage, leaving Portsmouth on 1 January 1837 and going via Rio and the Cape. It took 134 days to reach Hobart on 15 May. All the boys arrived safely. The master was Thomas Welbank and the surgeon-superintendent was Alex Nesbit, MD, who left a complete record of the journey in his log and in a letter to the Colonial Secretary, dated 2 June 1837:

HM Government having determined to transport boys by themselves as a trial by removing them from immediate contact with hardened offenders. Some specially selected adult convicts accompanied them; who were constantly to be with them whether on deck or below to check any impropriety and report immediately any disorder, also to superintend their washing and cleanliness generally, both of clothes and person; no power of punishment was allocated to them. Other men were appointed to take charge of the school and one to the hospital to look after the sick and finally one general superintendent of both boys and men who received orders from me and saw them carried into effect.

The boys were divided into 'messes' of eight and a monitor appointed to each to look after the conduct of the mess when assembled together and to report to the man of his section any improper conduct or language on the part of any individual in the mess; when the boys were in bed a monitor was nominated for each sleeping berth of four and held accountable for any noise or disturbance in the night. The system worked well and boys were only too pleased to become monitors.

Schools were established after the long period of cold tempestuous weather before clearing the channel permitted. Each section formed one class and was sub-divided again into five; four reading and spelling and one did arithmetic; we could not teach writing because the government did not supply any slates. The classes were under instruction for about one and a half hours in the afternoons and on Saturdays they were examined as to their progress. While one third of them were at school the remainder were on deck where they were allowed and encouraged to amuse themselves. We had a violin player on board and dancing was permitted after school hours. There was a religious service on Sundays and boys were encouraged to read the Bible.

The boys rose at daylight, each section being mustered on deck by the men. Clothed only in their trousers which were rolled up to the knees, they washed their faces, hands, bodies and feet in a large tub of salt water. Afterwards they went below and dressed themselves and attended to their bedding; they then cleaned the prison. In fine weather dinner was taken on deck. At night the prison gates were locked.

Some of the boys were allowed to take part in the watch. I allowed a watch of eight boys to be kept during the night and it was continued during fine weather. It was an object of great ambition to be enrolled in the watch and was used to reward monitors and other boys.

As the voyage advanced their behaviour greatly improved. Theft was exceedingly rare, immoral language and behaviour had entirely disappeared and the offences which were committed seemed more to depend on the ebullition of youthful feeling than on any inherent depravity.

I consider the experiment, so far as it goes, has been successful and I feel that the manner in which these unfortunates have been disposed of in this colony seems to bid fair to complete what has been contemplated – to withdraw them from the fangs of vice and render them useful members of society.[17]

Life on board a transport ship with a good surgeon-superintendent was considerably better than that which prisoners found when they were mustered at Sydney or Hobart, feeling dry, solid land under their feet for the first time after four or five months at sea; for on arrival the quality of life became something of a lottery.

Male convicts were removed to special barracks where requisitions for convict labour were sifted through by the Assignment Board and the men were legally assigned and delivered to their masters for work. Any girls on board would either be assigned as domestic servants or sent with the women to the female factory to spin wool until they were of marriageable age or got their 'tickets of leave'. Only a few of the arrivals, the known difficult and recalcitrant individuals, were sent on immediately to penal settlements.

The Comptroller of Convicts kept a register in which all names were registered with the name of the ship on which they arrived and their destinations in the colony. The greater portion of newly arrived convicts were thus distributed to the free settlers as assigned servants. The remainder were retained to work for the government on public projects. All were under some sort of surveillance and had to report regularly to a local controller. This assigned forced labour was regarded as part of the punishment. All convicts faced the same prospect: they either worked for the Crown or some private person for a given number of years in bondage. If they worked well and obeyed the rules they could be recommended for a pardon or 'ticket of leave', either of which allowed them to sell their labour freely, choose their place of work and receive wages.

Absolute pardons were very rare; they restored all rights to the convict including that of returning to Britain. *Conditional pardons* gave the transportee citizenship of the colony but not the right to return home. *Tickets of leave* meant that the convict no longer had to work as an assigned servant or government labourer but could spend the rest of his sentence working for himself, so long as he stayed in the colony. The 'ticket' had to be renewed every year and could be revoked for bad behaviour. When a convict had served the full term of his sentence, he became completely free.

There were government regulations with respect to the convict labourer's food and clothing. For instance, there was a stipulated amount of food which every master was bound to supply to his servants. This included meat, flour, salt and sometimes tea and sugar. However, it was a matter of luck as to whether an assigned prisoner went to a good or bad employer; one who kept or disobeyed the rules. He could be fortunate and find himself well-clothed, well-fed and treated kindly. On the other hand, he might end up with a harsh master, made to work hard and for any small offence reported and sent to a penal settlement to work in chains. With a bad master it was highly unlikely that he would ever receive a recommendation for a 'ticket of leave' and would therefore have to tolerate the bad conditions until his term was served.

Settlers were very reluctant to take on juvenile servants, thinking perhaps that they would not get so much work from them and the Convict Comptroller had great difficulty in assigning them. In 1820 a special barracks for boys was built at Sydney, called Carter's Barracks, in an effort to keep transported boys together in a place of discipline. This idea was not a success, as the institution developed a bad name and employers would not take on any boy associated with it, so in 1832 a semi-apprentice system was adopted. Boys were assigned directly from the ships, legally indentured and remained for seven years in service, which in most cases would have been their full sentence. Under this system they became fully-trained workers and, because it was such a long engagement, masters were more careful to train the boys to be useful to them and to try to make them respectable members of the local society. Under this scheme there were many more applications to take on boys.

Carter's Barracks as an establishment for detaining juveniles who had not been assigned never succeeded and was broken up in 1836. The main cause of its failure was given as 'the association of a body of young criminals together and the incorrigible effects of their example and communications on each other'.[18] Although Carter's Barracks proved a failure it was effective for a time in separating the boys from the men in a continuing attempt to avoid contamination problems. After 1836 it seems that the juveniles were once more kept in the Hyde Park men's barracks at Sydney and some inevitably suffered the consequences.

In his evidence to the Molesworth Committee on Transportation in 1837, James Mudie of Castle Forbes, New South Wales, a landowner and employer of convicts, admitted that he had heard reports from the prisoners' barracks at Sydney of boys going by the name of 'Kitty' or 'Nanny':

> There is a great deal of unnatural crime among the convicts. It was not safe to let a convict boy associate with convict men, nothing can save them being corrupted; every species of vice they glory in; and it is the glory of men convicts to corrupt a boy.

Ernest Slade, a superintendent of the Hyde Park Barracks, confirmed the problem:

> Sodomy is common in the barracks, some boys complaining that they could not remain in the rooms along with men. Many young boys complaining of men taking liberty with them. I appointed two overseers in each dormitory as a kind of watch but they only visited at certain times so the experiment was not successful. If a man was caught he was given fifty lashes.[19]

The following year on 8 February 1838 the Rev. William Ullathorne, whose title was Vicar General of New Holland and Van Diemen's Land, told the committee:

> On board ship they are together four on the same couch and I think that a great deal of evil, not only in their conversation, arises from that. The boys have a separate apartment below but they mingle on the decks with men and are much corrupted by the converse and remarks of the prisoners on deck. The huddling of boys together below is likewise accompanied with a great deal of moral pollution. The boys are separated from the men in the barracks but again they mix with them during the time of recreation ... In most ships there are sixteen to twenty boys in a ship with the men. I used to caution boys, particularly young boys on the very day of arrival of the temptations

to which they would be subject in the barracks; and remember being told by one young boy, a very young boy, he could not have been more than ten or twelve at the most, that very morning he had been attacked by a man in the barracks and the boy observed, very simply, that such crimes were never known in Ireland from whence he came.[20]

Ten years later the thorny problem was approached again by Francis Russell Nixon, Bishop of Tasmania, who in his letters to Earl Grey wrote:

I now approach a subject so revolting, so abhorrent to our social and Christian feeling that nothing but an imperative sense of duty would induce me to notice it ... During a short stay at the coal mines on Tasman's Peninsula I made some extracts from the hospital books of cases of acute disease resulting from constant indulgence in unnatural crime ... I also went down the shaft to the mines to ascertain what were the facilities for such practice of the atrocious crime. It was within a few weeks of the execution of two prisoners who had been convicted of an offence unheard of in a Christian country, that of the rape of a boy ... In scarcely any part of the mine could a prisoner stand upright and imperfectly lighted so as it would be impossible for the two constables (who after this crime were stationed to guard the prisoners) effectively to watch over or to prevent such crimes taking place amongst the seventy to ninety prisoners, even supposing the constables would have the courage to interpose when surrounded by such ungodly and desperate men.[21]

The mines on the Tasman Peninsula at Saltwater River were first excavated in 1833 and used as a means of punishing the most iniquitous convicts, who were forced to labour in terrible conditions in a poorly managed mining operation. Among the miners were those who had committed crimes after they had been transported, had resisted authority, attacked officers or fellow prisoners or tried to escape. Working in the mines was a second punishment for some who had been transported to Van Diemen's Land. The alternative was to be sent to a place where the punishment was even more dreadful.

Prisoners who were re-convicted of a colonial offence could be sent to the penal colony of Norfolk Island, where punishments were pushed to the last severity. Just as men were transported from Britain to Australia, if they reoffended, they were transported from Australia to Norfolk Island. It was the ultimate punishment. A volcanic island of just fifteen miles in circumference, as remote from any land as it was possible to be, it did not even have a harbour – merely a place for landing boats at particular times through the reef. Escape was impossible and discipline brutal.

It was described by Dr Robert Willson, who was the first Roman Catholic Bishop of Tasmania and who first visited the colony in 1846:

> The population of Norfolk Island is composed of all classes of persons; some have been sent from Van Diemen's Land doubly convicted, many of them are of a tender age; some of them could hardly have shaved before they landed on the island and their appearance young and fresh was very striking in the circumstance ... In the large prison there were 800 men, 500 old prisoners and 300 fresh men all mingled. They slept in large buildings containing from sixteen to eighty men and were shut up in the darkness without supervision from 8 o'clock at night to 5 o'clock in the morning.[22]

There were indeed children of a 'tender age' in this odious place, whom the authorities must have considered as too dangerous to be allowed through the normal channels, such as JM, aged ten when first convicted in 1832, originally transported for seven years, must have been very disobedient for was sent to Norfolk Island on a life sentence; CB, aged eleven when convicted, re-convicted and sent to Norfolk Island for life; JW, aged twelve, originally seven years, misbehaved and sent to Norfolk Island for life; WS, aged fifteen, was sent there for life but was stabbed to death whilst trying to escape.

From the 1845 Report on the Conditions of Prisoners on Norfolk Island, the following extract shows the original and colonial sentences and ages of fifteen boys aged under fifteen: [23]

Age	Original Offence	Sentence	Colonial Offence	Sentence
13	Robbing master	7 years	Aiding	Life
12	Stealing instruments	7	Burglary	Life
10	Stealing harness	7	Bushranging and robbery	Life
12	Stealing boots	7	Highway robbery	Life, not to return
14	Stealing kerchiefs	7	Burglary	Life in chains
12	Housebreaking	7	Burglary	Life
14	Larceny	7	Horse stealing	Life
14	Stealing watch	14	Felony	Life not to return
14	Arson	Life	Killing cattle	Life

Age	Original Offence	Sentence	Colonial Offence	Sentence
14	Horse stealing	Life	Burglary	Life
14	Picking pockets	Life	Having firearms	7 years
13	Picking pockets	Life	Highway robbery	Life in chains
13	Street robbery	Life	Cattle stealing	15 years
13	Housebreaking	Life	Having firearms	7 years
14	Housebreaking	Life	Robbery	7 years

A term on Norfolk Island was an extreme punishment and only affected relatively few of the young transportees. But in the mainstream system those apprenticed or assigned could also be punished harshly for seemingly minor offences. In some places where the settlers complained and brought children before a magistrate the children received the same punishments as the adult convicts; a flogging up to a maximum of fifty lashes. They were reported and flogged for quite trivial offences. Frequent reference is made in magistrates' returns to laziness, insolence and insubordination as reasons for flogging which they ordered and supervised. The ages of the children are not given and their names are abbreviated to initials only, but some entries indicate that some of them were very young. 'AB sentenced to thirty lashes. The boy cried out so much. Back turned blue at the twentieth stroke.' [24]

The Report of the Select Committee on Transportation of 1837/8 concluded by condemning the system absolutely as being unequal, without terror to the criminal class, corrupting to both convicts and colonists, and extravagant from the point of expense. Despite this condemnation, 'transportation beyond the seas' continued to have plenty of defenders who were determined to get rid of a vicious criminal population and who thought that the only means of achieving this was the entire removal of the offending class as the only security to society against their future crimes. The general consensus in Britain was that the system should continue, but in Australia, which attracted more and more free settlers as the century progressed, popular opinion turned against it. New South Wales became well-settled and too civilised to remain a penal colony and the transportation of convicts was abolished there in 1840.

Before this date most offenders were sent to New South Wales and those with worse records or guilty of more serious crime went to Van Diemen's Land, which now became the destination of all prisoners.

Between 1841 and 1850 approximately 2000 convicts a year arrived in Hobart,[25] a tremendous number for the available resources and organisation to cope with. All the problems which had manifested themselves on the mainland now had to be faced on this sparsely populated island. The government already had a system of dealing with the transportees which they expanded after 1840, setting the male convicts to work on extensive programmes of civil construction and building a factory for the women. Recalcitrant prisoners were sent to special penal colonies at Macquarie Harbour, Maria Island and Port Arthur.

To avoid the contamination of the juveniles, young prisoners were rarely put into work gangs or assigned, but were sent to Port Arthur where, in 1834, Governor George Arthur had established a penal establishment especially for boys known as Point Puer (*puer* – Latin for 'boy'). Point Puer was in essence a prison for children aged between nine and seventeen years who had been transported to Van Diemen's Land. Governor Arthur was faced with the problem of what to do with the ever-increasing numbers of young felons arriving on every convict ship. In 1834 out of 1434 convicts who disembarked at Hobart between January and September, 240 were juveniles. Boys such as these were of no use in the civil constructions gangs and would have been difficult to assign to the few settlers on the island. They could not be accommodated in the prisoners' barracks at Hobart without problems, so he decided to establish a special barracks for them, far away from civilisation and strictly separated from the main penal settlement by being on a peninsula one and a half miles from Port Arthur but close enough to the main settlement to share its resources and be efficiently managed and easily supervised.

The commandant at Port Arthur at the time Point Puer was established was Captain Charles O'Hara Booth, a tough disciplinarian with a name for justice and humanity, who was interested in the juvenile problem and strived hard to make Point Puer a success. A good description of the juvenile prison is in a letter from Booth to John Montague, the Colonial Secretary, on 24 July 1837:

> The juvenile establishment at Point Puer was formed in January 1834, the system with little variation, has not departed from that which was first established. The daily routine of duties are as follows viz: the boys rise at 5 o'clock, roll up and stow their hammocks and bedding; this done they are

assembled together, when a portion of scripture and a suitable morning prayer is read, after which the boys leave the barracks, wash and amuse themselves within the prescribed bounds (extending about a quarter of a mile) preparatory to being inspected for cleanliness, previous to breakfast which takes place at 7 o'clock. Muster for the labours of the day commences at 8, they continue work till 12 when a bell rings for leaving off, they then prepare and wash themselves for dinner – this meal consists of three-quarters of a lb fresh or salt beef or half a lb salt pork, 10 oz pudding made from flour and fat, or 1 pint of soup thickened with flour, 1 lb of cabbage or turnip or half a lb potatoes in lieu of other vegetables. They are mustered again at half 1 o'clock and work until 5. Their rations are the same as for the men at the penal settlement – and their Sunday indulgence is 2 oz raisins given to the boys for pudding. But these are withdrawn for any who had misbehaved during the week.

Boys are divided into messes of ten to twelve and corporals appointed to each mess who are responsible for seeing that their respective mess gets its proper rations. At 6.15 the boys are mustered for school for one hour after which a portion of scripture is read and a prayer and then bed. Lights are kept burning in the barracks all night and a watch is kept constantly.

On Saturday afternoons all boys are examined by a surgeon to ascertain if they are fit for the work assigned to them.

On Sundays missionaries come from Port Arthur to take services and examine boys on their religious knowledge. There are plenty of religious books, Bibles and religious tracts to be read during their leisure hours.

The trades taught are such as are most likely to be useful in a new country and consist of boot and shoemakers, carpenters, blacksmiths, nailors, tailors, coopers, bakers, gardeners and sawyers and a few are taught bookbinding; a number of boys go to Port Arthur to learn stone cutting and boat building.

Boys on arrival are employed in a 'labour gang' breaking up new ground, cultivating the Government garden, carrying sawn timber, making roads, splitting timber for firewood and washing, cooking and cleaning in and about the barracks. All boys are taught how to use husbandry tools, axe, saw etc. In 1837 some boys were employed in making fittings for the church which is being erected at Port Arthur and several articles of furniture for various Government buildings; boy stone cutters are also employed in cutting the stone for the church.

Their clothing is the same as for the other prisoners, two jackets, two pairs of trousers, two pairs boots, two striped cotton shirts, one cloth waistcoat and a cap annually. Their bedding consists of one rug, one blanket, one bed tick or hammock; boys who conduct themselves well are given an extra blanket for the winter.

Outside working hours boys amuse themselves in their leisure time in any innocent and rational manner within the prescribed bounds. Most trivial crime or irregularity is punished in proportion to the nature and degree of the offence; for minor offences they are confined to the muster ground during leisure hours where no amusement is allowed and have to do the duty of scavengers. The next grade of punishment is to be placed in a solitary cell when labour has ceased and to receive their meals therein. The next grade is confinement in a solitary cell with bread and water and no labour. For serious offences, which are rare, corporal punishment is practised.

A new gaol is being erected to be occupied by boys whose conduct is likely to contaminate the better disposed; they will have no connection with the others until their conduct has improved. Each month a Return is made to the Chief Police Magistrate of offences committed and punishments awarded also a Return to the Principal Superintendent of Convicts showing the manner in which each boy is employed and each half-year a Report is made to the Governor of the general conduct of each boy upon which the recommendation for assignment is based.

Recommendations for Improvement

That the library be increased with cheap, suitable and useful works for the purpose of lending to the boys to read during their leisure hours.

That two teachers be sent out in each vessel with the boys, conversant with the National School system, whose services would be found advantageous and would accordingly establish more efficient teaching in the gaol.

That a clergyman should be resident at Point Puer who would occupy the whole of his time and attention on the boys.

That a Bible and prayer book may be presented to each boy on leaving the establishment; donations of this kind appear to be greatly prized by most of the boys.

That some small portion of the value of each boy's estimated labour be invested in a Savings Bank, the accumulation and interest to be handed over to them on expiration of their sentences or obtaining a 'ticket of leave'. This would give them a strong stimulus and an interest in what they were doing, at the same time amassing a small sum for them on becoming free.

It would be recommendable that materials for clothing throughout the colony should be sent out from England to be made up in this establishment. it would be advantageous that the cloth be sent out in one piece and leather in hides. This would afford some the opportunity of being taught to cut out, one of the most particular branches of the shoemakers and tailor's trade.

The bedding having been found generally insufficient, an extra blanket is recommended as an additional comfort to the boys who are well conducted.

A towel and suspender (braces) annually are strongly recommended to each boy, very many of the minor crimes originate from the want of these articles.

A jacket, waistcoat and pair of duck trousers, are recommended for Sunday's use only, with a small portion of oil for cleaning boots.

It has been observed that boys under sentence of transportation for 'Life' have generally conducted themselves in a reckless manner, under the impression that their situation cannot be worse. I have endeavoured to impress upon them that this is a very erroneous supposition but would beg to recommend that some prospect might be held out to them, beyond that of adults under similar circumstances.

The Return to the Chief Police Magistrate referred to:

Return of Offences Tried at Point Puer Half Year to 30 June 1837

	Jan	Feb	Mar	Apr	May	Jun	Total
Average Strength	226	235	215	194	214	276	–
Absconding	9	1	4	8	2	–	24
Articles in possession	6	14	12	13	25	17	87
Bathing without permission	–	–	4	5	–	–	9
Destroying property	1	3	6	3	6	5	25
Fighting	4	11	7	5	4	7	38
Gambling	5	2	–	–	4	2	14
Insolence	10	2	7	19	8	26	72
Misconduct in barracks	1	2	1	–	1	7	12
Misconduct in Divine Service	3	2	3	1	2	9	20
Misconduct in gangs	–	2	–	2	2	13	19
Misconduct in school	–	–	2	1	1	3	7
Misconduct in general	3	9	7	27	4	19	69
Profane or obscene language	11	5	9	2	5	20	52
Privately working	3	2	–	–	–	–	5
Talking or singing in cells	4	–	2	–	19	1	26
Indecent conduct	–	1	–	1	–	2	4
Total Offences							483

Depending on the severity of the offence they received up to five days on bread and water in solitary confinement or from ten to twenty-five strokes of the birch.[26]

The boys who ended up at Point Puer were the same class of children who would certainly have experienced life on the streets. They would have known about low lodging houses, local gaols and maybe even conditions on a hulk; so by the time they reached Van Diemen's Land they would, each in his own way, have been fairly hardened. They knew how to behave when it was necessary for survival but amongst themselves the law of the gutter would have prevailed. As with the lads previously described by Mayhew, bad exploits would have been cheered, telling lies expected and the odd flogging praised. Likewise, as experienced on the hulks, a boy who 'squealed' would have been persecuted. Booth wrote in his journal that he was 'sick at heart from the number of boys I am obliged to punish'. In 1840, 351 out of 494 were punished for a total of 1011 offences, suggesting that there existed a desperate and unscrupulous element who would never have improved.[27]

Among such individuals there were cases of vicious boys attacking their gaolers. Two of these incidents were described by a Mr Stonar to the Select Committee on Criminal Law in 1847:

> I remember the case of a boy of sixteen who had been accused by his overseer. He watched his time and came behind the overseer with a hatchet in his hand and hacked him down with it. He hit the man's leg so severely that it had to be amputated. That boy was tried and executed. I remember another case at court at Point Puer in 1843 where there were three boys on trial. The head of one of them hardly rose above the bar of the court. In that case the overseer was destroyed with a stone hammer; a small hammer used for breaking stones. The boys concerned hacked him for a long time and a great many other boys were looking on and not interfering. Their defence was conducted by one of the barristers of the Supreme Court and he was very severe in cross-examining the witnesses. He asked each one of them what was the reason which prevented his coming forward and interfering. One of them stated that his only reason was that if he had he would have been called a dog and his life would have been rendered miserable by the gang. Another said it was no concern of his; and the other answers given by the boys were equally brutal and unfeeling. The boys were acquitted of murder but found guilty of manslaughter.[28]

During 1842, a total of 716 boys passed through Point Puer. The

seditious and unscrupulous among them would have been weeded out
and sent on to penal colonies, the mines or other places of punishment.
The remainder were well-disciplined and well-trained and opportunities
given them to learn skills and trades which would benefit them and the
colony when they were considered worthy of a conditional pardon, an
apprenticeship or release. There was by this time a special hiring depot
for youngsters established at New Town, Hobart, where arrangements
were made for their employment and thus their future.

The most popular training for boy convicts was that of stonemasonry
and associated building skills, including stone-cutting, brick-making and
brick-building; in fact the boys of Point Puer were responsible for much
of the stonework and fittings of the church at Port Arthur. There is a
poignant reminder of this calling in the present-day museum at Port
Arthur where there is on display a brick, found recently at the site of
Point Puer, on which a boy convict had found time to inscribe his name
– 'Jeremiah'. If Jeremiah had managed to keep out of trouble, on release
he would have found ready employment in the rapidly growing construction industry, which in the late 1840s was generated by a colonial
administration intent on creating substantial buildings, bridges and
engineering works.

This building work and general opening up of the island attracted a
new generation of settlers who resented the idea of convict labour, so
much so, that on 10 August 1853 transportation was abolished. On
1 January 1854 the much disliked title Van Diemen's Land, which carried
the stigma of the penal colony, was altered to that of Tasmania.

In the 1840s boys with a good recommendation from their governor
or chaplain were not generally sent to Van Diemen's Land. There were
two other destinations in Australia where, although labour was in short
supply, local authorities would not accept convicted men. The fertile
land around Port Phillip Bay, near the growing town of Melbourne,
was attracting increasing numbers of settlers who desperately needed
workers but who would not condone transportation. In 1844 Earl Grey
hit on the idea of sending out 'trusty' convicts who would receive
conditional pardons on arrival and be referred to as 'exiles'. This arrangement was reluctantly accepted and for a time proved successful.
It appeared to the prison authorities an excellent way of disposing of
well-behaved juveniles and between 1844 and 1849 many young lads

embarked for Port Phillip with the hope of starting a new life. The scheme, however, was short-lived and stopped in 1849 when a boom in free emigration meant that there were plenty of new emigrants to take up the labour opportunities.

The final destination of some juveniles originally sentenced to transportation was the Swan River, the original area of settlement of the region which became Western Australia. It had been founded as a free colony with a stipulation that no prisoners should be shipped to it, but being so remote even free immigration had failed to satisfy the settlers' demands for labour. In 1843 some young inmates from Parkhurst prison were dispatched to Western Australia, where on arrival they were indentured to colonists and euphemistically termed 'Government Juvenile Emigrants'. They were not to be considered as convicts. This experiment proved so successful that the government soon appointed a Guardian of Juvenile Emigrants who supervised their apprenticeships and systematically checked that the conditions of their indentures were fulfilled. He wrote annual reports which confirmed that, after a shaky start, the scheme worked well and the boys were hard-working and popular with the settlers, who were particularly in need of help on their farms. The Guardian reckoned that only 3 per cent relapsed into crime.[29]

In 1849 the Surveyor General of Prisons, Lieutenant Colonel Joshua Jebb reported:

> For the past five or six years boys from Parkhurst have been sent to Western Australia. They have been apprenticed and a superintendent was appointed who disposes of them and looks after their welfare and interests. In 1847 the superintendent stated that in March a large addition was made to the number of his charges by the arrival per *Orient* of fifty-one lads from Parkhurst. They arrived in good health and were all provided with suitable situations within three weeks of landing, the great number being sent into the country as farm servants. A further draft of a large number has been sent for which will be, I have no doubt, as readily disposed of. During the year thirty-four lads have completed the period stipulated for their apprenticeship and have been discharged. All of them have readily obtained employment.[30]

More information about boys sent to Western Australia from Parkhurst is contained in the Governor of Western Australia's Report for 1850. A letter from Governor Charles Fitzgerald, Government House, Perth to Earl Grey, dated 22 January 1849 states:

I have the honour to transmit a report of the Guardian of Government Juvenile Migrants which I am happy to find generally satisfactory as to the conduct of those committed to his charge, only three of whom out of 107 in number have been charged with offences of a serious character last year.

I lament the death of one boy, John Davis, after a long illness of three months consumption; otherwise general health is good. I have also to report the desertion of five from the colony within last year. The American whalers who dock at our outports for supplies offer great facilities for escape.

In conclusion, I have no hesitation in saying that the experiment of sending these lads to Western Australia has proved in its results eminently successful and highly creditable to the fostering institution at home; as, while the services of these lads have proved of the greatest benefit to the settlers in the present state of the labour market, you will be glad to learn that each of them on the expiration of their apprenticeship are gladly hired either by their old masters or other parties as farm servants or shepherds at wages (with board and lodging) ranging from £1 10s. to £2 5s. a month and that very few of them evince any wish to return home or leave the colony.

At the end of his report for 1850, Captain George Hall, Governor of Parkhurst, attached a letter which he had received from a former inmate. He must have felt it touching and important enough to send on to the prison authorities, just to let them know that, perhaps, after all, the work he was doing at Parkhurst was right, and that some boys had discovered a better life for themselves as a result.

23 December 1846. To the Governor of Parkhurst:

Dear Sir, I take this opportunity of writing these few lines to you hoping you are quite well as I am at present. I hope you will excuse me for not writing to you before but the reason was this. I was stationed in the Bush and had not the opportunity. I suppose you know I left the Isle of Wight on 24 August and we got to this colony on 11 December. I had not been long in the colony before I got a place; myself and Chifney went to one place together and have been on it until now and I have not the least doubt but what we will serve our time on it; my employment has been as a shepherd and Chifney is herding cattle. I expect my time will be up twelve month next May and I shall be very well able to get my living at shepherding for I shall be getting £30 a year. I have a few sheep of my own that my master gave me. This is a very hot climate and since I have been in the colony I have seen nearly all the animals that are in it; there are oppossums, wombats, two sorts of kangaroos, native cats and squirrels and native dogs which are very troublesome to a shepherd for they kill the sheep whenever they get a chance and especially the lambs but they are very frightened of any person, they are something like a fox and are a pretty good size.

There are some nice fur skins here. I have very often thought of collecting I have no means of sending them home on account of not being able to pay the expenses but if you have any wish for them and will pay the expenses I will collect a lot for you and send them home, you will like the fur skins they will make very nice tippets and muffs and such like.

Chifney sends his love to you and please give our love to Mr Knott and Mr Daintry and Mr Young. Please write to me again and direct your letter to John Scholes, Perth, Swan River, Australia, putting my name first. So no more from your humble servant,

Terence McGrath [31]

8

Missions of Mercy

'The enormity and amount of juvenile depravity is a subject which now most painfully engages the public mind.'

Mary Carpenter [1]

Until the advent of universal education in the 1870s and 1880s, multitudes of dirty, ragged children could be seen every day on the streets of British towns and cities. Without a caring state welfare system to guide them, these impoverished youngsters had to support themselves as best as they could and many of them did. Some managed to make a living by selling small items in the streets like lucifers (matches), watercress, flowers and fruit; others found they could earn money by entertaining the public in the streets – juggling, tumbling, singing. Many more employed themselves by holding horses or crossing sweeping – brushing away the horse droppings left by carriage transport so that people had a clear way to cross the street. An easier way of getting a living was by 'lifting' the property of other people, however, and street children were forever on the look-out for thieving opportunities.

By 1850 this manifestation of the young urban poor on the streets had begun to alarm the burgeoning middle classes and led to a genuine fear of mob rule – and of the uprisings that had broken out throughout Europe. This dread of the swarming numbers preying on society and threatening social order, combined with the abolition of transportation, had two notable effects.

First, it produced a new breed of literate social reformers, like Mary Carpenter and James Greenwood, whose ideas on saving children from vice and a life enmeshed in crime struck a responsive chord in the Victorian consciousness. Those who actually came into professional contact with young criminals took a serious interest in the problem and in the 1830s and 1840s articles on juvenile delinquency frequently appeared in periodicals. This concern set in motion several attempts to try more constructive action with young offenders than just whip them and send them on their way. These brave experiments led to some of the most innovatory aspects of nineteenth-century practices in the treatment of criminals.

Secondly, the general fear of the underclass led to an increase of benevolence as more and more people turned to giving to charitable institutions as a means of helping the poor and, no doubt, their own souls. The extension of private charity had, in fact been partly necessitated by the complete breakdown of the Poor Law system in the destitute areas of London. The system had operated on the assumption that there would be a mix of rich and poor in each area, but this ceased to be the case with the separation of the classes into their own distinctive districts. With each Poor Law Union responsible for the relief of its own poor, the result was that the poorer districts, with a necessarily greater number of paupers in need of relief, paid the highest rates and the richer districts the lowest. Inevitably, crisis point was reached and the system collapsed under the strain. Private charity became necessary to fill the gap. Children's charities attracted the most money, particularly girls' orphanages, and the setting up of refuges as a means of keeping the young out of gaol gradually gained in popularity. The number of such charitable institutions founded between 1800 and 1850 was 279; in the ten years between 1850 and 1860 another 144 came into being.[2]

All these charities relied on public support. They were generally financed by contributions, donations and subscriptions paid on an annual basis, or by legacies. Another source of income in many places was from regular contributions made as a result of sermons preached in local churches specifically for the purpose. The public would be informed that on a certain Sunday a sermon would be preached in aid of a certain charity and that collections would be made at the church door. Of course, this would only be appropriate for institutions which were properly run by governing bodies and committees and for which reports and accounts were readily available.

However well-run and well-intentioned, these institutions only scraped the surface of the problem. There are no accurate records of the number of homeless children living on the streets of London in the middle of the nineteenth century and it was often a matter of luck rather than need to get any help from the charitable organisations. What help would a runaway workhouse boy like Oliver Twist have received if he had not met the Dodger? What might they have offered Jo to replace his precarious existence on the streets? Neither of these two could possibly have become one of the 450 inmates of the Foundling Hospital because it only provided for 'poor, illegitimate children, whose mothers are known'. The number of orphan asylums steadily increased but acceptance was generally by the recommendation of subscribers and patrons. It would have been almost impossible for a homeless child, particularly one with a prison record, to know anyone among subscribers who would have been prepared to give him or her a recommendation. Some orphanages made a point of NOT taking the most needy, like the one where:

> The description of children which this asylum profess to receive are those from honest and respectable parents who have brought up their families *without parochial relief* and who have always set their offspring an example of sobriety and moral behaviour and surely they must ever claim the protecting shelter of the asylum and will become good and useful members of society.[3]

In fact, no child would have been considered by that orphanage if either parent had at any time been in a workhouse or received parochial relief of any kind. This rule cut down the eligible candidates to a very small number and was a far cry from the original idea of such charities, which was to civilise the poorest of children and save them from falling victim to vice.

There was, of course, class distinction among schools and charities. Mary Carpenter mentions the Rev. William Quekett of Christchurch, who proudly told her that the whole of his parish did not know of the criminal classes and he never remembered any child from his schools being in prison. When asked, 'Supposing a child who had been in prison applied to one of your schools, would you admit him?', he replied, 'Certainly not'.[4] For parents would not have approved of a boy who had been in prison being admitted. By this time even the Sunday Schools refused admission to young criminals. It seems that those who had no dealing with the lowest class of society did not wish to be associated with its members.

Fortunately, most of those who did have such dealings professionally showed more of a social conscience. Sir Richard Birnie, Chief Magistrate at Bow Street and successor to Henry Fielding, not merely in respect of his office but also in his deep concern that young boys should be protected and removed from a way of life which was none of their choosing and which was almost inevitably bound to corrupt them, said:

> To get away those boys before they are completely contaminated would be a great national object. I am talking of children aged eight to twelve; that if they could be taken from their parents when they are found in the streets and put in some asylum, it would be an immense thing and then the gangs would want recruits and would fall into decay.

When questioned as to how he would compel these children to enter such an institution Sir Richard went on to say:

> There is an unrepealed Act of Anne, which authorises every magistrate, with the consent of the churchwardens of the parish where the delinquent is found, who either begs or his parents beg, who cannot give a proper account of himself, to bind that boy to sea service.[5]

A good proposition in its time but the great difficulty of such a scheme was that, by the nineteenth century, masters of merchant vessels had become reluctant to accept such boys as apprentices.

Richard Birnie appreciated this problem and in 1828 suggested using an old 'Indiaman' moored at Woolwich, with a master, governor and carpenter, binding street boys for three years disciplined training after which they would have been ready for sea faring and merchantmen would be more inclined to take them. It would be another thirty-eight years before such a scheme finally materialised, when Lord Shaftesbury took up the idea of fitting out an old ship and filling it with 'boys of the ragged type' and training them for a seagoing life. On 14 February 1866, 150 homeless boys were collected at the St Giles's Refuge, in one of the poorest areas of London, and invited to train as seamen. The notion of a training ship caught the imagination of the public, funds were soon forthcoming and the frigate *Chichester* was bought from the Admiralty for the purpose. In 1874 Lady Burdett Coutts gave the sum of £5000 to fit out another ship the *Arethusa*. Lord Shaftesbury presided over the inaugural ceremony at Greenhithe on 3 August 1874 when 300 ladies and gentlemen were present.[6]

After the Poor Law Amendment Act 1834, boards of guardians were empowered to set up district workhouse schools. Although these were humane in intention, they still bore the Poor Law stigma, were very few in number, poorly organised and it proved difficult to find teachers willing to serve in them. One of the most successful of the workhouse schools was the one at Quatt, a village in the Severn Valley near Bridgnorth. In 1851 it housed 130 children consisting of forty-six orphans, forty-three children of widows, and twenty-one deserted and twenty illegitimate children. The object of the school was to provide a home and education for children who had neither. Those who were old enough did school work and labour equally. They grew their own food and from one cow got 180 lbs of butter and 540 gallons of milk in one year. The guardians noted an improvement in their characters, appearance and physical power; the children were healthy and contented and anxious to get positions for themselves.[7]

Boards of guardians frequently approved funding pauper families with the means to emigrate. They realised that it would be cheaper to the parish in the long run than looking after them in the workhouse, particularly where children were involved. In 1848 Anthony Ashley Cooper, the future Lord Shaftesbury, saw emigration as a partial answer to the problem of destitute children. He brought in a motion asking for an annual grant from Parliament, pointing out that, apart from the benefit to the colonies and to the children themselves, the scheme made good economic sense. The children would be spared from a life of crime and money spent on emigration would be money saved on prison expenditure. He was granted £1500 for one year only, but the following year the grant was withdrawn and Ashley Cooper depended on what he could raise by private donations.[8] People obviously approved of child emigration, as the scheme prospered and over the years many youngsters were sent to Australia and Canada.

City workhouses were desperate places and only resorted to by the street children when they were ill, starving or cold. The casual wards, where people were only allowed to spend one night, were used more frequently for a night's food and shelter. Henry Mayhew, who spent years bringing the plight of the destitute to the public attention, interviewed some boys in the casual ward of a London workhouse; their stories were typical of the problems of destitute juveniles.

One had originally come from Wisbech, Cambridgeshire, where his mother had died when he was five years old and his father remarried. Obviously unhappy, he had run away and lived by begging and sleeping rough until he reached London:

> I slept on doorsteps or anywhere. I was sadly hungered, regularly starved. I got crusts but I can hardly tell how I lived. One night I was sleeping under a railway arch and a policeman came along and asked me what I was up to. I told him I had no place to go and he said I must go along with him. In the morning he took me and four or five others to a magistrate, who heard what the policeman had to say – he said there were always a lot of lads under the arches, young thieves, they gave a great deal of trouble – and I was one associated with them ... I got fourteen days of it. After I came out I carried on begging and going from union to union to sleep ... I am unhappy but I have to get used to it.

Another boy in the same ward, who thought he was about thirteen, was barely clothed. He had no shirt and no waistcoat; all his neck and a great part of his chest being bare. A ragged cloth jacket hung about him and was tied together with bits of tape. What he had wrapped round for trousers did not cover one of his legs while one of his thighs was bare. He wore two old shoes; one tied to his foot with an old ribbon, the other a woman's old boot. His features were distorted through being swollen with the cold:

> I was born in Hadley in Kent, my father died when I was three days old. My mother went about begging, sometimes taking me with her. She died last year ... I came to London to beg thinking I could get more there than anywhere else ... I have been begging about all the time till now. I am very weak – starving to death. I never stole nothing, I always kept my hands to myself. A boy wanted me to go picking pockets with him, he did it to get into prison as it was better than the streets. I know it's wrong but I would do anything to be out of this misery.[9]

Many children who had not actually committed criminal acts found themselves in prison. Just being a vagrant was enough. In 1876 Dr Barnardo estimated that about 30,000 neglected children aged under sixteen years slept out in the streets of London. It was probably an underestimate. Vast numbers of these children were without friends, without any means of subsistence, and genuinely did not know right from wrong. Prison governors found their young charges not only neglected but untaught, unfed, unhoused, unwashed, uncared for, some hardly able to speak and some never having heard any kind words before they came to gaol. These negative conditions were bound to generate future criminals and it was reasoned that these children required humanising rather than deterring from crime.

An enlightening case came to light during the examination of witnesses before the Select Committee on Criminal and Destitute Juveniles on 25 May 1852. The man being interviewed was John Ellis, a shoemaker who lived in the poor district of Albany Street, London, who, on his own, at his own expense, had rescued fifteen criminal boys and by his kindness and example had trained them to his profession and enabled them all to make an honest living.

David Power, the Recorder of Ipswich, discovered this phenomenon. He was having problems with juvenile delinquency in his own area, particularly after a return from the Town Clerk and Superintendent of Police showed forty-seven convictions of those aged under sixteen; of whom twenty-two were either thirteen or under. Twelve of these juveniles had been transported or were bad characters in Ipswich; thirteen had left the area; two were in the union workhouse and only three out of the forty-seven were improved characters in any way. He had visited Ellis, examined his system and left with a full assurance that the boys were reformed criminals. A journal of their current activities showed that each one was getting his living in an honest way without being the slightest expense to the community. Seeing this induced Power to start a similar institution in Ipswich, based on the simple principles of the London shoemaker.[10]

As well as running his shoemaking business, John Ellis found time in the evenings to help out at a Ragged School in Brook Street which was near to his workshop. This brought him into contact with the lowest class of criminal children. Being a man of strong religious conviction, he became interested in juvenile crime and its causes. One night in 1848 a youngster with a particularly bad record was brought to the school by Mr Platt, a Ragged School organiser. At first he seemed like another hopeless case but, on talking to the boy, Ellis found out that, despite his wretched background, he genuinely wanted to leave his criminal life and go to work. On hearing this the teacher realised that a major cause of crime was want of employment and resolved to take the boy into his business and train him to make a useful living. The following morning two of the boy's comrades in crime joined him and by the end of the year Ellis had the management of fifteen young criminals.

> I trained them in shoemaking and found they were very good at it, I used to sit with them for two or three hours a day and talk to them, reading passages from the Bible sometimes, I taught them that it was wrong to break the social laws which bind society together and also the laws of God. Apart from teaching I provided them with food and gave them clothes to wear. These were children who had been destitute all their lives, called lawless children, chained, whipped, confined and subjected to every punishment without effect; poor, ignorant wretches and still children. I thought to supply them with the necessities of life, a bed to lie on, water to cleanse themselves, a fire, a clean place to sit down, good conversation, interesting books. It is surely as spring follows winter and harvest follows seed-time their moral wilderness would become a fruitful garden. And we have seen it.
>
> With regard to their morals I thought I could not do better than set them a good example myself. I ate with them, slept with them and asserted myself in every way, I tried to show them the law of the gospel as well as I could, although I am not much of a scholar myself.[11]

Ellis was a widower and his only son, who was aged seven in 1848, was brought up with the trainees. There was no punishment involved in his methods: he believed that kindness was enough to reclaim all juveniles and the boys thought so much of their master that they expressed a wish to pay him back for their lodging and training. The chairman of that Select Committee, C. B. Adderley, later Lord Norton, was so impressed with John Ellis that, when he founded the Birmingham Reformatory in 1853, he appointed Ellis as the first superintendent.

Birmingham was the centre of two other early experiments in treating juvenile crime in a more humane manner. Matthew Davenport Hill, a brother of Sir Rowland Hill, was the Recorder of Birmingham from 1839 to 1866 and in this capacity did much to reform the criminal law. He was, for instance, a pioneer in the informal use of probation for children. Some magistrates on his Midland Circuit had been in the habit of sentencing very young offenders to one day's imprisonment on condition that they were more carefully watched and supervised by their parents in future. Beginning early in 1841 Hill took this idea a step further and, when there was ground for believing that the child was not wholly corrupt, when there was reasonable hope of reformation and when there were parents or persons qualified to act as guardians, and kind enough to take charge of the young convict, he felt himself justified in handing over the young offender to their care, in the belief that there would be a better chance of amendment under such guardians than in the county gaol. At unexpected periods a confidential police officer would visit the guardian, make enquiries and note the facts of the case in a register.

Results from the first years, 1842–46, showed that out of 117 prisoners who were given up to their guardians only forty-eight turned out well, twenty-nine were 'doubtful' and forty remained bad. There was a more favourable result from the years 1849–51 when out of sixty-six probationers forty-four turned out well, eleven doubtful and eleven reoffended. Hill attributed the better results to the character of the master or guardian to whom the youngsters were entrusted. Those who reoffended, of course, would have been subjected to much heavier sentences.[12]

When a young offender had no family or employer to look after him, rather than commit him to prison the Birmingham magistrates had another option open to them; they could send the boy to an asylum in the village of Stretton-on-Dunsmore near Warwick. This institution had been established in 1818 by a group of Warwickshire magistrates as private individuals, not as an exercise of magisterial power, for the care of poor young offenders, its income depending on subscriptions and any profits of the boys' work on their smallholding. Up to 1835, 197 boys had been received into the asylum and 114 had been reformed; twenty-four of these children had been received without spending any time in prison. These obviously destitute children were sent from the courts by Birmingham magistrates and a few came directly from Warwick gaol. There was no legal power of detention but a system was worked out whereby the master of the asylum 'hired' them as servants, so that if they did run away, magistrates had the power to commit and punish them.

This small organisation could only accommodate twenty at a time so those sent there were those most deserving benevolent care. Magistrates were aware that it was not a prison and that the principles of the establishment relied on gentleness and good treatment; a house of refuge rather than punishment, aimed at a transformation of the boys' lives. From the year of its foundation up to 1827 only forty-eight boys out of 100 had been reformed; by 1843 56 per cent had improved; and in 1847 the proportion was 65 per cent which Matthew Davenport Hill thought 'was a very encouraging state of affairs'.[13]

The asylum at Stretton-on-Dunsmore was not the first institution of its kind. That honour goes to the refuge of the Philanthropic Society founded in 1790 for children of criminals who had been hanged or transported. By the early nineteenth century the society had an establishment in St George's Fields, Southwark, which contained three distinct and separate departments: a manufactory for sons of convicted felons; a female school for daughters of convicts; and a 'place' for very criminal boys. The criminal boys were not allowed out for two years, during which time they received secular and religious instruction. When they were considered ready they went to the manufactory to serve apprenticeships. All the children were aged under thirteen.[14]

A Report of the Philanthropic Society gives a list of the sixty-four inmates and their state.

The following were received from 31 March 1832 to 31 March 1835:[15]

Sons of Convicts (12)

Age	Condition
10	Father transported, mother left with four children
9	Father transported, mother of bad character
10	Father transported for life, mother dead
10	Father executed, mother dead
9	Father transported, mother left with three children
9	Father transported for life, mother dead, stepmother blind
10	Father transported for life, mother left with five children
9	Mother transported for life, father unknown
9	Father transported, mother dead
11	Father transported for life
12	Father transported for life, mother dead
9	Father transported for life

Daughters of Convicts (19)

Age	Condition
9	Father transported for life
10	Father transported, mother left in distress
9	Father transported for life, mother dead
11	Father transported for life, mother left with three children
9	Father transported
11	Father transported, mother dead
9	Father transported
9	Father executed for murder, mother in great distress, near confinement with her eighth child
9	Father transported, mother dead
9	Father transported for life, mother left with six children
9	Father transported, mother left with three children
9	Father transported for life
9	Father transported
10	Father transported for life, mother left with four children
10	Father transported
9	Father transported for life
9	Father transported, mother dead
11	Father transported for life, mother left with six children
10	Father transported, mother dead
10	Mother transported, father dead

Criminal Boys (31)

Age	Condition
10	Boy of vicious character; father transported
11	Boy of very depraved habits; charged with stealing five silver spoons and other property
10	Charged with stealing money and various articles; had been for two years constantly guilty of theft
10	Charged with theft and stated to be so depraved as to be hopeless unless admitted
11	Had been twice charged with stealing various articles and frequently guilty of acts of delinquency

Age	Condition
10	A very bad character. Twice charged with theft
9	Recommended by a magistrate before whom he had been charged with stealing a watch
11	A very depraved character, convicted of felony at Middlesex Sessions
9	A boy of very bad habits, charged with stealing a piece of woollen cloth
11	Sentenced to be imprisoned and twice whipped for felony and again committed for three months in the same year
10	Convicted of felony before the Recorder
12	A vagrant in the House of Correction, father and mother dead
10	A boy incorrigibly dishonest and depraved. Charged with stealing money
11	Twice committed to prison guilty of various thefts
12	Charged with feloniously stealing various articles
12	Four times charged before a magistrate. A boy of depraved habits
11	Recommended by the mayor and corporation of Plymouth having been confined in the Borough Gaol for larceny
9	Frequently guilty of theft and bad conduct; father transported
12	A boy of bad character. Charged with stealing various articles
11	Certified to be a bad character, charged with Intent to Commit a Felony and sent to Brixton
11	Charged with embezzling various sums of money. A boy of very depraved habits
9	Charged with stealing a pair of boots and frequently guilty of theft
12	Several times charged before a magistrate or in custody for theft
12	Frequently guilty of theft
10	Recommended by magistrates after been tried for theft
10	A destitute orphan of very vicious habits, one month in the House of Correction
10	Continually guilty of theft and other bad conduct
12	A boy of very vicious habits, guilty of several thefts, father transported

Age	Condition
12	Imprisoned in the House of Correction and certified to be of vicious habits
10	A depraved boy confined in Brixton for stealing boots, father and mother dead
10	A vicious boy, lately in Clerkenwell prison; father and mother dead
12	Convicted of felony at Horsemonger Lane Sessions

One of the most experienced and enlightened of the chaplain/superintendents of this refuge was the Rev. Sydney Turner, who in 1846 accompanied by Thomas Paynter, a London magistrate, visited a similar French refuge at Mettrai known as the 'Colonie Agricole' for delinquent boys. They were so impressed by what they found that on their return they recommended five of the French principles:

The employment of trained staff.
The division of inmates into family groups living in a homely setting.
The use of persuasion rather than force.
Active outdoor employment.
Using the charity of individuals with the support and sanction of the government.

This last point was adopted almost immediately and by receiving government support meant that some deserving children who had been committed to London prisons were recommended for conditional pardons on condition that they went to a charitable institution.[16] The Philanthropic Society's refuge was by then the biggest and best-known of these institutions. In April 1849 the organisation moved from London to a 200-acre site in Redhill, Surrey, where it transformed into a farm school for criminal boys aged over thirteen.

A different approach to the problem of saving destitute children from a life of crime was adopted by the Children's Friend Society, which was established in 1830 by Captain Edward Pelham Brenton RN. After he left the navy Brenton took an interest in juvenile crime and the terrible condition of vicious and neglected children in the city excited his pity. He had small means in the form of a naval pension but with the support of a few tradespeople, started a school at Hackney Wick, where boys received moral and religious instruction combined with manual employment under strict superintendence. Most of the early labour consisted of building the school which, when first occupied was in a ruinous condition. This taught the children to make mortar, set bricks, to saw, plane and drive in nails – skills which would be useful to them in the future. They even built their own sleeping quarters where Captain Brenton insisted on rigid simplicity. The shed was arranged like a sailors' cabin with three rows of hammocks one above the other. If he was told that the boys should be made a little more comfortable he always replied: 'They are much better off than our brave lads in His Majesty's Navy'.[17]

From the rules of the asylum at Hackney Wick we learn that

> Each boy upon admission to be washed in a warm bath under the direction of a medical assistant and to have his hair cut short.

> Boys to be numbered from one upwards and entered upon a roll, the name, age, size, previous mode of life to be noted, reference being had in their arrangement of the moral conduct and habits of each. All to be divided into three classes lettered, A, B and C, – Class A being those who had a parent or guardian who were too poor to look after them, Class B were workhouse boys and Class C those absolutely destitute usually picked up on the streets.

> Any boy guilty of a falsehood or improper language to be placed in solitary confinement for a short period. For a serious offence from six to twelve hours solitary on bread and water. Flogging and blows are strictly forbidden.[18]

Captain Brenton's efforts in rescuing vagrant boys were brought to the attention of Miss Amelia Murray, grand-daughter of the Duke of Atholl and a lady-in-waiting of the young Princess Victoria. After visiting the boys' school in 1832, she founded a similar institution for girls at Chiswick and persuaded her royal mistress to be the patron. The Royal Victoria Asylum of the Children's Friend Society was under the separate management of a committee of ladies and the destitute girls were taught household skills, until 'good and respectable habits had been acquired'.

The main difference between these two asylums and similar establishments was that the Children's Friend Society made emigration its main object. Brenton really believed that this class of child would stand a better chance in the growing colonies than they would if they returned to the streets of London with their temptations of crime and vice. The aim was to train the children and then send them to British colonies where they would be apprenticed or found positions as domestic servants. Most of them went to South Africa, where a committee of influential gentlemen in Cape Town set up an apprenticeship scheme; the others were sent to Canada.

During the year 1835, ninety-three boys and twenty girls were sent abroad. One group of children sent to Cape Town included:

Name	Master	Employment
Daniel Golding	William Dickson	Storekeeper
John Bolter	John Upjohn	Gardener
Charles Ratert	John Saunders	Cook and confectioner
George Pelteret	R. W. Eaton	House servant
Edward Morris	Joseph Lawton	Tinsmith
Charles Hatchett	Thomas Matthews	Cooper
Edward Gorman	William Hutchons	Sailmaker
Louisa Thomas	D. I. Cloete	Servant
Mary Conway	G. Hodgskin	Servant
Mary Litchfield	F. G. Landsberg	Servant
Mary Williams	D. G. Foek	Servant
Ann Field	H. Leatt	Servant
Mary Dixon	E. Holt	Servant
Sophia Duffy	E. Goodison	Servant

In 1833 a boy named Henry Powell had been found in the Old Kent Road nearly starving and some charitable people took him to the Hackney Wick asylum. It was discovered that he had a sister some years older and that the latter had struggled to support her little brother in vain. When the boy recovered and was about to be sent abroad, the girl turned up at the asylum and asked if she might go with him. Although Martha Powell was rather beyond the usual age, she was enabled to join her brother on the voyage to Cape Town.

Later from Cape Town on 17 September 1834, she wrote a letter to a member of the Ladies' Committee of the asylum:

Madam, I have taken the liberty of writing these few lines to thank you for your kindness to me and my brother. We both have good places and are very happy. My brother is with a doctor's family and is behaving very well; we are near each other so that I am able to see him. I hear that the other emigrants who came out with us are behaving well, although a few of the boys ran away from their masters at first, all but three have returned. There is an evening school here three times a week and a penny library. We had a very pleasant voyage but a great deal of sickness. The Captain was kind to us and we all arrived in Cape Town in good health, I remain, your obedient servant, Martha Powell.[19]

Another interesting letter regarding the children who were sent to Canada was received in 1834 from Mr Washburn, Clerk of the Peace for Upper Canada:

> The usual method of binding children in Canada is this: the child being bound, the master, together with the usual covenants of lodging, clothing etc enters into another, that if the apprentice (being a male) shall behave properly during his apprenticeship he shall receive at its expiration a new suit of clothes, a pair of oxen, yoke for the same, an axe and any other small matters that may be thought of, to enable him to go on his land; or in lieu of these a certain fixed sum of money, say $60–100. In the case of females the covenant is to give a feather bed, bedding, a cow, spinning wheel, new dress etc as it is supposed she will immediately marry, a matter which of course so often happens that it is considered a matter of course.[20]

The Children's Friend Society continued to function successfully until 1840, when rumours began to circulate indicating that some children were being badly treated in South Africa. It was discovered that some of the young emigrants had been apprenticed to Dutch Boer farmers who did not speak English, leading to unforeseen difficulties which caused some boys to run away. One boy actually managed to get back to England, where he returned to his old life as a thief. When he was caught he gave a full account of his bad experience in South Africa to the judge at his trial. Following this revelation there were accusations of atrocities and slave labour and a public clamour arose against the society. Many supporters withdrew their subscriptions. The scandal damaged the society tremendously and, when Captain Brenton died in 1841, the asylum was closed down due to lack of funds.

After a visit to Newgate gaol in 1825, where she found four girl inmates aged under thirteen, Elizabeth Fry started an asylum for criminal girls, known as the School of Discipline, in Paradise Road, Chelsea. It catered mainly for female children who had been committed to prison but whom magistrates thought it better to send to an institution. Girls aged between seven and thirteen were kept for up to two years and, if suitable, were found positions as servants. The regime was strict and austere as Mrs Shaw, secretary of the school in 1835, describes:

> For half an hour in the morning, half an hour in the middle of the day and an hour in the evening children are allowed time for air and exercise. We do not call it 'play' in a house of discipline. They eat meat four times a week and on other days broth and potatoes and for breakfast and supper bread and milk. We do not allow beer, tea, butter or sugar as we consider these to be luxuries. I am sorry to say that some of these children aged eight or nine come in most dreadfully addicted to beer and spirits.
>
> Expenses are by subscription and the British Ladies' Society for the Reformation of Female Prisoners give us a grant every year, if there are parents they pay between sixpence and four shillings a week, but with most we do not know their parents.
>
> We have had only two thorough failures, one was sent to a refuge for the destitute and turned out very bad. The other was a desperate girl who set fire to our house seven years ago with a view to escape; after consulting Mrs Fry and some of the Ladies' Committee she was sent into solitary confinement where she remained for three months.[21]

The poor backgrounds of the girls are revealed by three cases who were received into the School of Discipline in 1834.

> EG, aged twelve, and greatly addicted to stealing; her thieving propensities are so great that she has been expelled from a charity school where she was placed by her parents.

> AW, aged ten, expelled from a charity school for stealing, she broke open a box and stole the money it contained and by her own confession 'let it out in gin', which she drank and was found in a state of intoxication.

> H, aged eleven, addicted to lying and thieving, frequently leaving her home for weeks together and gaining her living by false pretences; she has been eight times before magistrates for various offences and lately for stealing the keys of an empty house.

Girls like these spent their time in the institution learning to sew and making fine shirts, coarse shirts, night shirts, petticoats, pocket handkerchiefs, cambric handkerchiefs, night caps, pairs of sheets, pillow cases, table cloths, towels, cravats, aprons and pairs of pockets.[22] When they

were considered ready for the outside world the Ladies' Society would
find them suitable positions and, for a time, follow their progress.

The original Bridewell institution in London, which was founded in
the sixteenth century for 'rogues, vagrants and disorderly persons', was
still active as a House of Correction in the nineteenth century but by
then it had developed many departments catering for different needs.
One section was the House of Occupation which housed 'inmates of
both sexes of the younger sort who were taught various trades and their
letters with the prospect of being returned to society'. In 1834 this applied
to ninety-eight males and forty-four females aged fourteen and under.

Nathaniel Nicholls, Steward of the House at that time described the
four classes admitted:

1. Offenders from the House of Correction who show signs of contrition so
   desire to reform their lives; a chaplain or prison superintendent must
   recommend them.

2. Those who their relations or friends find it impossible to control. If they
   are addicted to pilfering, staying away from home, associating with bad
   characters or getting into vicious courses, the governors decide if they can
   be taken into the House.

3. Very young girls who have been deserted by their parents or their parents
   are so dissolute that they are quite certain to run into the paths of vice, the
   governors extend the benefit of instruction to them without the children
   themselves being in any way offenders.

4. A class of young girls who have been on the streets and become diseased
   and admitted to St Bartholomew's or St Thomas's or any other hospital in
   the city of London. They were admitted when they had been declared cured.[23]

The boys were taught tailoring, shoemaking, ropemaking, baking, brew-
ing and mat making while the girls were occupied with needlework,
washing and household work. The ropes and mats were sold on the
open market to help finance the project, but all the clothes, shoes, bread
and beer were used by the House of Occupation, Bridewell Hospital or
the Bethlem Hospital (Bedlam).

Of the fifty-one boys who were inmates on 9 July 1835, twenty-three
had been brought in by relatives, like the eleven-year-old brought in by
his father for pilfering from his parents and keeping bad company;

another eleven-year-old was committed by his sister for robbing her, keeping bad company and being addicted to bad habits; a twelve-year-old was brought in by his mother for pilfering from her; another twelve-year-old was also brought in by his mother for pilfering from his parents; and a twelve-year-old was brought in by his mother for being prone to wicked pursuits from the example of vicious associates.

Among the forty-eight girl inmates on that same date, thirteen had been sent from hospitals as victims of venereal disease. Others included a ten-year-old brought in by friends, being deserted by parents and in a destitute condition; a twelve-year-old brought in by friends who was taken by the police from a brothel at the request of those who brought her in; a thirteen-year-old brought in by an aunt, an orphan of wild and roving disposition and likely to fall victim to vice if not placed under control; a twelve-year-old sent from St Thomas's Hospital who, cured of venereal disease, was of loose habits, depraved and from the lowest class of society and a thirteen-year-old whose father 'suffered' her to go on the streets.[24]

Refuges like these for criminal, destitute and diseased children were few and far between, they were the least popular of the charities as, generally, people did not want to be associated with this class of child. Throughout the country social reformers and magistrates continued to find difficulty in dealing with the problem of how to keep these juveniles out of gaol – but they kept on trying.

In 1848 the magistrates of Durham adopted a system whereby each member of a gang associated in committing the same offence was sentenced to a different term of imprisonment. By this system the magistrates tried to make the prison the effectual means of breaking their evil association. The expiration of sentences would not be on the same day, preventing them from meeting at the prison door and relying on each other for support, which usually meant returning to their original way of life. For instance, in the case of a gang convicted for stealing a till, the boy who actually stole the till would receive the longest sentence, the boy who received the till outside the shop the next longest, and the boys who received a certain proportion of the money, but who were aiding and abetting, a lesser term; other distinctions, such as age, were also taken into account.

The chaplain of the county gaol at Durham, the Rev. George Hamilton, was very concerned about the plight of young prisoners on discharge and tried several ways to either restore them to their relations or help them to earn an honest living. One of his methods was what he called his 'Chaplain's Charter', which was a letter sent to the parent or nearest relative of an underage prisoner one week before their being discharged from gaol. This was the form of the letter:

> I write to inform you that your ... will be discharged from this prison on ... day next, the ... day of ... at 8 o'clock in the morning. I beg you will come to meet h ... at the above place and endeavour by your influence to keep h ... from following into further crime.

The following table shows the results of 749 copies of the charter being sent to relatives of young criminals discharged from Durham Gaol in 1851 and 1852:

	1851	1852	Total
Special answers from parents, masters or relatives	96	28	124
Answers containing money to take prisoners home	42	21	63
Met by parents or relatives on discharge	116	158	274
Returned undelivered	27	19	46
Unnoticed by parents, masters or relatives	187	55	242

Of the 749 children discharged from the gaol in those two years, 288 of them were totally ignored by their relatives. These were the ones whom Hamilton was most anxious to help. He set up a refuge in Durham for young, discharged prisoners, both male and female, and managed to support it by voluntary contributions. The chaplain interviewed each prisoner personally, previous to discharge. If they were contrite, and indicated that they would like to adopt an honest living, he would attempt to help them.

The refuge for girls could only accommodate four at a time, but they did not stay long, before being found employment either as servants or in a factory. Before starting their new job, each girl was given a new set of clothing. With regard to the boys, Hamilton realised that many of them would benefit from a seafaring life so he devised a scheme whereby on discharge a boy would be given a note to a shipping agent in Sunderland, marking it with the gaol stamp and 'County Gaol' written across it, least the lad should make improper use of it by begging or showing it to others than the agent to whom it was directed.

As a 'test' of his good intentions the boy was required to walk the twelve miles from Durham to Sunderland. If he delivered the note to the shipping agent employed by the managers of the refuge, he was received into his house and taken care of by his wife and in a few days would be bound apprentice and sent off to sea. In 1852, nine boys failed the 'test' of walking to Sunderland.[25]

These refuges and asylums could only benefit a very small number of those who needed help. The vast majority of young offenders continued their existence of crime and punishment because it was the only life they knew.

On 12 April 1851, Mr Crowder, the Recorder of Bristol, in addressing the Grand Jury of the Quarter Sessions, said:

> In twenty-four cases there have been prior convictions, I am sorry to find from the great number of cases of this description in which young persons have been brought before me for the second, third or more time, that the punishment awarded has not had the effect of reforming them. It is an evil greatly to be lamented because it was hoped that punishment would have the effect of reform and I am very sorry to find in so many cases that it has failed to do so.[26]

The experience of magistrates all over the country was the same, imprisonment and punishment were not deterring youngsters from further crime. The question was: what could be done with the persistent juvenile offenders?

9

A Leap in the Dark

'The truest mercy is to prevent a child from continuing in the habits of crime – the greatest cruelty is to permit him to continue in crime if it can be prevented.'

Thomas Lloyd Baker [1]

The situation became so grave that a parliamentary select committee was formed to report on the whole question of criminal and destitute children. From evidence taken between 3 February to 1 July 1852, the final general consensus was that special schools should be established to reform, educate and train young people convicted of criminal acts.

In the spring of 1852 while that select committee was in session, and unknown to anyone but those involved, an experiment was taking place in the English countryside that anticipated the recommendations of the committee. In her evidence Mary Carpenter had commented that 'The idea that charitable individuals might run the schools is so peculiar a case that it has never occurred in any Government measure, it is impossible to predicate what would be the result'.[2] But that is just how the reformatory movement started. The charitable individual was Thomas Barwick Lloyd Baker of Hardwicke Court, near Gloucester, a country squire of moderate wealth who, as a county magistrate and prison visitor, developed an interest in the causes of crime. Among his other work he was a Poor Law guardian and was drawn into personal sympathy with the poor, outcasts and destitute particularly among the young. It saddened him to see so many children in the county gaol and houses of correction. In his book *War with Crime* he wrote:

On the imprisonment of children it is very commonly said that it must be wrong to send a child to gaol; first because the poor child knows no better; it is the fault of the parents who have brought it up badly and they ought to be sent to gaol instead; secondly because of it being sent to gaol and herded with older criminals the child must be corrupted; and thirdly that if the child once has a prison brand upon him he is marked for life and will never again be able to obtain honest employment, and must fall from bad to worse.

Children born to dishonest parents brought up in poverty and squalor. It is not their own fault and to send them to gaol and thus destroy their self-respect, sour their feelings and stamp them as felons for the rest of their lives is a wrong course when we could try to save them.

What are we to do with the rising generation of juvenile offenders? Where can we now transport them? What shore will receive them? The earth is saturated with British criminals and at home we are full to overflowing. We must begin at the fountain head and reform those whom we cannot transport or shut up.[3]

The idea of reforming criminal children had been in his mind for many years. In the 1830s he had met Amelia Murray, founder of the Royal Victoria Asylum of the Children's Friend Society, who called his attention to the possibility of reclaiming vicious children and told him about the school run by Captain Brenton, who took destitute boys from the streets, trained them and sent them off to the colonies to earn their living in a new environment. Baker visited the school and was greatly impressed by it. He talked to friends of the possibility of founding another similar institution but at that time they thought his idea 'grand and wild' and paid little attention to it.

It was not until later when he had had some years experience as a magistrate and prison visitor, and encountered the pathetic young in-mates, that he became convinced of the truth of his early ideas. The thought slumbered in his mind for many years to start a school to 'reform' these criminal children but it would be a difficult task to carry through on his own with no support. At last, in 1851, he formed a friendship with George Bengough, a young man with property adjoining his own, who encouraged him to go ahead and start such a school. At that time Baker was actively engaged in many activities and told Bengough that it would be necessary to find a man who could devote his whole time to the task. To his astonishment Bengough declared that he would like to undertake it, if Baker would help him. George Ben-gough, then aged twenty-three, was heir to a fortune of £10,000 a year and could easily have spent his time in hunting and other leisure pursuits, as many young men of fortune then did, but he chose instead to become involved in an experiment to reform young criminals.[4]

The two men must have spent many hours discussing the subject of the care and reformation of children convicted of a criminal act: what to do and how to do it. The only precedent they knew of was Captain Brenton's school and that had long since ceased to function. The select committee had not even started when they decided to go ahead privately and find a building to use as a school and to find some boys who would benefit from their attention. Baker later said, 'We had no idea how it would all turn out, it was truly a leap in the dark.'

Thomas Lloyd Baker and George Bengough provided the money themselves to start the school and they became its first managers. They found an old labourer's cottage on the Hardwicke estate, in the area between the River Severn and the Gloucester and Sharpness Canal, which was situated on poor land, therefore not suitable for letting, and this became the basis of their 'reformatory'.

At first they must have felt very unsure of themselves and their scheme, for they decided not to start the experiment with local boys. Instead they contacted Lieutenant Frederick Tracey, governor of the Westminster House of Correction, and he recommended three boys who were about to be released whom he considered would be suitable candidates for such schooling. All three had been convicted from four to eight times and, undeterred by periods in prison, were hardened in crime. The life in London to which they would have returned was so very grim that they offered themselves willingly for the experiment. The prospect of being taken to the country to be reformed must have seemed the lesser of two evils. On 24 March 1852, his twenty-fourth birthday, George Bengough travelled to London himself to collect the young thieves. He had no experience in handling young people, and his friends and relatives were very concerned, expecting he would be murdered or robbed, for no one could envisage what difficulties he would encounter. However, he found the boys 'weak in health' and only too pleased to go with him. What an experience it must have been for the three boys, who had never been out of the grime of London, to travel by Great Western Railway and carriage through the countryside to their new home.

Matters progressed quickly. One week after the first admissions on 31 March 1852 a committee meeting was held at which the name the Children's Friend School was adopted and a constitution drawn up. One member of the original committee C. Jellinger Symonds, who was the Government Inspector of Workhouse Schools, gave evidence to the Select Committee on Criminal and Destitute Juveniles in June 1852, in which he stated:

> If you confine a child to prison you must have walls and I think a very different establishment would be more suitable for the purpose of reformation. I would recommend a small farm, a farm of some ten to twelve acres to be cultivated by spade labour and as remote from a town as could be. I have some means of ascertaining that there is no need for confinement.[5]

Although he did not mention it by name, surely he was referring to Hardwicke, which was at the time still a private experiment.

The Children's Friend School was on Baker's estate, situated four miles from Gloucester and just across the canal from the church. Originally it was a small, red-gabled, brick building with just a few rough sheds around it and six acres of land. At one end was the cottage of the bailiff and at the other the schoolmaster's room. At first George Bengough took on the role of schoolmaster himself; this young man with his own fortune actually moved into a room at the reformatory and for two years worked as its schoolmaster.

Once the three London boys had settled down they were joined by four young thieves from Cheltenham and in October of that year another four local boys were admitted. These youngsters were aged between eleven and fifteen and all of them had been in prison at least twice in their lives. It was intended that the institution would admit only those who had been convicted of a crime, by due process of law, and who would benefit from reformatory treatment, although at the time they entered the school they were free boys and were committed by their parents or guardians who should have been responsible for paying their maintenance. At the end of October 1852 George Bengough reported to the Gloucestershire Michaelmas Quarter Sessions 'It is early days yet but we feel we have kept, for so many months, out of mischief and at a very small expense, boys who would otherwise have been doing a good deal towards filling our prisons at a considerably greater cost'.[6]

In those early days the Children's Friend School was a private institution, financed purely by subscriptions, donations and any maintenance money which could be secured, but with responsibility for eleven children and with so many people now involved the experiment was no longer a secret. The message had now to be got across to magistrates, police and those who came into contact with criminal juveniles that the school existed and that it was not solely a charitable institution for the purpose of relieving parents from the duty of taking care of their own wayward children, nor to relieve parishes of supporting their own poor, but that its purpose was to decrease juvenile crime – first by lessening temptation to the innocent and secondly by preventing those who had commenced crime from continuing in it.

The first results of the reformatory experiment were encouraging and during 1853 the school was extended to include accommodation for twenty-five boys, with ten acres of land under cultivation. In a report dated December 1853,[7] it was stated that there were twenty-four boys in the school. Seven had left during the year, two had gone into service and one had joined relatives in America and were all doing well. Four had left in unsatisfactory circumstances; either visiting parents and not returning, or relatives taking them away. It must be remembered that at this time the school managers had no legal power to retain boys at the school, which was all voluntary. The only authority they had was the signatures of parents or guardians for attestation and consent to the boy being kept during the managers' pleasure as required by the rules. A few parents managed to pay the maintenance but most never contributed anything at all.

As a result of the recommendations of the select committee, the Bill for the Better Care and Reformation of Juvenile Offenders, known as the Juvenile Offenders Act 1853, was passed. This Act, however, was not very clear as to the sort of children to be sent to reformatory schools. It mentioned those 'never before convicted' or 'in a destitute or neglected state' and these were not really the children for whom the reformatories were established, but, as a result of the Act and the publicity generated by the Hardwicke experiment, similar schools were soon established in Bristol, London, Droitwich, Birmingham and Newcastle-on-Tyne. After a time of obvious frustration, magistrates managed to send some of the really deserving cases to the reformatories by evoking the Act of 1838,[8] under which the Crown could grant pardons to young criminals on condition of their going to some charitable institution approved by the Secretary of State. The powers of this Act too were very obscure, however, and more legislation was badly needed.

During 1853 and 1854 meetings were held throughout the country to petition Parliament that schools to reform juvenile criminals should be 'fostered and multiplied'. Baker spoke about his experience at many such meetings as well as writing numerous papers on the subject. On 20 December 1853 the largest of these meetings was held in the Town Hall, Birmingham, in order to discuss the necessity of reformatory schools and to 'promote such schools throughout the kingdom both by legislation and some pecuniary assistance'. Thomas Lloyd Baker gave a full account of the Children's Friend School and among other speakers were Sir John Pakington, MP for Droitwich, and Lord Shaftesbury – such was the support that the reformatory movement now had. The result was the passing of a second Youthful Offenders Bill on 10 August 1854.[9] This gave more definite guidelines. Section II of this Bill reads:

> Whenever after the passing of this Act any person under the age of sixteen years shall be convicted of any offence now punishable by law either upon indictment or summary conviction before one or more JPs, then in every case it shall be lawful for any court, judge, police magistrate, stipendiary magistrate or any two JPs before or by whom the offender shall be convicted, in addition to the sentence passed as a punishment for his offence to direct any such offender to be sent at the expiration of his sentence to any Reformatory School and there to be detained for a period of not less than two years and not exceeding five years and such offender shall be liable to be detained pursuant to such direction.

Section III set out how the Treasury would be responsible for paying maintenance fees if the parents were unable to do so. The Bill also stated that, if a child absconded from that school, he or she would be liable to imprisonment and gave guidance on establishing reformatory schools. Finally, it stipulated that the schools would be subject to the inspection of HM Inspectors of Prisons.

Government help with maintenance must have been good news to the managers of the Hardwicke school. In 1854 this was five shillings a week for each convicted boy and in January 1856 the amount was raised to seven shillings. The Children's Friend Reform School in Gloucestershire, had been the first county reformatory. Although it was approved by the Secretary of State in 1853, it received no help with maintenance until it admitted its first convicted boys in 1854. The school received its first certificate as a reformatory school on 4 October 1854 and only then did it have a legal power of detention. It was the first reformatory school in the country to be so certified. In 1856 it was renamed the Hardwicke Reformatory.

For over two years the managers had struggled along, commencing with no assured prospect of success; experimenting, bearing costs, and gradually forming the seeds of an idea into an accepted method of reforming delinquent children. As Thomas Lloyd Baker's school became known, managers from all over the country wrote to him for advice and he continued to lecture and write papers on the subject for the rest of his life. George Bengough helped to start another reformatory school at Kingswood, Bristol, but sadly contracted tuberculosis and died in 1861, aged thirty-three.

Once the school was licensed to accept convicted offenders, it began to attract attention and received visits from those interested in social reform, including Members of Parliament. In January 1854 *The Times* published an account of the school:

There are at present seventeen inmates, who are properly taken care of, and taught and employed. A recent visitor states that when he went there most of the boys were at work at spade husbandry, but two or three were occupied at household work. One was sitting cross-legged, mending his trousers. The history of this boy is a melancholy one. Although only fourteen, he was seven times convicted as a thief in London, and was brought to Hardwicke by Mr Bengough. The boy seemed willing to answer questions, but did not exhibit the least compunction for his misdeeds. He was neglected by his father and in order to indulge his taste for cheap theatres he began to rob shop-tills, which soon procured him a cell in the Westminster House of Correction. A note is taken of the character and conduct of the boys and the utmost exertions are used to reform them. The boys have a regular routine of duties to perform, but time is allowed for recreation. They are, of course, instructed in religion. Their studies comprise, writing, reading, and elementary geography. On one day a week drawing is also taught. Their work consists of outdoor agricultural labour and in wet weather they are employed at basket-making indoors and some of them at tailoring and shoemaking. They are punished if they behave badly and rewarded for good conduct.

The article attracted considerable attention and was reproduced in many other newspapers throughout the kingdom. Juvenile offenders were a national problem and in London alone there were estimated to be 20,000 children who lived by criminal activities. In a quiet rural backwater a start had been made to help some of these children and it began to look as if the experiment was going to be a success.

At first the managers decided to send boys out to the colonies, but this was quickly dismissed as it was felt to be too drastic a measure. Instead it was decided to train them to be useful farm labourers. So the boys were introduced to agricultural employment which, according to Baker, was peculiarly adapted to institutions whose aim was to unite real advantages to the boy with the absence of all that might appear, even to the ignorant, to make the effects of crime desirable. He thought that the mind of a boy fresh from the excitement of life on the streets of a town – alternating crime and idleness, the lavish expenditure when lucky and the cold want when unsuccessful – was in a state of feverish restlessness which required to be calmed before it could be safely operated on. There was no other occupation which allayed this excitement and tranquillised the mind like hard steady digging. Boys came to the school quick and energetic by nature with a restless craving for change and excitement caused by long vagabond and lawless habits. By putting them to hard bodily exertion, the energy expended itself not only harmlessly but profitably and the very feel of fresh air and the appearance of liberty was thought to tranquillise and allay that feverish excitement. When the labour of the day was over the boys enjoyed their rest. At first some were disgusted by the hard work and threatened to run away, but the bailiff was always in sight and the other boys prevented their escaping, as they did not like runaways. Escape would have been difficult as the school was situated between the River Severn, which was wide and dangerous at this point, and the canal, where bridgekeepers would have been on the alert. Seeing others around content, the young inmates soon settled down to regular habits.

Most of the boys came from towns. If trades had been taught to them, they would have returned back to towns and the vices of the streets would again have become a temptation. Placed with a farmer in the country the lifestyle would remind them of school life where they were reformed rather than of their former evil days and the broken thread would not likely be renewed.

The educational condition of the boys when admitted was various, many having been taught reading, writing and elementary arithmetic, ranging down to a complete ignorance, even of the letters of the alphabet. Some knew a great deal of scripture while others did not know the first elements of religion. In the school, two hours at night were devoted to secular instruction in reading, writing, arithmetic, geography and general knowledge. Those who were very backward had a short time of additional teaching during the day. Religious instruction was by a short practical lesson at the daily morning prayers. The catechism of the Church of England was taught one day a week and the boys were all taken to church twice on Sundays where they came in after the congregation was seated, stood at the back during the service, and left before the congregation.

The lads must have looked forward to the walk to church. It gave them a welcome change of scenery and an opportunity to see other people, and, although they were forbidden to talk to the villagers, they must have lost no opportunity in contacting some of them. An entry in Mrs Mary Baker's journal for the 22 July 1852 reads: 'A fracas at the new school, the boys have been writing love-letters to the girls in the village'. And in Thomas Lloyd Baker's journal for the same day: 'Row about love letters.' But that seemed to be the end of the affair.

From an inventory of 1853 we know that in the schoolroom there were two deal tables, six benches, one shoemaker's bench, three maps, one stove and pipe and one easel and blackboard.[10] The sleeping room for twenty boys allowed a space of 3 ft by 6 ft for each, leaving a narrow passage down the centre of the room, just room for their hammocks on which was a straw stuffed 'mattress', a pair of sheets, a blanket and a counterpane.

The same inventory lists fifty-nine shirts, fifty-eight pocket handkerchiefs, fifty-eight neck cloths, fifty-eight pairs of stockings, twenty-nine caps, twenty-nine pairs of boots, thirty-one jackets, sixteen sleeved waistcoats, twenty-nine pairs of trousers and some material not made up. The school uniform consisted of a suit of cord and a jacket replaced on working days by a short smock of duck worn over the sleeved waistcoat.

The school diet consisted of skimmed milk, bread (about 10 oz at each meal of which it formed the main part), vegetables, rice, cheese, soup, meat in small quantities three times a week (4 oz cooked to each boy) and occasionally about half a pint of common cider, and a little tea and butter on Sundays.

The timetable changed very little over the years. Hygiene was not a strong point in those days, the boys had baths once a fortnight except during the summer months, when they were allowed to bathe once or twice a week in the canal and to learn to swim.

General Timetable

Weekdays		Sundays	
5.30–6 am	Rise, Dress, Private Prayers, Wash, etc	7–8 am	Rise, Dress, Private Prayers etc
6–7.45	Schooling, winter months. Summer – work	8–9	Breakfast, Family Prayer etc
7.45–8.45	Family Prayers, Psalms for the day, Breakfast	9–10	Religious instruction
8.45–1	Employment. On wet days, schooling	10–1	Church
1–2 pm	Wash, Dinner, Recreation	1–2.30 pm	Dinner and Recreation
2–5.30	Industrial Employment	2.30–4.30	Religious instruction, Collects and Gospel or Church in winter
5.30–6.30	Wash, Supper	4.30–5.30	Supper and Recreation
6.30–8.30	Schooling	5.30–6	Prepare for Church
8.30–8.45	Family Prayers, Private Prayers, bed	6–8	Church or Religious Instruction, Singing Hymns, Reading, bed
*	Stock boys, Cooks, Tailors, rise at 5.30 am, in charge of Officer and changed alternately		Stock boys rise at 6 am, with Officer, also Cook and Post Boy

Note: On Saturdays the boys cease to work out of doors at 1.30 pm. Saturday afternoons and evenings are spent in preparing for Sunday – bathing, changing linen, recreation, Scripture, and learning Collects and Gospels etc.   .

Every inmate is thoroughly bathed once a fortnight, and during the summer months the boys are allowed to bathe once or twice in the Canal, and learn to swim.

August 1870   Thomas Gee, Governor [11]

In the summer of 1861 the school received a visit from Professor von Holtzendorff, a German philanthropist, who had met Thomas Lloyd Baker at a conference in Dublin. By that time Baker was universally recognised as having established the first reformatory school for young criminals which had turned the tide of legislation in favour of such schools. Von Holtzendorff gives an engaging description of his visit to the school:

> After we left the house the squire explained the principles of his agricultural work to me in the quarter of an hour in which it took us to reach the reformatory. The superintendent expected us and had assembled his lads, most of them between twelve and fifteen. Their tools were lying near them and they had just begun digging. We went among them. Baker raised his finger and conducted a song which was given in unison and with spirit. Then we went into the simply furnished schoolroom. The result of an examination in elementary subjects was to obtain accurate and ready answers to our questions.
>
> After the lapse of an hour the field work, which had temporarily been suspended, was resumed. In a brief address the boys were to prove themselves worthy of the honour shown to them by the visit of a foreigner, and with a 'Hurrah' we left.
>
> What struck me most was the unmistakable look of cheerful industry and the shade of complexion which made such a striking contrast to the pale, cadaverous, expressionless faces of the young boys in the industrial reformatories in the towns.[12]

What effect did the reformatory have on its earliest inmates? Of the three original boys brought from London, the boy who had been neglected by his father and robbed shop tills was aged twelve on admission. He had then been convicted seven times as a thief. In the report of the school for January 1854 Baker describes him:

> A repeatedly convicted boy who at his first coming was a shameless liar thoroughly intractable, frequently obliged to be locked up and exceedingly irreverent in his general behaviour; but within six months he became amenable to discipline and desirous of doing better for his own sake. I watched

this poor boy gradually becoming obedient, steady, truthful and trustworthy to a degree which gives us hope that he and others may yet be saved from their own destruction.

This boy spent twenty-seven months in the school and was then helped to emigrate to Australia, where he did well. The second London boy spent nineteen months at Hardwicke at the end of which he was apprenticed to a farmer and he too did well. After sixteen months at the school the parents of the third boy asked if he could visit them in London but unfortunately the boy absconded whilst there and returned to his old associates.

After the passing of the Juvenile Offenders' Act in 1853 the Hardwicke Reformatory began to receive boys sent by the courts on conditional pardons, the condition being that they be sent to the institution for a certain number of years, and for the first time names appear in the records. The first boy admitted this way was Daniel Wayman, aged fifteen from Cheltenham, who on 26 December 1853 was found guilty of stealing hay and sentenced to three months hard labour. He received a conditional pardon on 10 February 1854 and was immediately collected from Gloucester gaol by George Bengough and taken to Hardwicke. On 21 February, Robert Emmerson and Thomas Hayes, both aged thirteen, were charged with stealing and sentenced to three months hard labour. After one month they were given a pardon and sent to Hardwicke. Ragan Williams aged ten, was charged with setting fire to a hayrick and sentenced to four years penal servitude, but on 10 May 1854 he too received a pardon and went to the school; and on 17 October of that year George Dee aged nine, was charged with stealing, sentenced to four months hard labour but soon received his pardon on condition that he went to the school.

Daniel Wayman spent only eight months in the reformatory, probably because of his age. He was apprenticed to a local farmer later in the year and apparently did well. Another boy who was apprenticed in 1854 was George Cole. He first appeared in the Gloucester gaol records on 17 March 1850, then aged ten, when he was charged with breaking and entering and was sentenced to three months hard labour, the first and last three days to be in solitary confinement. By 1854 he was an inmate of the reformatory and obviously worthy of trust, for the managers apprenticed him to a local farmer. The third boy apprenticed in 1854 was Stephen Philpotts, aged thirteen, from the Cotswold village of Moreton-in-Marsh, who on 5 February 1853 had been found guilty of stealing a fowl and sentenced to one months hard labour. His mother was dead and his father was about to be transported for life. A letter concerning this boy from Thomas Lloyd Baker to his legal adviser Rob Wilton reads:

> Dear Wilton, I accept gladly your offer of assistance to the school. Will you kindly draw the indentures according to the enclosed form binding Stephen Philpotts as Farm Servant to Thos Pipon, Joyce Grove, Nettlebed. I enclose his Note thereto. Philpotts' father was I believe sentenced to transportation for life for an abominable crime this Assizes, so the son is well to be out of it. Poor fellow, he showed excellent feeling towards his beast of a father. Thank God he is likely to turn out well.[13]

With the passing of the second Juvenile Offenders Bill, in June 1854, magistrates had the power commit children to reformatories at the end of the gaol sentence. Gaol records reveal that the first boy recommended for this treatment was Benjamin Cummings, aged ten, who on 17 October 1854 was charged with stealing a mare. He was sentenced to three months hard labour and at the expiration of this sentence was sent to the Reformatory School at Hardwicke for two years. In January 1855 John Cox and William Priest, both aged fourteen, were charged with stealing sweetmeats and sentenced to fourteen days hard labour in a house of correction followed by two years at Hardwicke. On 12 June, Charles Workman, aged twelve, was charged with breaking and entering and had a similar sentence, as did Alfred Betteridge, aged fourteen, who was charged with stealing from his master.

Save for a few exceptions, such as that of Stephen Philpotts, parents of the boys were expected to pay the maintenance fee, as laid down by the Juvenile Offenders' Bill. One shilling a week was the standard fee but this seemed too much to some poor families. Alfred Betteridge's father, Thomas, objected to paying the fee and was summoned to appear at the Upton Petty Sessions in August 1855; he was in employment and earning ten shillings a week, out of which he had to support three children. After hearing the evidence, the magistrate ordered him to pay the shilling. It was the first case of its kind to be tried in the country.[14]

Thomas Lloyd Baker had strong views on the subject of parental contributions. They were expounded in the school report of 1859:

> Payment of maintenance must be guided solely by the magistrates of the district in which the parents live. If they are kindhearted and say 'Here is a poor man earning ten shillings a week, I do not see how he can live on it; we will tell him to pay sixpence a week and not enforce it.' Depend on it! Manage the school as we will some parents will try to get the children off their hands. If on the other hand, the magistrates say TB has ten shillings a week, two shillings for rent and fuel which are not ceased by taking the boy away; that leaves two shillings for the man and his wife and one shilling each for four children, therefore he can pay one shilling a week for his boy *without being any the worse*; but he ought to be worse off than the man who had brought up his children well; therefore we would suggest his paying one shilling and sixpence a week. Were this done, although there might be a parent here and there who did not know the facts and might wish his son in a Reformatory, the number of such would be small and decrease rapidly.[15]

By January 1856 the school had received ninety-four boys; of these, five had absconded, three had been removed without consent, seven apprenticed, eight in trade, three in service, six at sea, one emigrated, six returned home, thirty-one removed to other schools and twenty-four remained in the school.

The 'thirty-one removed to other schools' needs some explanation. Baker knew from his own experience that when starting a new school it was difficult to get what he termed 'a good moral tone'. Where all the boys were unruly it was difficult to tame any of them, but when once habits of order and discipline had been imposed on the majority it was easier to pacify and train newcomers. Acting on this idea, he suggested to managers of new schools in several counties that taking a number of his boys who had been partly trained in his establishment would help to form the nucleus of the new school. When this idea was accepted and boys were taken, Baker received half the number of newly convicted boys in return. Thus the reformatory techniques first used at Hardwicke spread all over the country. Thomas Lloyd Baker's idea of reforming criminal boys and giving them a chance in life rather than punishing them had caught the mood of the age.

There were, of course, failures, like the one described in the report of 1861:

Relapse is occasionally found in a boy with a violent and passionate tempera-
ment; this is sad because the boys often have much good feeling in them and
a wish to do right. I received one boy of this character and I allowed him to
go into service in a large town where I afterwards found he had been in the
habit of going when the police were in pursuit of him. In this town he well
knew every den of iniquity and yet he continued honest to his employer for
more than twelve months; at the end of this time some of his old associates
found him out and drove him into leaving his service. The moment he again
embarked in crime he became perfectly reckless and broke into a house where
he could not have hoped to escape detection. He was sentenced to seven
years penal servitude. I saw him on his return from the Bermuda hulk,
apparently hard and reckless but with the aid of others he was persuaded to
emigrate and I have ever hoped he would do well.[16]

This was the fate of boy Number 7, one of the original four young
Cheltenham thieves brought in to join the three London boys at the
start of the reformatory experiment.

10

Off to the Reformatory!

'Reformatories are like hospitals – most valuable for serious cases;
that is for cases where other remedies have been tried and failed.'

Thomas Lloyd Baker [1]

Punishment in the first half of the nineteenth century was based on
retribution, with sentences being given which were in proportion to the
gravity of the offence. The belief was held that every individual had
the same powers of resisting temptation and therefore deserved the same
punishment for the same crime, whatever the circumstances. It was
during the 1850s that exceptions began to appear to this rigid formula,
particularly with respect to young offenders. Children coming before
the courts were no longer regarded in the same light as adults but were
seen as a distinct class in their own right and entitled to special care
because, it was deemed, they lacked full responsibility for their actions.

The most constructive change was accomplished by the introduction
of reformatory rather than punitive treatment for juveniles, a discipline
which also involved new powers of intervention in the relationship of
parent, or guardian and child. The reformatory system, which significantly distinguished the offences of young offenders from those of
adults, quickly replaced a penal system which had up to then had made
little provision for children.

Reformatories were not refuges open to anyone; nor were they
charities maintained at great cost by the state for the benefit of wayward
children and idle parents; nor were they for saving parish rates; nor
were they a moral mill through which evil children passed and ground
out perfect beings at the other end. The main aim of these institutions
was the diminution of juvenile crime which at the time had reached
alarming proportions.

The first consideration of this aim was to decide how the classes who were liable to criminal activities could be acted upon. The Youthful Offenders' Act 1854 gave the courts authority to send anyone aged under sixteen years to a reformatory school at the expiration of his or her sentence, creating a dual track system: prison sentence first and reformatory treatment after.[2] The offender could be kept for two to five years in the school but the Home Secretary had the power to order his or her discharge at any time and could also transfer an offender from one school to another. By the same Act the state was empowered to make a 'per capita' grant to those schools which were inspected and certified by one of Her Majesty's Inspectors of Prisons. Absconding or refractory conduct could be punished by a sentence of up to three months in gaol.

According to the reformatory managers the successful working of a school depended on three objectives: Deterrence, Reformation and Detention. Deterrence was in the form of a sentence meted out by magistrates, according to the gravity of the crime – between seven days and three weeks imprisonment. As a general rule, when a boy was brought before a magistrate for the first time he would be sentenced to one week in gaol with a caution that, if he was convicted again, he would be sent to the reformatory and his parents made to pay the fee. If that child did appear a second time the threat was carried out and he was sent to the school for two to five years.

Parents were compelled by law to contribute, if they were able, up to 5s. a week. This provision was strengthened by an Act of 1855 which, in cases of failure to pay, gave the courts power to summon parents, to make an order for payment and to distrain upon their goods, or commit them to prison if necessary.[3] Those receiving parish relief had their benefits reduced. This involved the parents or legal guardians in the child's crime, with the intention of stimulating them to their best efforts to keep their children honest.

As for the young offender, a week 'inside' might appear to be rather a slight deterrent but conditions were so harsh and the diet so meagre that any child experiencing it would regard it as a very bad place and report such back to his associates. One boy told his friends, 'It half killed me', and really believed that a month inside would have done so. So boys came out impressed that prison was a most disagreeable place and would try to avoid a return, especially if they knew that the next offence would ensure at least two years in a reformatory for which their parents would have to pay.

Thomas Gee, who after the 1854 Act was governor of Hardwicke, expressed the opinion:

> In common with almost all persons interested in reformatories I believe that the fear of prison is a powerful deterrent and that the severity of a short imprisonment is a good preparation for the steady but less severe discipline of the reformatory.

Thomas Lloyd Baker agreed with him:

> I have always advocated a short imprisonment, not in order to complete punishment and wipe off the debt to society, but to impress on the boy's mind the feeling that he has done wrong and to prepare him to receive the milder discipline of the reformatory.[4]

It was not until 1893 that reformatory places became available to children who had not undergone a sentence of imprisonment.

Reformation was of great importance in the diminution of crime but it was a difficult objective. In a letter dated 6 December 1856 to the Chairman of the Gloucestershire Quarter Sessions: Thomas Baker wrote,

> If a boy, in spite of his first warning does commit another crime, he will merit a very heavy punishment and the longer his sentence the more likely he is to settle into the school discipline and the better his chance of refor-mation. However, we do not propose to be infallible in turning bad boys into good. We may bend nature but we cannot transform it. Some boys have minds hopelessly deformed and the evil principle at the end of two years is only suppressed but smouldering and ready to break out again at any moment. Others are hopelessly weak, full of good intentions but incapable of resisting temptation, they are 'as unstable as water'. Whether four or five years of discipline might enable them to become stronger, I know not. Still, if we cannot reform them we can give them a fair opportunity for amendment.

Relapses were to be expected in boys who had led undisciplined lives without any moral training. It was possibly detention – the two to five years of institutional life – which had more effect than anything else on the really hardened cases. The reformatory was not like a refuge: disci-pline was absolute, work was hard, and freedom could be curtailed for very young offenders for up to five years. However, at the end of that time the boy had a chance of maintaining himself honestly and during his confinement he would have received a decent education, had moral training and would have discontinued the practice of crime and probably forgotten his former bad associations.

Between 1853 and 1858 statutes applicable to juvenile offenders in reformatories laid down practices for ordinary cases which included:

That no juvenile offender be for a first offence sent to a reformatory. That every male juvenile offender on a second or subsequent conviction be sent to a reformatory.

That the imprisonment for the first offence be so short as to ensure the lowest scale of prison diet.

That when any juvenile comes before a magistrate the clerk should communicate with the managers of the Reformatory in order that the court which tries may have the means of knowing to what Reformatory to send him, if convicted.

That in every case of sentence to a Reformatory notice be sent immediately by the Petty Sessions Clerk to the Managers.

That in every case the police take every available means to procure the attendance at the trial of the parent.

That on conviction the court distinctly informs the parent that, it being the child's first offence, he will be sentenced only to a short imprisonment but that the parent must take care that the child does not offend again; that if he is convicted of a further offence he will be sent to the Reformatory and the parent made to contribute for his maintenance and a note should be entered on the proceedings of court that the parent has been cautioned.

That in every case of a second offence the attendance of the parent in like manner is procured at the trial.

That immediately on receipt of a certificate of conviction the Petty Sessions should take proceedings at once against the parent.

The person appointed by the Secretary of State to receive the contribution is HM's Inspector of Reformatories who usually selects as his agent the Superintendent of Police of the district.

The rate of contribution may be revised from time to time and the payments to be made to the person appointed to receive same and are liable by default to ten days imprisonment.

It is recommended that under similar circumstances girls should also be sent to a Reformatory, for which purpose the term of preliminary imprisonment will probably require to be longer as it may take a longer time to ascertain what Reformatory can receive them.[5]

The cost of these proceedings under the appropriate Act was defrayed out of the rates of the county and in Scotland out of the 'Rogue Money' of the county or police rates of the burgh.

Sometimes managers refused to accept cases which they considered had been convicted for very trifling offences. For instance boys 'sent down' for stealing bread, fruit or cake which they then ate, or for 'stealing' some small article found in the street, or the case of a small child picking the lead out of a cottage window – not exactly house-breaking; or the boy playfully knocking some coins out of another child's hand in the village street – not exactly highway robbery. Such children could be sent to a reformatory for three years, costing the nation £180 each, so managers occasionally decided that the money could be better spent on more vicious children and refused to take them.

In the late 1850s it cost £60 a year to keep a boy in a reformatory, but that was a bargain according to James Greenwood:

> It would come as much cheaper to the country if these budding burglars and pickpockets were caught and caged up before their natures became too thoroughly pickled in the brine of rascality. Boy thieves are the most mischievous and wasteful. They will mount a house roof and for the sake of appropriating the half-a-crown's worth of lead that forms its gutter, cause such damage as only a builder's bill of £20 will set right. The other day a boy stole a family Bible valued at 60s. and after wrenching off the gilt clasps, threw the book into a sewer; the clasps he sold to a marine store dealer for two pence halfpenny. In the case of boy thieves, who are in the hands of others, before they can make 10s. in cash, they must as a rule steal to the value of at least £4. Let us put the loss by exchange at its lowest and say that he gets a fourth of the value of what he steals before he can earn 1s. 6d. a day, he must rob to the amount of two guineas a week or £109 a year! Whatever less sum it costs the state to educate, clothe and teach him, the nation would be in pocket.[6]

Within four years of the 1854 Act authorising their establishment there were fifty reformatory schools catering for juvenile offenders who were legally detained. In 1857 the Rev. Sydney Turner, who had done so much to transform the Philanthropic Society's institution, was appointed as the first Home Office Inspector of Reformatory Schools. Under his guidance the system continued to expand and develop and by the end of 1865 there were sixty-five certified reformatory schools accommodating 4915 children.[7]

In the early days reformatories had a religious bias. Although most of them were run under Church of England guidance, the committing authorities tried to ascertain the religious persuasion of an offender or his or her family, and, if possible, to select a school conducted in accordance with that persuasion. For instance in the Bristol area the Hardwicke reformatory followed the principles of the Church of England while the Kingswood reformatory, near Bristol, was for 'dissenting' or nonconformist boys; the surrounding area being a Methodist stronghold. For girls, Mary Carpenter's Red Lodge was nonconformist and Arno's Court reformatory was for Catholic girls, this establishment being managed by Ann Parrish, the mother superior of an associated convent.

Besides religious differences, schools varied in their selection of occupations and in the way the 'houses' were organised. In a report read to the Statistics Section of the British Association at Glasgow, in September 1855, the Rev. A. K. McCallom, governor of the Glasgow House of Refuge, which had just been certified as a reformatory, described his system:

> In the school, reading, writing, arithmetic, grammar, geography, music and scientific and scriptural knowledge are taught. The time is divided into two divisions, morning and afternoon, four classes in each. The boys are found to be very ignorant when admitted. Out of 286, seventy-nine on admission could read tolerably, 119 could read little words and ninety-seven did not know the alphabet.
>
> Idleness is the bane of the juvenile population and almost inevitably leads to crime. It is vitally important to train boys to the usual trades carried out in society, farming, tailoring, shoemaking, weaving, joining and wood splitting are the principal occupations of the houses.
>
> It is hoped that the houses will soon be able to accommodate 450 boys and be one big, happy, Christian family with the governor and his wife acting in the place of parents. The law of love should pervade the youthful community. Restriction and restraint should be unknown. A newly admitted boy has preliminary training, separately, under the care of the governor and by degrees is permitted to associate with the rest. Thus admitted he is absorbed into the habits and feelings of the rest and soon moulded by them. At the close of each day three marks, one for obedience, one for truthfulness and

one for industry are given to each boy by his master according to how he has behaved. These marks help to determine the length of time a boy will be detained in the House. In the summer the boys have excursions down the Clyde and to the Botanical Gardens etc.

Of 225 boys dismissed during the last five years after the most rigid of examinations we can discover but nine cases who have fallen into the hands of the justices. The following are some of the occupations of the boys on leaving: thirty sailors, six soldiers, nineteen tailors, sixteen shoemakers, fourteen farmers, two mechanics, three iron founders, four wrights, five message boys, three shop boys, three brass founders, one baker, one carver, four office boys, three carters, one shopkeeper and one clerk.

Boys are taken from the age of six to fifteen. On 1 July 1855 there were three aged six, five of seven, six of eight, fifteen of nine, thirty-six of ten, twenty-six of eleven, fifty-six of twelve, fifty-seven of thirteen, fourteen of fourteen and twenty-two of fifteen. Of boys admitted during the year, 124 had parents who were drunkards, forty-eight had parents who had deserted them, sixty-one were orphans, seventy-nine father dead, forty-two mother dead and fifty-six parents both alive'.[8]

By 1857 this reformatory had accommodation for 400 boys.[9]

In Aberdeen, the first governor of the Oldmill Reformatory, James Meeston, ran his establishment like a factory and had workshops for tailors, web shoemakers, ordinary shoemakers and weavers, employing between ninety and a hundred boys. The emphasis on industrial work continued successfully and as a later governor, R. Simpson, indicates in a paper which he read at a meeting of the Masters and Mistresses in Scotland in 1876, they kept up with the technology of the times:

> The introduction of new industries requires grave and serious consideration unless the articles made are for home use. The simplest, most useful and profitable industries carried on in the neighbourhood of a school should be tried – boots should be made on the riveted principle which for many reasons is preferable to the handsewed work for the boys. At riveted work the boys become very useful in one year and by the time they are out on licence are able to earn a good deal more than will keep them decent and respectable; whereas at sewed work they are only of any use in the school and unable to keep themselves when let out. Boys may also be employed profitably at power loom work.[10]

That year, 1876, the 130 inmates made a profit of £1550. By January 1878 they had an engine to supply power to several machines, including a webbing shop, where about thirty boys were employed making carpet and webbing and carpet shoes, both sewn and riveted. They were sold to wholesale merchants in the city of Aberdeen. Another machine was used for weaving stockings; a complete stocking could be made in a few minutes. The weaving department employed another thirty boys making shirting, sheeting, a fluffy material called wincey, and girths for carpet shoes. But it was not all work, the school also had a band and music was high on the agenda for entertainment.[11] Other reformatories concentrated on farm and outdoor work, for instance at the Wellington reformatory school at Penicuik, twelve miles south of Edinburgh, the boys were originally engaged in digging peat.[12]

More unusual reformatory establishments were reformatory ships, like the *Cornwall*, moored at Purfleet on the Essex bank of the Thames, and the *Akbar*, moored off Rock Ferry on the Cheshire side of the Mersey near Liverpool. These were by no means in the same class as the hulks as they had to conform to the standards and aims set out in the Youthful Offenders' Act before they could be certified.

The *Akbar* was certified and ready to receive boys on 8 January 1856. With a full complement of 300, it was quite a problem for those in control to supervise and keep the lads busy for fifteen hours a day. Of course they spent many hours scrubbing decks and keeping the ship clean; besides this, it seems that by 1858 most of the boys were employed in tailoring. They made and repaired all their own clothes and also took orders from other establishments, including making the uniforms for young naval officers on a nearby training vessel.

In order to add a little interest to the otherwise tedious system, in 1858 the governor, Captain Fenwick, decided to buy such musical instruments as might be necessary for a band and to hire a bandmaster. As a result a full brass band was formed and soon its excellence made it a popular attraction at bazaars and other functions in the area. Unlike their predecessors on the old hulks, boys confined to this floating reformatory did have the occasional outing on shore.

By 1863 the increase in the number of applications for the admission of Catholic delinquents was causing concern. The committee responsible for the *Akbar* refused to accept Catholic boys, ostensibly because of the difficulties of fitting in their religious requirements. The problem was resolved in 1864 when a number of prominent Catholic businessmen on Merseyside decided to provide a reformatory ship of their own and soon the *Clarence* took up a position alongside the *Akbar*.

The job of supervising these ships with their companies of young criminals under such cramped conditions required great strength of mind and a strong constitution. Applicants for the position of captain of the *Akbar* were told:

> The post is not an easy one. It requires tact, knowledge of character, patience, habits of order and the committee will not consider it right to appoint and retain anyone who does not conduct the duties of the vessel in a successful as well as a diligent manner.[13]

In 1898 out of 395 'old hands' of the *Akbar* heard of during that year there were: able seamen (71), apprentices (2), army sergeants (2), bandsmen (2), boatswains (2), captains (1), carters (4), chief mates (1), colliers (1), contractors (1), cooks (1), engine drivers (2), firemen (3), first mates (3), fish hawkers (1), greasers(1), labourers (114), lance corporals (2), leading stokers (1), letter carriers (2), master mates (1), ordinary seamen (76), painters and decorators (4), policemen (1), privates (8), quartermasters (3), railway porters (2), sailmakers (1), second mates (4), shoe blacks (4), stewards (3), stokers (7), stone cutters (1), third mates (3) and tradesmen (55).[14] It is not surprising that many of the boys had chosen a seafaring life, but there was a good variety of other occupations as well.

The *Akbar* had a good disciplinary record and was one of the most successful of the floating reformatories; others were not so effective. The difficulties of keeping so many wayward boys usefully occupied in such a confined space as a ship naturally threw up problems. At the Hull police court on 21 January 1874, five lads were charged with attempting to destroy HMS *Southampton*, a reformatory ship lying on moorings in the Hull Roads. The evidence went to show that two of the lads, Pidgeon and Maddon, attempted to scuttle the ship by sawing in two a lead pipe that could be used for flooding the ship in the case of fire. The other prisoners were ringleaders in attempting to set the ship on fire. The superintendent, Captain Pollard RN, informed a meeting that several of the lads were returning to the ship from work when they used revolting language to his daughter that so irritated him that he flogged several of them severely. There had been great discontent on board and on the previous Friday officers of the ship found that an attempt had been made to set the vessel on fire. The lads were so excited that it was deemed advisable to send for a body of policemen and thirteen of them were placed under arrest. One of them, named Hatton, said he saw Pidgeon give a saw to the prisoner Maddon and he afterwards witnessed Maddon set fire to a pile of wood on board. Pidgeon also sprinkled oil on the sides of the ship and Maddon took the paraffin feeder out of the lamp locker before tea and placed it close to the fire that was made before supper. Another boy, Harrington, was seen to heat a poker to redness and then dip it into a cask of tar and his accomplice, Brown, was seen to take oakum, coal and oil which he placed on the lower deck. The prisoners were remanded and eventually committed for trial at the quarter sessions on 17 April where they were severally sentenced to eighteen months, twelve months and six months imprisonment. At the expiration of the sentence they were to be sent to Stranraer Reformatory for five years.[15]

It was not only on ships that problems occurred. On the night of 13 November 1875 a mutiny occurred at Mount St Bernard Roman Catholic Reformatory near Ashby de la Zouche, Leicestershire, when about 160 of the 200 inmates escaped. They were all recaptured the following day.[16]

There was a riot too at the West Riding Reformatory for girls, Doncaster, on 24 July 1876, when several of the older girls refused to go back into the house. At the same time nearly all the inmates turned out and began to smash the windows. They were ordered in but refused to obey. Police were sent for and eventually succeeded in getting the girls back into the house. Mr C. E. Palmer, secretary of the institution, then reasoned with them and order was restored. Ten of the ringleaders were taken into custody and one of them sentenced to imprisonment with hard labour for three months; of the others, six girls were sentenced to ten weeks, two for six weeks and one for a month. The girls smashed thirty-eight panes of glass in the course of their proceedings.[17]

Despite the odd hiccup, the new system forged ahead and even by 1860 the idea of deterring would-be juvenile offenders was beginning to take effect. The school managers soon realised that crime could be reduced dramatically by detaining 'often convicted' boys, the professional boy thieves who operated gangs with the help of apprentices.

Thomas Lloyd Baker helped to bring this fact to the attention of the public:

> My object has always been not so much a mere reformation of boys who have fallen into crime as to preventing others hitherto uncontaminated from catching the infection. It is known to all who have studied the subject that boys almost always learn crime from other boys. I do not mean to deny the existence of a 'Fagin' but I cannot think but such are extremely rare in all but extremely large towns. All the boys in this county who have had any education in crime have learned it from boys under 16.[18]

The spa town of Cheltenham, which attracted well-off residents and visitors, produced as many young thieves as the rest of the county of Gloucestershire together. During the year 1852, forty-five boys were imprisoned and four years later fifty-three. After long endeavours the police found out who were the leaders and who were the apprentices and in 1856 the two master thieves were caught. They confessed to having trained eight young boys in the year. After a short imprisonment they were sent to the Hardwicke reformatory. Of their apprentices, some were frightened by the loss of their leaders and left the neighbourhood; the others turned more or less honest. During 1856 the last of the gangs and their apprentices were sent to reformatories. The following year only fourteen boys overall were convicted. In this case, at least the principle of catching the trained thieves with a view to preventing them from corrupting others had proved successful.

In general, all over the country, the experience was the same, with figures for juvenile crime beginning to fall.

Counties of England and Wales: Abstract of Criminal Returns, 1854–59

	Boys committed to prison				Girls committed to prison			
	1856	1857	1858	1859	1856	1857	1858	1859
Bedfordshire	46	42	25	28	2	3	5	4
Berkshire	68	62	62	45	18	17	7	12
Buckinghamshire	46	38	40	42	5	4	2	2
Cambridge	52	62	35	46	5	8	4	5
Cheshire	242	179	149	117	47	31	18	20
Cornwall	31	40	29	16	12	3	12	13

	Boys committed to prison				Girls committed to prison			
	1856	1857	1858	1859	1856	1857	1858	1859
Cumberland	44	22	41	23	9	11	5	6
Derby	79	69	49	39	10	12	4	23
Devon	202	188	153	159	34	36	35	22
Dorset	52	47	38	22	8	7	12	6
Durham	73	213	158	137	20	37	39	39
Essex	175	163	128	86	17	13	15	12
Gloucestershire	183	122	110	130	41	19	7	19
Bristol	199	175	116	129	20	29	18	12
Hereford	18	18	14	25	5	7	4	3
Hertfordshire	94	58	65	49	12	4	6	1
Huntingdon	11	9	23	9	4	5	6	1
Kent	285	279	225	236	53	50	34	40
Lancashire	279	210	217	228	63	23	30	29
Liverpool	708	502	387	404	285	152	99	87
Manchester	751	827	622	401	82	101	73	55
Leicestershire	84	110	139	89	16	16	18	11
Lincolnshire	63	89	77	77	25	20	39	25
Middlesex	3606	3133	2644	2281	642	398	368	278
Monmouth	42	35	42	21	34	13	14	10
Norfolk	187	188	147	116	15	15	11	8
Northamptonshire	79	63	64	67	10	9	9	8
Northumberland	220	162	188	150	79	36	33	46
Nottinghamshire	119	134	132	88	17	23	17	13
Oxfordshire	44	43	53	23	7	7	6	5
Rutland	4	4	2	1	-	-	1	-
Shropshire	67	28	31	46	20	17	12	8
Somerset	171	142	100	132	35	36	28	15
Southampton	239	255	189	144	42	23	27	31
Staffordshire	209	222	189	179	77	22	26	37
Suffolk	123	104	79	78	15	7	21	11
Surrey	1317	1437	968	701	161	144	117	143
Sussex	150	146	94	107	31	38	23	26

	Boys committed to prison				Girls committed to prison			
	1856	1857	1858	1859	1856	1857	1858	1859
Warwickshire	91	65	78	80	14	7	11	18
Birmingham	265	244	143	119	49	38	17	21
Westmoreland	12	12	9	8	8	1	3	5
Wiltshire	37	56	47	59	9	12	7	15
Worcestershire	80	61	75	74	29	22	27	18
Yorkshire (W)	372	226	219	154	58	35	52	39
Leeds	129	98	79	103	15	24	36	24
Yorkshire (E & N)	295	244	212	186	38	35	41	33
Totals for England	11,652	10,626	8686	7454	2198	1567	1399	1260

In England and Wales the total numbers of boys and girls under sixteen committed to prison were: [19]

1856	1857	1858	1859	1860
13,981	12,501	10,329	8913	8029

With a few exceptions, in counties like Durham which nearly doubled its population at this time, the statistics suggest a large decrease in the number of children committed to prison. How much of it may be attributed to the work of the reformatories and how much to other causes is a fair matter for debate. But it does appear that within five years of the Youthful Offenders' Act there was a noticeable diminution in juvenile crime, which had been the original aim of the pioneer schools. By this time most English counties had a reformatory and there was one in Wales and five in Scotland.

Reformatories in Ireland were established later than those in England. In 1863 Patrick Murray, Inspector of Reformatories in Ireland, made a report stating that on 31 December 1862 there were nine institutions in Ireland dealing with 591 juveniles. He gave two examples of the problems they faced: a boy of eight years of age when first charged, had forty-two convictions before he was fourteen; imprisonment, hard labour and whipping had been tried in vain. A girl of nine years when first charged had nine sentences of imprisonment by the time she was fourteen. Murray said 'For her and the boy gaol held no terrors, it had become familiar, crime became more attractive after each recommittal. The children were hardened in vice by contact with their fellow criminals.' These examples were given by Patrick Murray to show the uselessness of such prison sentences and the enormous cost of crime in Ireland before the establishment of reformatories in that country.[20]

It had been the intention of the early reformers that reformatories should independently and individually develop their own systems, but at the same time they were well aware of the advantages of the exchange of information and experience among those engaged in the day to day operation of the schools. To achieve this in 1856 the Reformatory and Refuge Union came into being, its motto was 'To Seek and Save that which was Lost'. The union relied on grants, subscriptions and donations, with people contributing from between one guinea and £50, and the occasional legacy such as that from the late Robert Hanbury, manager of the Whitechapel Reformatory who had also been honorary secretary of the union, to which he bequeathed £500 when he died in 1867. The organisation had a threefold object:

1. To collect and diffuse information as to the operations and results of all such institutions; to afford a means of communication between their promoters and a concerted action with reference to the government, the legislators and public bodies in general.

2. To facilitate the institution of new institutions, the selection and training of efficient masters, matrons and assistants, the procurement of books and school material for educational or industrial work and the ultimate provision for inmates by emigration or situations of permanent employment.

3. To promote the religious, intellectual and industrial education of such institutions and without interfering in their management to encourage those who conduct them in every effort to elevate and reclaim the neglected and criminal class by educating them in the fear of God and the knowledge of the holy scriptures.[21]

The union provided a point of contact and a forum for the exchange of views and expression of opinions, especially through its *Reformatory and Refuge Journal* which commenced publication in 1861, quarterly at first, then monthly from 1864. In 1862 the Earl of Shaftesbury became its president.

This organisation found itself in a position to advise magistrates as to which reformatories were ready to receive and which were the most suitable for the various classes of criminal children. It published a classified list of reformatory and preventative institutions which contained particulars of each institution, contributed by the managers themselves: names and addresses, date of foundation, accommodation, ages preferred, class received and terms of admission, name and address of the honorary secretary, name and address of superintendent or matron, list of colonial institutions.[22] Over the years the organisation cooperated with magistrates all over the country in placing juvenile offenders in appropriate reform schools. The Union recommended the restriction of punishment for young children in reformatories but also advocated the establishment of special schools for refractory cases. It was also responsible for the setting up of 'half-way houses' to help those discharged on special licence.

In 1857 the Youthful Offenders' Act was amended to allow local authorities to contribute both to the establishment of reformatories and to the upkeep of children in them.[23] The Act also gave authorities the power to release on licence any well-disposed inmates after half the period of their detention.

The amendment relating to contributions gave local magistrates the authority to order monetary aid for a reformatory which could be used towards building a new school or extending existing buildings. No money could be granted to any establishment until it had been officially certified. The licensing of children who were considered to be ready for the outside world, after they had served at least half of their sentence, was on a three monthly renewable basis. If the child misbehaved in any way or absconded while out on licence, he or she would have been liable to a term of three months imprisonment. Once an offender on licence had proved himself worthy, the reformatory managers could bind him legally as an apprentice to any trade, or act as referee and stand security to any other employer for the term of the child's sentence.

When the time came for their release, most of the children were found suitable positions by the committee of management of the reformatories, many of whom were local businessmen, or by the Reformatory and Refuge Union if they came from a different part of the country. Those released were encouraged to write to their old schools to let them know of their progress. Many did.

For instance, Francis, who as a child had been picked up on the streets as a vagrant by the Liverpool police, remembered with appreciation the system which taught him to read and write and convinced him that, although he had entered this world as a nobody without a chance, aided by the reformatory system he became honest, obedient and industrious. On his release in 1872 Francis was helped to emigrate to America. Eight years later, a prosperous businessman in the mid-west, he sent a $20 bill to his old reformatory and found jobs for two boys in America.[24]

11

Bad Girls

'I believe that the experience of almost every parish priest in England would be that girls are kept straight, not so much by their own good principle, as by the check imposed on them through the dread of shame, the fear of fathers, mothers, friends and relations. Let that check be removed and their future progress is rapidly downward.'

Francis Russell Nixon, Bishop of Van Diemen's Land, 1846 [1]

Jane Cameron was born in Croiley's Land, Glasgow, an area described by the police as 'the worst place in the world'. She was born on a litter of shavings in the corner of a room on the third floor. Her mother, although not known as a professional thief, was well known to the police for keeping a disorderly house, being intoxicated in the streets and abusive to the public. In a room 8 ft by 7 ft she took in lodgers and frequently had it so full that her own child was turned out to sleep on the stairs. Not one sign of love or interest did she ever manifest towards Jane but treated her as an encumbrance. When the child reached about five years her mother sent her out to beg, telling her she was old enough to look after herself. Any money Jane received her vicious mother immediately took from her. When she was between seven and eight she experienced some friendly treatment from a mat maker and his wife, who took her in when she was shut out by her mother. They got behind with their rent and were driven out of their room, so Jane was on the streets and friendless once more. When she was ten she worked for a time in a cotton factory and earned 1s. a week, which her mother took and spent on drink. Her putative father told her, young as she was, of a better manner of making money on the streets and threatened her unless she adopted it. She was then induced to frequent the streets where she formed acquaintances, both male and female, who hastened her downfall. At a Penny Dance room at the age of eleven she met Jock Ewan, a lad of fifteen who belonged to a gang of thieves. By now she had left her 'home' and with Ewan commenced a life of thieving. She became an expert and more and more reckless, with the result that at the age of twelve she was imprisoned for twenty days. Unfortunately, as a consequence of the prison being full, she was placed in a cell with a old recidivist who was the means of hardening her against any advice offered by the chaplain and prison officers. When she left prison she and Ewan commenced living together, even though he was described as a cowardly lad without a single lovable quality. Unwilling to risk any danger himself, he sent Jane out to do the 'jobs', resulting in her being imprisoned a second time for sixty days with hard labour. The hard labour was not exacted, however, as by now Jane was pregnant. The birth took place soon after her discharge in the midst of the direst want and wretchedness. Jock Ewan had abandoned her for another girl. She lodged with an old Irish woman and was slow in regaining her strength after the birth of her child. She took her baby and begged in the streets for sustenance but this daily exposure to the cold made the infant weak and it soon died of scarlet fever. After this event Jane regularly associated with gangs of thieves. As a result at the age of fifteen she was sent to Glasgow gaol.[2]

A cautionary tale but very common in the mid nineteenth century. Throughout the country there were thousands of female children sent out to earn their living on the streets – legally or illegally – creating an outcast class of criminal girls which cost the country heavily in workhouses and prisons.

At a meeting of the Ladies' Association for the Care of Friendless Girls it was reported:

> It is necessary to consider how to meet the case of those girls who have already become mothers. It is a numerous class. There are many cases where a girl is induced to take to the streets from the necessity of supporting an infant which the father has abandoned ... At present parish guardians refuse any assistance to the support of these infants when the mothers are sent into Homes. But when the state pronounces the mother a criminal (for example for theft) and sends her to prison, her child is cared for as long as she is in prison ... If it be that hard upon ratepayers to support these children while

the mother is in prison, probably learning to be a laundrywoman or servant, let it be remembered that if the mother be left untrained and the child unsaved both will probably enter the criminal class and cost the ratepayers much more in the end as inmates of prisons.[3]

Criminal prisons were a man's world designed for men. Women in prison were seen as anomalous and therefore they were not always catered or legislated for. There was a well-held belief in nineteenth century society that women were naturally morally superior to men, so by descending into crime they became worse than men and deemed beyond redemption. Therefore, to reach a state of base criminal depravity women had to descend the moral scale a greater distance.

To prison officials women and girls presented more of a practical nuisance than a problem of discipline and training. They had to deal with the difficulties of caring for babies inmates brought in or gave birth to in prison, as well as moral and psychological differences which were just beginning to be recognised. Although, on the whole, their crimes were less numerous and less serious than boys, young girls in particular were found to be more difficult to control. Lieutenant Colonel Joshua Jebb, Chairman of the Directors of Convict Prisons, observed that:

> Because they are not so amenable to punishment, their offences are of a different character and depend very much on impulse. If they quarrel one with another they will set to work and break the windows of their cells and tear up their clothes all without assignable reason and then they will sit down and burst out crying. They are a difficult people to manage.[4]

As manager of a girls' reformatory, Mary Carpenter was also well aware of how far young women sank to reach the depths of criminality:

> The very susceptibility and tenderness of the woman's nature render her more completely diseased in her whole nature when thus perverted by evil and when a woman is thrown aside, the virtuous restraints of society are enlisted on the side of evil and she is far more dangerous to society than the other sex.[5]

In her book on reformatory schools she indicated that it was a known fact that young girls were generally less prone to crime than boys of the same age but that their tendency to it rapidly increased with age and once embarked on a criminal career they became more thoroughly hardened than boys. The truth of this fact had been attested to by Francis

Russell Nixon, the Bishop of Van Diemen's Land, who in 1846 testified before a Select Committee of the House of Lords respecting juvenile offenders and transportation. After speaking of the fearful conditions of the female convicts in the colonies, which surpassed in degradation and vice even that of men, he added:

> Female felons are so bad, because, before a woman can become a felon at all, she must have fallen much lower, have unlearnt much more, have become much more lost and depraved than a man. Her difficulty in regaining her self-respect is proportionally greater. There is nothing to fall back upon – no one to look to. I believe that the experience of almost every parish priest in England would lead him to the conclusion that there are many cases in which our village girls are kept straight, not so much by their own good principle, as by the check imposed upon them through the dread of shame, the fear of fathers, mothers, friends and relations. Let that check once be removed and their future progress is rapidly downward. When they go out as convicts everything is gone, every restraint is removed; they can fall no lower. (1)

Women convicts experienced very different, more restrictive, forms of imprisonment than men. They were subjected to longer periods of close confinement, sedentary forms of labour and an uncertainty about the duration of their sentences. These factors tended to make the time spent in prison more severe than a sentence of the same duration for a man. For a few the prolonged solitary confinement and the pitiless pressure of prison regimes proved intolerable and they attempted either to escape, or draw attention to themselves by bad behaviour, or to protest by self-mutilation or, in desperate cases, by suicide.

The Golden Bridge Reformatory in Dublin received prisoners from the notorious Mountjoy Gaol. In 1863 the superintendent, Sister Kirwan, offered the following reasons why it was imperative that females should be detained for a longer period of time than males:

> It is generally admitted that women are more difficult to reform than men. Upon release men and boys usually take outdoor work, whereas girls are generally engaged in household duties often with valuable property under their charge and therefore require more time for training and testing. They must be untaught and retaught since females of the criminal class are essentially idle and ignorant to helplessness.[6]

Girls were not expected to lead an independent life. As they were to be prepared to look after a house, a great degree of neatness, order and propriety of demeanour was expected of them. The 'idle and ignorant' had to be trained during their years of detention. In a paper read before the British Association for the Advancement of Science in August 1856, Mary Carpenter recommended the following important principles of management in dealing with girls in reformatories:

1. The physical condition of these girls will generally be found very unsatisfactory; and it is well known that the moral state is much influenced by the physical. All sanitary regulations for ventilation, regular and sufficient personal ablutions, suitable temperature etc. should be strictly attended to. The advantage of agricultural labour not being procurable, walks beyond the premises, as well as outdoor play, should be regularly taken and as much bodily exercise as possible should be devised for them in their daily industrial work, as an exercise of their physical energies. The food should be sufficient and of a more nourishing description than is allowed in most pauper schools.

2. The young girl must be placed, as far as possible, in the same kind of position as children in a well-ordered family in the working classes. She has been accustomed to be independent of authority and to do only what is right in her own eyes. She must now feel under steady, regular restraint, administered with a firm, equal but loving hand. Her irregular impulses must be curbed. She must insensibly, but steadily, be made to feel that it is necessary for her to submit to the will of others and especially to be obedient to duty.

3. Children of this class have hitherto felt themselves in a state of antagonism with society, and totally unconnected with the virtuous portion of it. They must, as far as possible, be brought to feel themselves a part of society, regarded by it with no unkind feeling but rather, having been outcasts, welcomed into it with Christian love and entering into it as far as their own conduct renders this possible. Nothing in their dress or appearance should mark them out as a separate caste; as far as it is found safe and expedient, they should be enabled to associate with others.

4. The affections must be cultivated as much as possible in a healthy direction. The love of their families must not be repressed and the natural ties must be cherished as far as can be done without evil influence being exerted over them. The school must be made a home and a happy one. Mutual dependence must be cultivated; and as in actual society, they must be made to feel that all must often suffer through the misconduct of one, while the good conduct of every individual is a benefit to the whole number.

5. The activity and love of amusement natural to childhood should be cultivated in an innocent and healthy manner. These cannot be repressed without great moral injury but they may be turned to good account and made the medium of conveying most valuable lessons on the rights of others and the nature of property and even of imparting useful knowledge. The children should be allowed to possess little toys and articles treasured by childhood, which they may be permitted to purchase with earnings awarded for work done. The valuable exhibitions now open to ordinary schools may be allowed to them occasionally, especially as a reward for good conduct. The Dioramas and Zoological Gardens may improve their minds and give a stimulus to the advancement of knowledge more than any other lessons.

6. All rewards and punishments should be the natural consequences of actions. Deceit or dishonesty will occasion an amount of distrust and watchfulness, which a judicious teacher may render a very severe punishment. The employment of bad language, and the indulgence of a quarrelsome disposition will require separation from the society of others as a necessary consequence. All punishments should be administered with the greatest caution and impartiality. There should be no bribery to do right nor deterring by fear only. Hence artificial stimulants to good conduct should be avoided in these schools; they foster many bad passions.

7. As much freedom should be given as is compatible with the good order of the establishment. Those who prove themselves deserving of confidence may have situations of trust assigned them and may be sent on errands beyond the premises. It is only in proportion as there is liberty, that security can be felt in the child's real improvement.

8. The intellectual powers should be steadily trained, though not superficially excited. It is only by giving the mind wholesome nourishment that it can be prevented from preying on garbage.

9. Every effort should be made to infuse a good moral tone into the school.

10. The will of each individual child must be enlisted in her own reformation and she must be made to feel that without this the efforts of her teachers will be useless. Such confidence must be awakened in the minds of the children towards their teachers as to lead them willingly to submit to all the regulations for order, neatness and regularity which are an important part of their training.[7]

In an age when few girls had the advantage of an education, and when they were expected to work and support themselves as soon as they could, the choices of employment were limited and without much prospect. Selling items on the streets attracted many city girls, who regarded this as better than sweatshop labour or crossing sweeping, but it was more difficult for country girls to earn an honest living, as farm labour was often seasonal and known to be arduous. For most young girls the answer was to leave home and go into service; to work in a household in return for wages, a roof over their heads and their keep. Once a family became rich enough to own a home it was not considered proper for the woman of the house to do her own housework. With the rise of respectable society, if you could afford a decent house, you could afford a few servants to run it.

The 1861 Census revealed that out of 2,700,000 women employed in Britain, 2,000,000 were in domestic service, which remained the largest category of employment for women until the Second World War. Servants made up a large proportion of the population. Nearly every house had at least one, including some young children. A 'child-of-all-work' could be employed for a few pence a week. Isabella Beeton described the 'maid-of-all-work' as 'deserving of commiseration; her life is a solitary one and, in some places, her work is never done. She is also subject to rougher treatment than the house- or kitchen-maid, especially in her earlier career'.[8]

Young female servants not only lived away from the influence of their family and friends but were generally ignored by their mistresses and higher servants of the house. They were also very poorly paid. Girls who worked day after day surrounded by the trappings of wealth were often tempted and succumbed to crime. Domestic servants certainly kept the police courts busy as they were constantly involved in crimes against their masters. In his evidence to a Select Committee a police constable pointed out:

> A thing which needs looking into; the easy mode servant girls have of turning anything they can bring into money. There is scarcely what is called a chandler's shop in any part of the metropolis but boys with bottles or linen or anything that a servant girl who, when she goes there to purchase things can take with her. The shopkeepers will propose things to them and many girls lose their reputation by the encouragement of such women. This is not a suspicion, it is a thing proved and known. This species of domestic labour

is increasing. Servants have become vile in the extreme, servant girls in particular are infamous.[9]

Dismissals were commonplace. If a girl found herself out of work, what could she do when she ended up in the street with only a few silver coins and a bag containing all her possessions? Without a reference she had little chance of finding a respectable situation and, if she had no friends or local connections, she was likely to drift towards the underworld. In a cheap lodging house a girl could turn her dismissal to good account. For instance, if her employer's house was worth burgling, a first-hand knowledge of its layout was an asset she could sell and, if she did want to go back into service, there were ways and means whereby she could 'buy' a reference. Girls learnt quickly that their best chance of survival often lay in striking up a connection with criminals, who gave them the impression that crime paid. There appeared, on the surface, to be far more to be gained by associating with a 'minder' than slaving away in a sweatshop all night or suffering the abuse of a bad household. It gave them a new sense of excitement and freedom, previously unknown.

As well as devising individual thefts, youngsters often worked together. Gangs of urchins could take goods worth as much as one of their fathers earned in a week off a badly loaded cart. To be caught was therefore a chance worth taking. The girls acted as accomplices in many ways. They were frequently used as look-outs and carried stolen property from place to place as the police were less likely to stop and search a young girl. Girls were also frequent customers of pawn shops, chandler's shops and marine stores, where stolen goods could be turned into hard cash. An intelligent girl soon learnt the business of survival on the streets and many of them became thieves in their own right and had the additional resort of prostitution when the need arose. As they grew older these prostitute-thieves derived most of their subsistence by robbery of those who came into contact with them, stealing money, watches and even clothes.

An account of the life of a runaway maid-of-all-work was given to Henry Mayhew by a girl whom he termed a female vagrant:

> I lived with my grandmother at Oxford who took me out of pity as my mother never cared for me. I remained with her until I was ten when

my mother came from Reading and took me away with her and my stepfather but they were badly off, they drank a good deal. I was with them about nine months when I ran away, he beat me so, he never liked me ... I was apprenticed a maid-of-all-work in Duke Street. My mistress was sometimes kind and she sometimes beat me. My master beat me and my mistress knocked me downstairs, so I ran away and stayed in lodging houses. I first went to Croydon begging my way and sleeping in workhouses, after that I went to Brighton again begging but couldn't get much, not enough to pay lodgings. I was in prison a time in Tunbridge Wells. I was constantly insulted in the lodging houses and in the streets ... I am sorry to say that during this time I couldn't be virtuous. I know very well what it means but no girl could be so circumstanced as I was. I seldom got money for being wicked; I hated being wicked but I was tricked and cheated. I am truly sorry but what could a poor girl do? [10]

It was all too easy for girls such as this to drift into prostitution as a means of survival and if they did they soon encountered the hostility which all the respectable classes of society directed towards them. People shied away from the subject and even Lord Shaftesbury, when approached on the matter, said that he knew little of it and wished to know even less. Religious bigots opposed preventative and sanitary measures on the grounds that syphilis was the 'penalty of sin' and was therefore a strong deterrent; others chose to deny its existence. It was very difficult to bring the subject into the open.

Of the character of Nancy in *Oliver Twist*, Dickens wrote in his 1841 preface:

The girl is a prostitute, though I endeavoured, while I painted the truth in all its fallen and degraded aspects, to banish from the lips of the lowest character I introduced, any expression that could possibly offend ... In the case of the girl, in particular, I kept this intention constantly in view.

But Nancy did indicate her dire background to Rose Maylie:

I, lady, am the infamous creature you have heard of, that lives among thieves, and that never from the first moment I can recollect my eyes and senses opening on London streets have known any better life ... Do not mind shrinking openly from me, lady. I am younger than you would think, to look at me, but I am well used to it. The poorest women fall back as I make my way along the crowded pavement. You were never in the midst of cold and hunger, riot and drunkenness and – and – something worse than all – as I have been from my cradle. [11]

If Nancy had not met a premature and violent death she would, no doubt, at some time have found herself in a police court. Many such girls spent some time in gaol. Oblivious of a child's age and circumstances, magistrates continued to use gaol sentences as a deterrent.

Margaret Cowan, aged eleven, from Bowmore on the Isle of Islay, stole a pair of shoes. She sold them for 1s. 6d. and was paid partly in cash and partly in oatmeal. Three weeks later she stole a pair of trousers which she exchanged for two biscuits. Margaret was a pauper child and illiterate but on 13 February 1857 she was sentenced to forty days imprisonment in Inverary Gaol, Argyllshire, followed by three years in a reformatory in Glasgow.[12] This harsh sentence for a simple girl would almost certainly have been carried out in full. Margaret would have served her sentence in the women's ward of the gaol. Other similar-sized establishments had the same arrangement as in Newcastle-on-Tyne gaol, where eleven girls aged under twelve were committed in 1836.[13]

Larger prisons had special sections reserved for girls, as did Liverpool Borough Gaol described by the Chaplain on 24 March 1851:

> In the girls' class there are this morning fifty-four children, we have occasionally sixty; for these we have only twelve cells, one cell is occupied by two children suffering from a cutaneous disease and through the other eleven, the remaining fifty-two children are distributed at night; nearly an average of five in each cell.

Mary Carpenter had visited this gaol on 8 August 1850:

> The matron appeared kind and cheerful, the girls were sitting at work; she said she was familiar with many of them as old offenders, though young. It was a melancholy sight to look upon those poor girls with the stamp of crime upon them; most seemed hardened; all looked mournful. I spoke to four of them who were sitting together, saying to each a word of affectionate encouragement and each thanked me as I said it; I found that all of these had been in prison six times or more; one of them, a sweet looking girl of only twelve years of age had the habit of picking pockets. They all seemed penitent. The matron said that to some prison was their only true home; she believes that a great reason of their so soon falling again into sin after their discharge is the want of any helping hand; tempters often lie in wait for them as they leave the prison. They know their character is already lost so they yield and are shortly again committed.[14]

A report of the Rev. John Clay, chaplain to the Preston House of Correction, confirmed the matron's point:

> Young girls have been met at the very gates of the House of Correction by women who were known to be keepers of disorderly houses; the deluded girls having been, it is believed, up to that time innocent of the profligacy into which they were about to enter. These meetings it is supposed were arranged between the parties by previously liberated women, whose contaminating influence upon the prisoners of their class is manifested in lamentable results. There needs to be a refuge for the destitute in several districts.[15]

In London where the problem of girl criminals was most prevalent, the Westminster House of Correction had a special girls' unit with the following commitments in the years 1851–1855:[16]

Girls under 17	1851	1852	1853	1854	1855
Total commitments	229	222	269	274	262

More than half of these girls were committed for short terms which rendered it impossible to make much impression on them and which served to make the prison more of a temporary refuge for the destitute rather than a place of penance and reformation. Henry Mayhew visited the girls' section of the Westminster House of Correction and wrote:

> The youngest girl was eight. A schoolroom with sixteen children, clad in blue and white spotted frocks and caps with deep borders, most of them at work plaiting straw. There was a young boy amongst them, the son of one of the prisoners, whose mother was serving four years penal servitude. 'Poor little man, in a few years you will probably make your appearance in the same prison, year after year by legal right; and a few years after that will doubtlessly be found among the convict troop at Pentonville and then soon labouring in the public dockyards or quarries and finally all trace of you will be lost in the gravestoneless burial ground of some convict prison.

The eight year old was in for stealing a pair of boots, sentenced to three months. Magistrates had put the brand of a thief on this mere child, it was infantile delinquency. When will legislators learn the iniquity and absurdity of sending mere babies to associate with older thieves as a means of teaching them right from wrong. A ten year old was in for passing bad money, her 'Aunt' had given it to her to buy fruit. A twelve year old was in for picking pockets, she had been in twice before. The schoolroom was for girls up to sixteen.[17]

During that visit Mayhew noticed in the prison nursery thirty-three infants, some under six months old, the babies of convicts. When a young prostitute became pregnant she usually had to resort to thieving to support herself and very often ended up in gaol, where at least she and her offspring would be cared for. In this House of Correction as well as the usual oakum picking and laundry work, girls were taught knitting and how to make baskets and straw hats from plaited straw. The knitting room was designed with a view to preventing the young prisoners talking and was always watched over by warders. The girls slept in dormitories where warders were constantly on duty throughout the night.

In Horsemonger Lane Gaol in London the female prison had an infirmary consisting of three rooms and a bathroom. These rooms were described by the matron:

> A lying-in room with three cells, furnished with bedsteads, tables and chairs. A 'Foul condition' ward for prisoners suffering from itch and vermin – some prisoners are in such a disgusting condition that we have to cut their hair off and others are covered in dreadful eruptions of the skin. Some of them are very young, young girls who are afflicted with a horrid disease and in a sad condition. We have such frequently remanded here for a few days or weeks. The third room was for prisoners who needed to be watched, such as those suspected of attempting suicide or subject to fits.[18]

Girls were liable to punishment if they misbehaved while in gaol. Whipping was forbidden for females and had been since 1820. The Record of Punishment in Millbank Prison for 1861 showed that:

Juveniles

Males		Totals
Handcuffs	4	
Dark and refractory cells	3	7
Females		
Handcuffs	11	
Strait waistcoat	116	
Dark and refractory cells	45	172

This staggering difference made Mary Carpenter object to 'The remarkable disparity in the punishments inflicted on the two sexes and the peculiarly severe punishments of the women'. A favourite means of punishing girls at this time was to restrain them in a straitjacket, which at Millbank was a stiff canvas jacket with black leather sleeves closed at the ends and straps which were fastened at the back.[19]

Child prostitution was an important facet of crime in nineteenth-century Britain yet until the 1880s the subject was ignored; not mentioned in respectable society and a blind eye turned to it on the streets. Into this ostrich-like situation a bombshell was delivered on Monday 6 July 1885 in the form of a report, in the prestigious *Pall Mall Gazette*, by social investigator, W. T. Stead. In his long report '*The Maiden Tribute of Modern Babylon*' he pointed out the 'crimes' of :

> The sale and purchase and violation of children
> The procuration of virgins
> The entrapping and ruin of women
> The international slave trade in girls
> Atrocities, brutalities and unnatural crimes
> That is what I call sexual criminality, as opposed to sexual immorality. It flourishes in all its branches on every side to an extent of which even those specially engaged in rescue work have but little idea. Those who are constantly engaged in its practice naturally deny its existence. But I speak of that which I do know, not from hearsay or rumour, but of my own personal knowledge.

In his report the whole subject of sexual criminality appertaining to children was laid down in no uncertain terms. Shocking stuff to reveal to Victorian society. Readers were presented with such evidence as:

> *A Child of 13 Bought for £5* One agent gave a woman a sovereign for her thirteen-year-old daughter. The woman was poor, dissolute and indifferent to everything but drink. The father was also a drunk and told his daughter she was going to a situation. The agent thus secured possession of the child then sold her to a procuress for £5, £3 paid down and the remaining £2 after her virginity had been certified. The girl was taken in a cab to the house of a midwife; the examination was very brief and satisfactory. But the youth and complete innocence of the girl extorted pity even from the hardened heart of the old abortionist. 'The poor little thing, she is so small, her pain will be extreme'. The procuress asked if she could supply anything to dull the pain and the woman produced a small phial of chloroform. One guinea

was paid for the certificate of virginity and £1 10s. for the chloroform. An arrangement was made that if the child was badly injured Madame would patch it up to the best of her ability.

Delivered for Seduction With offers of money to poor servant girls, procuresses had no difficulty finding willing victims. Bessie was an under-cook at a hotel, she came perfectly prepared to be seduced, apparently believing it was the proper thing to do, although her ideas were somewhat hazy. In conversation I found that the idea of being seduced never occurred to her until a month or two before when it was proposed by a Miss X as a thing everybody did and a convenient method of raising a little money. She was to have £2 10s. and said she did not mind the pain and would chance having a baby, for Miss X had told her that girls never had babies the first time.

The Ruin of the Very Young A girl who is now walking Regent Street had a little sister of five violated by a gentleman whom she had brought home. She had left the room for a few minutes and he took advantage of her absence to ruin the poor child who was sleeping in a corner of the room. As a rule children who are sent to homes as 'fallen' at the age or ten, eleven and twelve, are children of prostitutes, bred to the business and broken in prematurely to their dreadful calling. There are children of five in homes now, who, although have not technically fallen, are little better than animals possessed by an unclean spirit, for the law of heredity is as terribly true in the brothel as elsewhere. Sister Emma has at present more than fifty of these children in her home in Hampshire. The proportion of victims among the protected is comparatively small to those who have passed the fatal age of thirteen. If Mr Hastings, who would fix the age of consent at ten, or Mr Warton, who is in favour of an even lower age, were allowed to have their way, we should probably have to start homes to accommodate infants of four, five and six who had been ruined 'by their own consent'. What blasphemy! [20]

Stead gave an estimate of 10,000 child prostitutes in England, but of course the real number was impossible to calculate. Sexual intercourse with a girl less than twelve years old was illegal until 1871, when the age of consent was raised to thirteen. After 1885 girls were protected by law up to the age of sixteen but, as with juvenile offenders, it was often impossible to determine a street child's real age, so even the law gave inadequate protection. The Criminal Law Amendment Act of 1885 also made the procuring of young girls illegal, which meant that the whole profession then had to operate under cover.

Commercial prostitution was an urban rather than a rural institution; in country parishes it was just not possible to violate conventional morality. In the big towns and cities, however, in a world where many thousands of girls worked from early morning to late night for a pittance, it was easy to stray from the path of virtue. If a girl did give in and earned more in a couple of minutes than she normally did in a week, she might soon join up with others in her situation, frequenting known streets and known houses. There were plenty of women who procured young girls, some of them actually taking girls from workhouses on the pretext of training them to be seamstresses. Girls called these women 'aunts' and there were many such aunts who made money out of her 'nieces" virtues. Once girls had fallen into this precarious existence, they led a brutal life and often a short one.

Prostitution itself was not illegal. Girls who found themselves in prison were sent there for theft, displays of public indecency and public order offences relating to prostitution. Drunkenness was a big problem among this class, suggesting that the relationship between drink and 'the life' was a consequence rather than a cause.

A report of the London Diocesan Conference on the notoriously immoral conditions on the London streets in 1886 gave the following causes which they believed were leading to and swelling the amount of child prostitution in London:

Summary dismissal of servants and young girls in business.

Hard life of drudgery, the lot of many young servants in lodging houses.

Monotony and want of innocent recreation – the attractions of liberty and dress.

Temptation to prostitution from the example and counsel of their own sex.

Over familiarity and rough indecent play between boys and girls at and before the age of puberty.

Popular and dangerous custom of 'keeping company' when there is constant intimacy and no recognised engagement to marry.

Sanction and encouragement of prostitution given by parents to children.

Overcrowding.

Low tone and example of parents and neighbours.

The enforced association of children of good and bad parents in schools.

Familiarity with sin – children knowing and understanding how women under the same roof get their living.

That so many of the young have no wise poor relations as their friend and adviser in the difficulties and temptations of youth.

Seduction and abandonment.

Burden of child maintenance.

Increasingly low views of the sanctity of marriage.

Difficulties felt by men as to the ability to marry and maintain a wife and children.

Carelessness of parents as to the ways in which their children spend their evenings and of late hours at which they return home.

An increasing independence of parental control.

Very small wages earned by many hard working girls.

The bad influence and conversation in factories, workshops – carelessness and want of moral supervision on the part of employers and in some instances the wicked abuse of their position.

The difficulties and dangers of the position of a young servant in the establishment of the rich and upper classes.

The evil effect of low music halls and dancing saloons and cheap and unwholesome literature.[21]

Most of these causes had already been suggested earlier in the century by reformers, like Rev. John Clay, chaplain of Preston gaol, as factors relating to juvenile crime in general.[22] They stressed the obvious and by now well-documented evidence, that it was from among the poor that these children were largely recruited.

Immoral girls were a source of ambivalence to the magistrates and the reformers; some wanted them punished, others thought they should be rescued from the life they were leading and sent to a refuge where they could be trained and given an opportunity to lead a decent life. Reformatories, generally, did not accept girls who had been prostitutes, as they were established and licensed to reform children from thieving habits rather than vice. Even refuges demanded medical certificates from prison doctors to ensure that girls were free from venereal disease before they were accepted. If a refuge girl was found to be pregnant she would be sent to a workhouse or mental asylum as a long-term inmate.

After serving a number of years, girls were sent out from reformatories 'on licence' to work for the rest of their sentence. Back in the real world some girls inevitably went astray, like Eva from the Mount Vernon Girls' Reformatory, Liverpool, who picked up syphilis whilst out on licence as a parlour maid. The reformatory committee refused to take her back but paid for her to receive hospital treatment for six months. At the end of that time Eva still had syphilis and the committee ordered her discharged from their responsibility.

Mount Vernon Reformatory functioned between 1857 to 1906. During that time 1213 girls were received. Of these twenty-two died, nine were transferred, one sent to an asylum, 638 went into service, 357 to friends, thirteen emigrated, twenty-eight absconded, seven went to prison, forty-three were discharged due to disease and twelve by special warrant.[23]

At the start of the reformatory movement in 1852 criminal boys were the only object of attention but it was realised that there were a large number of girls marked with the prison brand, who, if left unreformed, would be the teachers of vice to the next generation.

In 1854 Lady Byron, the poet's widow, bought the Red Lodge, Park Street, Bristol, for Mary Carpenter to set up the first girls' reformatory in the country. Mary Carpenter was the eldest child of Dr Lant Carpenter, minister of Lewin's Mead Unitarian Chapel. Like many non-conformists of the time the family were devoted social reformers. While still a girl Mary had helped her parents by teaching in their private school. In 1831 at the age of twenty-four she became superintendent of a Sunday School in Bristol and it was there that she first became aware of the problems of the poor. Four years later she became secretary of the Working and Visiting Society which her father had established for visiting the homes of the poor. In 1846 she started a Ragged School in Lewin's Mead and it was there, among Bristol's most deprived children, that she became aware of the problems of young offenders, devoting the rest of her life to campaigning for their better treatment. The Red Lodge was opened to cater for the most difficult of these children and in the first few years faced the problems of pregnancies, riots, runaways and fire raisers; but, with a better diet and education, many of the girls did well and eventually found steady employment.[24] The second school opened in 1854 was at Camden Street, Birmingham. In 1856 Arno's Court, Bristol, opened to take Catholic girls, also in that year Toxteth Park, Liverpool, Allerley Farm,

Warwickshire and the Chelsea School of Discipline became certified reformatories.

Returns of Girls Sent to Reformatories
1 December 1854 to 31 October 1856 [25]

	Number of girls received	Now in schools	That can be received	Number who have left
Red Lodge	61	44	50	17
Birmingham	18	16	20	2
Arno's Court	26	26	100	–
Toxteth	25	19	30	6
Allerley Farm	5	5	8	–
Chelsea		45	46	–
Total	135	155	254	25

Most of these girls were under fourteen and their crimes included arson, horse stealing, picking pockets, false pretences, felony and petty theft. They were sent to these institutions from all over England and Wales from places as far apart as Berwick-on-Tweed and Devon, Merthyr Tydfil and Yarmouth. However, the fact that these six schools were capable of containing 254 girls and only had 155 in them suggests that in the early days magistrates and judges were reluctant to make use of them, even though a large number of girls were annually convicted of crimes. This situation would change as the century advanced.

Although the regime of reformatories was not as severe as that of prisons, girls were kept hard at work during their detention. In 1866 Miss Nicholl, superintendent of the Hampstead Reformatory said:

> Inmates of reformatories should be prevented from brooding over their former deeds, which only resulted in worthless reflections and a consequent longing to enjoy again their former wild independence. The key to prevent all this was hard work. The hardest work is in the laundry from which we raise about £600 a year. In addition to this there is all the industrial work in the house. At the expiration of their detention girls should be capable of taking situations in any part of domestic work.[26]

As well as domestic work the girls did have time allowed for schooling. An advertisement in the *Reformatory and Refuge Journal* in July 1862, read:

Wanted for the Doncaster Girls' Reformatory, a school mistress competent to instruct girls in reading, writing, ciphering and needlework and to assist in general superintendence. Salary £25 per annum with board and lodging. Apply enclosing testimonials

Reformatories were for girls who had been convicted by due process of law and sentenced to a number of years detention in an institution. There was very little chance of that sentence being reduced. Young girls who were found guilty of minor offences, particularly if it was a first offence, were often recommended by magistrates to be sent to a charitable refuge where they would be looked after and trained for domestic service. There were many such institutions all over the country; as well as Refuges they were called Home Missions, Homes of Rest, Houses of Rescue, Homes, Homes of Penitence, Houses of Mercy, Girls' Missions, Training Homes, Night Shelters – catering for Protestant and Catholic girls. These charities were aimed at rescuing girls who had not yet fallen into persistent crime or prostitution. Girls were trained in household labour to provide them with the background to fulfil the enormous demand for household servants.

One of the earliest of these institutions was in Scotland. Known as the Dean Bank Refuge, it was specifically for young girls below the age of sixteen who had committed petty thefts. Much of the work they did was productive, as they took in sewing, washing and ironing from local families, the proceeds from which nearly defrayed the entire cost of the institution. The matron of Dean Bank reported that 'she found no difficulty in getting situations in respectable families for such of the girls as she could recommend, the training which they receive being considered a great advantage and as to render the girls superior to the ordinary run of young servants.' [27]

Another well-established refuge for girls existed in Manchester and had functioned satisfactorily since 1845. In 1852 the manager, Thomas Wright, described it to the Select Committee on Criminal and Destitute Juveniles:

Girls are sent from the Borough Gaol, Liverpool and from Kirkdale Gaol; they are aged between eleven and sixteen and most of them have been convicted of dishonesty. The institute is supported by voluntary contributions. When they come in they are first taught to read and write and to sew, they are then taught to knit, to wash and to cook and after they have been there for some time they are sent out into service and a great number of them turn out well. Some of them call round to see me and my wife and tell us how they are going on and it is very gratifying to see them well-clothed and conducting themselves orderly.[28]

These charities were generally financed by subscriptions and donations but the inmates were expected to work to help with expenses. The most popular occupations were sewing and laundry work:

> Washing from London is much needed in a home for fallen girls lately started in Lewisham. The girls are taught by an experienced laundress and the work is thoroughly well done. Hampers should be sent to and fro by Carter and Paterson and the work returned by Friday evening. Apply to The Matron, 9 Church Grove, Ladywell, Lewisham.[29]

As Miss Nicholls of the Hampstead Reformatory had indicated, the hardest work was in the laundry, where household linen and clothes were washed in wooden or stone troughs and all water had to be heated in a 'copper' boiler and poured into these troughs, resulting in many accidents. The floor was always awash with water and suds and there were many instances of girls and staff slipping and breaking bones. The hard soap used in laundries peeled and reddened the skin of the hands and the dank atmosphere and fumes weakened the girls' lungs. Complexions were roasted from the heat of the ironing stove on which the large, heavy irons were heated up ready for duty. The fashions of the day involved endless cotton petticoats, underskirts, tucks, frills and trimmings, making ironing a gruelling and lengthy task, particularly to achieve the high standard demanded by the ladies. Dirty washing arrived in giant hampers which had to be lugged around. The check on ownership of the garments was a unremitting process, for nothing could be lost, mislaid or damaged without serious repercussion. As well as private laundry these institutions took in washing from hospitals, hotels, schools and some military establishments.

Refuges were run by appointed committees; usually two. A gentlemen's committee which looked after the finances and made the important decisions and a ladies' committee which ran the institution. They were responsible for seeing that the girls were kept clean and tidy and possibly with providing each inmate with a uniform. For example, an outfit for the girls as supplied by the committee of the St Giles's Girls' Refuge, London was:

> 3 cotton dresses, 1 stuff ditto, 2 bonnets
> 4 caps, 6 collars, 1 pair of gloves
> 1 shawl or mantle, 1 necktie
> 3 pairs of boots, 1 pair of shoes (house)
> 3 chemises, 2 night jackets, 3 ditto caps
> 2 flannel petticoats, 2 top ditto
> 3 pairs of stockings, 1 pair of stays
> 4 white aprons, 2 coloured ditto, 2 coarse ditto
> 6 pocket handkerchiefs, 1 hairbrush, 2 combs
> 1 clothes bag, 1 shoe ditto, 1 comb ditto
> 1 workbox or bag fitted
> Bible, Textbook and prayer book
> Box with tray and lock and key [30]

One of the more interesting of these charitable institutions was Urania Cottage, Shepherd's Bush, London, which was opened in 1847 and sometimes referred to as the Home for Homeless Women. This refuge was planned and virtually run by Charles Dickens – with the help of Angela Burdett-Coutts, later Baroness Coutts, who paid most of the bills. His visit to the women's prison in Newgate obviously excited his pity and was probably the stimulus for his charitable involvement with young prostitutes and delinquent girls in Urania Cottage. His principal adviser in establishing the unit and suggesting how it should be run was the governor of Coldbath Fields House of Correction, Captain G. L. Chesterton, and several features of the regime were copied from Coldbath, including the girls' histories being kept secret, even from the staff. This gaol was the main source of recruits for Urania during its early years. Chesterton and Lieutenant Tracey of the Westminster House of Correction also urged Dickens to admit girls who had not yet been tried and imprisoned. So, although many came straight from prison or the police courts, others were passed on from other institutions like Magdalen asylums. Dickens found some girls, too, by visiting ragged schools or by speaking to them in the streets. For almost twelve years, between 1846 and 1858, Dickens was associated with this refuge and many of his ideas were put into practice. These included a 'cheerful' uniform; books to be read aloud to girls as they did their needlework;

the cultivation of flower-beds; and a marks system for good behaviour. Up to four marks a day could be earned under nine separate headings – Truthfulness, Industry, Temper, Propriety of Conduct and Conversation, Order, Punctuality, Economy, Cleanliness and Temperance.[31] As with other similar institutions, the girls were found suitable employment when they were considered ready. It is not known whether there were any special incentives at Urania Cottage to encourage girls to keep their jobs as there were at some reformatories and refuges.

The School of Discipline at Chelsea took great care to place girls in suitable situations. Girls put into service from there received a reward of one guinea for continuing in their first place of service for two years, on producing a certificate of good conduct from their mistresses, and 10s. at the end of each year until the seventh when they received £1 and a certificate from the committee and for every subsequent year to the fourteenth another 10s. The committee also had discretionary power to pay the same reward to girls who by general good conduct had deserved it but who had been prevented by circumstances over which they themselves had no control from remaining from the first in the same place of service.[32]

By the 1880s there were charitable refuges for young girls in all parts of the country, even in the Channel Islands. In January 1887 the First Report of the Jersey Refuge Committee reported that fifty girls had been sent to the home and then on as servants in England. The refuge at Glengarry Cottage, St Clement's Road, was open to any girl from all parts of the island at any hour of the day or night.[33]

By the last decade of the century there were even special refuges for girls with illegitimate children, such as Queen Charlotte's Convalescent Home at 20 Victoria Road, Kilburn, which was a temporary refuge for girls with their first child who had nowhere to go and who were still too weak to look after themselves.[34] Such a place would have been useful to Jane Cameron, who had suffered such a miserable and fraught childhood and was in and out of gaol throughout her teens, but, even she was eventually rescued by a refuge and ended up being sent to New York, where she died.

12

Perishing and Dangerous Children

'There is but one way to empty the prisons and that is by paying attention to outcast children. So long as the state forgets its paternal duty, just so long must it expect its offspring to grow up vicious and dishonest. It is because of our neglect of the poor, desolate and destitute little creatures about us that our country swarms with what is termed the 'dangerous classes'.

Henry Mayhew [1]

The rapid increase in population, particularly in urban areas, created a great amount of juvenile destitution, for which, by 1850, no adequate remedy had been provided. The ever-growing number of refuges and other charitable institutions could not cope sufficiently with the huge numbers of underprivileged children involved in petty crime, and parochial overseers often refused to have anything to do with them. If the authorities had adopted appropriate measures, a large proportion of that crime could have been prevented. Thousands of youngsters, who had nothing before them but a hopeless career of misery and vice, could have been converted into virtuous, honest and industrious citizens. The children who became criminals by exposure to the dangers and temptations inevitable in their position were punished for their transgressions when what they needed was systematic education, care and industrial training to help them earn a living and support themselves.

Sergeant Adams, Chairman of the Middlesex Quarter Sessions, had pointed out in his evidence to the Select Committee on Criminal and Destitute Juveniles of 1852 that – 'idleness is the parent of all vice' [2] – and so was ignorance. Lack of work was indeed the root of much mischief. Her Majesty's Inspector of Workhouse Schools, Jellinger Symonds also gave evidence to that committee:

There was one case of a man who was convicted for a disgusting offence, with a group of little boys around him, in a state of perfect idleness, having been recommitted. This was before trial. Those boys and the man had nothing to do, they had no work of any kind, there was nothing to employ them, they were left to conversation. I asked the governor whether he did not think that it tended very much towards the corruption of children and he said, 'Undoubtedly, but we have no means of checking it'. I have a good means of investigating juvenile offences since I became inspector of workhouse schools. In some large towns in England, it appears to me that there is a class below that poor class who come within the means of civilisation and who have been called the 'dangerous classes': therefore I do not think the existing schools are sufficient; they do not meet the class of those who come below the ordinary scope. Those who are more degraded.[3]

Mary Carpenter, whose work among this degraded class enabled her to understand the situation at its roots, added to the debate:

That part of the community which we are to consider consists of those who have not yet fallen into actual crime, but who are almost certain from their ignorance, destitution and the circumstances in which they are growing up, to do so, if a helping hand be not extended to raise them; – these form the *perishing classes*: and of those who have already received the prison brand, or, if the mark has not been yet visibly set upon them, are notoriously living by plunder, who unblushingly acknowledge that they can gain more for the support of themselves and their parents by stealing than working, – whose hand is against every man, for they know not that any man is their brother; these form the *dangerous classes*. Look at them in the streets, where, to the eye of the worldly man, they appear the scum of the populace, fit only to be swept as vermin from the face of the earth; see them in their homes, if such they have, squalid, filthy, vicious, or pining and wretched with none to help, destined only, it would seem, to be carried off by some beneficent pestilence; and you have no hesitation in acknowledging that these are indeed dangerous and perishing classes. Behold them when the hand of wisdom and love has shown them a better way and purified and softened their outward demeanour and their inner spirit, in schools well adapted to themselves and you hardly believe them to be separated by any distinct boundary from the children who frequent the National and British Schools. Yet there is, and long will be, a very strongly defined line of separation between them and which requires perfectly distinct machinery and modes of operation in dealing with them.[4]

There were emphatic differences between the lower classes. The respectable poor would have nothing to do with the perishing and dangerous classes, even to a point of moving away from an area as its standards declined, leaving some streets inhabited exclusively by the degraded class. The police did not patrol these districts, where fights and disturbances were commonplace and children grew up regarding such happenings as ordinary events. Some brave citizens did venture into these 'no go' areas, mostly on missionary work, but they were not well received, as this extract from the *Sunday School Teacher's Magazine* of April 1850 suggests:

> On the way to school in company with ... who has been appointed to act as my assistant we were saluted by women and boys as we went along in a most singular manner. I cannot say that the exclamations and gestures of these people were significant of displeasure or the reverse, however, their coarse and brutal manners had a most disheartening effect on me. I looked in vain for some manifestation of feeling that would enable me to 'Thank God and take courage'. It was a dismal scene, no appearance of thrift or industry, nothing but squalid wretchedness and dirt and idleness, the lanes were full of men, women and children shouting, swearing and laughing in a most discordant and noisome manner. The whole population seemed to be on the eve of a great outbreak of one kind or another; ready for anything but work. These lanes are a moral hell. The place and people beggars description. No school can possibly by worse than this. It were an easy task to get attention from savages; a white man's appearance would ensure him some sort of regard; but here the very appearance of one's coat is to have a badge of class and respectability; and although they may not know the meaning of the word, they know very well, or at least feel, that we are representatives of beings with whom they have ever considered themselves at war. This is not theory but fact. Fearful scenes soon occurred. After separating two girls who had been fighting and yelling most furiously and sending one home who was severely hurt, after about ten minutes a fearful outbreak took place. Seven women ran into the school and outside at least fifty women had collected. These were the mothers and friends of the girls who had fought. Having abused me in no measured terms they proceeded to fight ... remonstrated with one woman and I with the others; so we stopped the battle. The boys cheered most tremendously. The women swore and shrieked. Those outside responded. Never, surely, was such a noise heard before. I did not believe that human beings resident in a Christian metropolis could so behave.[5]

Social reformers all agreed that so long as the young were growing up under such influences juvenile crime was bound to continue. Combined with their compassion was a strong belief in education and training as a means of reclaiming the underclasses. Education and occupation were envisaged as the fundamental ways to get youngsters off the streets and able to support themselves in an honest and satisfactory manner.

One of the reasons why there were so many children on the streets in the nineteenth century was that few of them had any regular schooling. The movement to educate the masses of the poor had been started in the late eighteenth century by Robert Raikes, who had been appalled by the behaviour of children who worked in a pin factory in the city of Gloucester during the week and who ran riot on their one day off – the Sabbath, so he started Sunday Schools, which not only taught them religion but also taught those wild children to read. Most provision for weekday schools for the poor was left to dame schools and charities. In 1808 the British and Foreign School Society was founded by Joseph Lancaster, to educate nonconformist children. This was followed in 1811 by Dr Bell founding the National Society for Education of the Poor, which followed the principles of the established church. These societies provided schools where education was given for a modest weekly charge. That weekly payment, however small, was an obstacle to those families who required all their money for physical needs or who were unwilling to spend it on something they did not value. These families also discovered the exclusivity of the British and National Schools which, for reasons of poverty, behaviour or appearance, did not admit the lowest social ranks. By the mid-century even the Sunday Schools were largely confined to the more industrious and respectable classes.

There were also prison schools, for those who had been convicted, workhouse schools and ragged schools. The schools provided by workhouses catered for those who accepted the assistance of the Poor Law authorities; these pauper schools provided very inadequate education and guardians found it difficult to find teachers willing to serve in them – but they were for honest pupils. There was a distinct line between honesty and dishonesty; by breaking the law the delinquent, however destitute, cut himself off from the pauper. The poorhouse was, in theory, a refuge for the destitute – victims of misfortune and not tainted by association with victims of vice however similar their situations appeared. Moral deprivation required separate treatment.

To cater for the dishonest and degraded children, ragged schools started to appear in 1840. In origin they were not part of an organised effort but sprang up wherever devoted enthusiasts set to work to meet an obvious need. For instance Ethel May, a fifteen-year-old girl with a capital of 15s. 6d., started such a school in a neglected area for children too dirty and ragged to be admitted to the neighbouring National School. Anthony Ashley Cooper, Lord Shaftesbury, came into touch with ragged schools in 1843 when he saw a notice in *The Times* asking for help for Field Lane School, which was situated in a notorious district nicknamed 'Jack Ketch's Warren' because so many of its inhabitants ended up on the gallows. When the Ragged School Union came into existence in April 1844, Lord Shaftesbury became its first president.[6] The honorary secretary of that organisation, William Locke, was one of the four founding fathers, four men who wished to form a union which would give permanence and regularity to existing ragged schools and promote the formation of new ones. The union was supported by voluntary contributions and actually encouraged the schools to receive boys and girls who had frequently been in prison. William Locke described the schools:

> The ages of children received are between four and sixteen, half are under ten. Destitution is the condition on which the children are admitted. Daily routine varies according to circumstances, generally a system of education and industrial training pursued in the morning schools.
>
> Food is occasionally given to children as they are sometimes so destitute that they cannot be taught until they are fed; lodging is also provided for some of them. At Grotto Passage, Marylebone, they lodge twenty boys and feed all who come to the school. The results of the entire system are gratifying; great numbers of these children are sent to the colonies and enabled to gain an honest livelihood instead of living dishonestly at home and being a burden on the community at large. Another good result has been the employment afforded to some of the children by cleaning shoes in the street.
>
> ... the boys who have been frequently in prison, though many of them have at first behaved in a most disorderly and insulting way, through honest and kind treatment they have almost invariably been brought in subjection and obedience and many of the very worst boys have turned out to be better men.[7]

By 1852 there were 110 such schools with 600 voluntary and 200 paid teachers, instructing 13,000 pupils. There were also special Sabbath Schools for children who had weekday jobs.

Ragged schools did not stop their pupils from committing crimes. It was estimated that one-third of the children in these schools were connected directly or indirectly with the criminal class. Those who were known thieves would go to their schools for a couple of hours and then go out to pilfer again. Mayhew thought that:

> However well-intentioned such instructions were, they must be, from the mere fact of bringing so many boys of a vicious nature together, productive of far more injury than benefit to the community. If some boys are rescued – and that such is reputedly the case, is cheerfully and fully conceded – many are lost through them.[8]

The system was by no means the perfect answer to the problem but, despite the criticism, on balance the ragged schools probably did a good job. They provided some education for those who would otherwise have received it in gaol, and the teachers, who had to be dedicated to the job, took an interest in them. It was probably from the social side that most of the benefits came. John Ellis was a ragged school teacher.

The establishment of free day schools for the destitute and those living in such circumstances that they appeared in imminent danger of transgression became a crucial factor in the fight against juvenile crime. It was agreed that the ragged school system needed extending and improving in quality. Even the term 'ragged school' was disliked and misleading. The Recorder of Birmingham, Matthew Davenport Hill, who had already experimented with alternative methods of dealing with juveniles, suggested the name Industrial School for the Training of the Young. He also advised on the establishment of such schools with a legal compulsion for:

1. Very young children convicted of criminal offences.

2. Those who had been committed as vagrants.

3. Children whose parents had lost control over them.

4. Those whose parents from moral depravity were incapable or unwilling to take care of.

Hill made the point that

> In the industrial schools it must not be supposed that a stay be an inducement
> to crime, care should be taken that the diet there afforded should be such as
> should not induce a desire on the part of the children, or the parents to send
> them there. I would keep the diet very moderate indeed. The dietary on
> which I am most qualified to comment at the industrial school in Birming-
> ham, run by Mr Grantham Yorke, costs 7½d. per week per head.[9]

Before any such schools could be given government sanction, there
had to be an incentive to get the appropriate children to attend. Mary
Carpenter came up with the notion of industrial feeding schools with
boarding potential. First of all, unlike the reformatory schools, which
were far removed from society and in rural areas, these new schools
needed to be in towns where the majority of the poor lived. The idea
of feeding the children of the neglected class was to appeal to their want
of sustenance and to entice children to present themselves, attend and
become subject to the discipline of the particular school. Industrial
feeding schools were duly set up in several cities, first known as industrial
training schools, then just industrial schools; some were partly day and
partly boarding schools depending on the circumstances of destitution.
There was no separation on religious grounds, as most of the children
involved came from a class with no religion at all. Until 1857 they were
dependent on voluntary support.

The majority of the young criminals coming before the courts were
known to be utterly ignorant of all means of getting their own living
legitimately. Thus the two main objects of industrial training became
to teach habits of industry and to develop the potential powers of the
degraded child. The trades taught to them would have to have some
meaning and appeal; the stimulus being that if they succeeded at school
they could gain an independence and become useful and respected
members of society.

The idea of teaching children work skills was not new, in fact it was
as old as the Poor Law itself. In Elizabethan times a compulsory poor
rate provided not only relief, but the overseers of the poor were compelled to buy material to enable the paupers to work. A statute of
1601 prescribed – 'a convenient stock of flax, hemp, wool, thread, iron
and other stuff to set the poor to work'.[10] Workhouses were basically

industrial schools for adults and children, although the system, which held out no hope of improvement for the inmates, was lamentably inefficient and bore the pauper stigma. One of the earliest attempts at initiating an industrial feeding school for the young destitute was in Aberdeen in 1841. Its sixty original pupils were neglected boys who had been found guilty of petty offences. Once a suitable arrangement for them was running smoothly an equivalent school for girls was opened. In 1846 another school, called the 'juvenile school', was established there under a Local Police Act which declared begging to be an offence. On a certain day every little boy or girl found begging in the town of Aberdeen was arrested under the sanction of the magistrates and taken to the 'school'. In 1846, 120 children were treated in this manner, which was probably illegal; but the general opinion was that it did a great deal of good. After their initial capture the children were treated kindly, given food and told that they had the option of returning the following day. Of the original seventy-five captives, seventy-two came back the next day and the school continued its work successfully.[11]

One of the recommendations contained in the Report on Criminal and Destitute Juveniles of 1853 was:

> That the ragged schools, especially the ragged feeding schools at present supported by voluntary contributions, have produced beneficial effects on the children of the most destitute classes of society inhabiting large towns. That voluntary contributions have been found inadequate to supply the members of such schools at present required in the metropolis and other cities and towns and therefore should not be excluded from the aid of the National Grant under the distribution of the Committee of the Council for Education; great care being necessary in framing the minutes applicable to this description of schools so as not to fetter private exertions or to exclude men imminently qualified to fill the laborious and difficult position of teachers by the requirement of too high an educational certificate.[12]

As the ragged and early industrial schools struggled along on voluntary contributions, many of them could not afford to employ well-qualified teachers, and many made good use of the monitor system whereby older pupils taught younger ones. To improve the quality of these schools in any way government sanction and funding became essential. Social reformers pleaded for legal powers to aid or establish industrial schools where young children who had been found guilty of vagrancy, begging or petty infringements of the law would be compelled to attend and the cost of their maintenance recovered from parents where possible. The Scottish pleaders obviously had a louder voice than those south of the border for in 1854 an Act, limited to Scotland, provided that a mendicant or homeless child, under fourteen, could be sent by any sheriff or magistrate to an industrial school; while parents could be sued for the child's support and that the cost of maintenance was otherwise to be borne by the parochial board.[13]

Three years later, in 1857, the Industrial Schools Act was passed in England which empowered magistrates to sentence children aged between seven and fourteen to industrial schools.[14] The sentence was not preceded by imprisonment, as this Act dealt only with children charged with vagrancy. Voluntary management of the schools was again combined with state aid. In 1861 a further Act extended the range of industrial schools and the following categories of children became eligible for training.[15]

Any child apparently under the age of fourteen found begging or receiving alms.

Any child apparently under the age of fourteen found wandering and not having any home or visible means of support, or in company of reputed thieves.

Any child apparently under the age of twelve who, having committed an offence punishable by imprisonment or less.

Any child under the age of fourteen whose parents declare him to be beyond their control.

Reading through this document it becomes evident by the statement 'apparently under the age of ...' that by 1861 the 'age problem' had still not been resolved. An extract from the Report of the Reformatories and Industrial Schools Commission informs us that 'In all cases, where children are represented to be less than sixteen, the court should have the power to decide the child's age, which shall be the true age for all purposes under the Act'.[16] Children could still lie about their age to their advantage or some genuinely did not know it – it was not until 1875 that birth registration became compulsory.

The most important Act concerning industrial schools was that which consolidated all English and Scottish Acts in 1866.[17] It stated that the classes of children to be detained in certified industrial schools would greatly exceed in variety those liable to commitment to a reformatory.

Section 14 of the Act concerned children, apparently under the age of fourteen, found begging; receiving alms (whether actually, or under pretext of offering anything for sale); found wandering without a home or proper guardianship and without visible means of subsistence; or found in the company of reputed thieves. Such children were to be brought before two justices or a magistrate and sent to an industrial school. This Section also applied to any child who was found destitute, an orphan, or having a parent undergoing penal servitude or imprisonment. Children, apparently under the age of twelve, who had been charged with an offence punishable by imprisonment and who had not been previously convicted, could be sent to the schools if the committing authority considered them suitable. Another Section concerned refractory children. If the parent, step-parent or guardian of a child stated that he or she was out of control, or if a workhouse guardian charged a young inmate with being unruly or disobedient, they too would come under the auspices of the Act and be recommended for an industrial school.

The period of detention was left to the judgement of the committing authorities. No child could remain in a school once they had attained the age of sixteen but in most cases it seems that, once sentenced, the children remained there until they had reached that age.

In addition to these specific Acts there were from 1870 onwards provisions contained in various Education Acts. The new school boards were given much the same powers in relation to industrial schools as had been in the hands of prison authorities, they were empowered to establish, maintain and control this new stratum of the educational system.

The wild and destitute children on the streets caused a financial worry to all who had to deal with the problem. The union workhouses often ignored street children, looking on them as a financial drain on parochial resources. Mary Carpenter related a relevant case:

> On coming out of prison the master of St James's Back Ragged School, Bristol, went with him to apply for admittance to the workhouse and they refused

to have him saying that he was a bad boy and they would have nothing to do with him. The boy was left wild in the streets for the whole of a year and at last returned to the school where the master once more made another effort to get him into the Union. He applied several times and they refused saying that if they were to take in all the boys who were on the streets they should soon have to lay a very large rate on the city and besides the boy would corrupt others. He had at one time been in the workhouse and had run away. Seeing him again wild and vicious in the streets I asked the master to ask the authorities to catch him and take him before the magistrates for stealing the workhouse clothes. They laughed at the master saying they were glad enough for him to run away, clothes and all. I asked the governor privately and he confirmed 'Yes, they were glad enough to have him run away'.[18]

Due to rapid expansion, the funding of industrial schools soon began to cause anxiety. The most important problem, as far as the government was concerned, was the soaring costs, which the system of per capita state contribution did nothing to abate. The more children in the schools the more the expense, and the number of children sent to these schools depended not on the Home Office but on the courts. After 1861 if a young child was found guilty of vagrancy or a minor crime the courts had a choice between imprisonment or sending to a school, with the latter option gaining in popularity. Corporal punishment could still be administered but was known to be ineffective. There remained only the lesser penalties of fines and binding over, neither of them very useful where children were involved. Parents and guardians were supposed to contribute towards their child's maintenance, as was the case in reformatories. The word 'parent' included the mother of an illegitimate child and the putative father of any illegitimate child against whom an order had been made for maintenance of such child; but as most of the children who were taken into industrial schools came from a vagrant or destitute background, not much was collected from this source. It was sometimes the case that industrial school managers declined to receive children, particularly under Section 16 of the 1866 Act, for children sent by parents who could not control them, because the managers knew that they, in particular, would not contribute to the child's cost and they also knew that the authorities often failed in their duty to compel them to do so.

An Act was passed in 1880 which finally placed outcast girls on the same footing as boys, enabling magistrates to commit to industrial schools children who were being brought up in the society of disreputable women and in houses of bad repute;[19] but its recommendations were very rarely acted upon because of the high costs involved, as pointed out in the journal of the Home Mission, *Seeking and Saving*:

> The Act has remained almost a dead letter. Why? Not because there were no such children to be found – they can be counted by the hundred in London – not because they have not been brought before a magistrate – but because the expense would be so great; so many more industrial schools would have to be provided. The present accommodation in industrial schools is for boys 19,037 and for girls 4656. Boys are to be rescued from thieves and bad company; girls may rot and die because it is too expensive to train them in the right ways. Girls are considered able to take care of themselves; boys must have every care taken of them. Which is the most expensive, the prison or the industrial school? [20]

Costly though the schools appeared, their benefits to society were appreciated by an increasingly literate public and their expansion continued. Nearly all the children who were sent to industrial schools would, in former times, have been permitted to remain at large until they committed some criminal offence. These children, who would otherwise have swelled the prison population, were guided to better courses by the training they received.

As with other nineteenth-century institutions the schools 'disposed' of their pupils at the end of their training. Those showing promise were sent out on licence or apprenticed; others were sent to sea or helped to emigrate as was thought best for them. Parents of children sent to certified industrial schools were not allowed to interfere with the apprenticing of their children by the school managers who had had the training of them during the greater part of their childhood. The state felt that when a child was discharged from an industrial school, trained and educated, the worthless parents might try to resume their authority and interfere with or injure the child's future prospects. After rescuing the child at an early age and training it, nothing was allowed to hamper the apprenticing or other disposal of the child in accordance with the wishes of those who had taken care of it during that period.

While at a school, life followed a well-worn routine. The work was not so arduous as in the reformatories and the discipline not so severe. However, any child absconding from an industrial school or being particularly refractory was liable to be sent on to a reformatory.

Timetable for Certified Industrial Schools, 1864 [21]

BOYS

6 am	Rise; private prayer; wash and dress; beds made
6.30	School
8	Family worship. breakfast and play
9	Work in garden, housework, tailoring, shoemaking and other trades
12.45 pm	Wash and prepare for dinner
1	Dinner and play
2	Work as before; those indoors in the forenoon, now in garden
4.45	Wash and prepare for supper
5	Supper and play
6	School; family worship
7	Bed

GIRLS

6 am	Rise; private prayer; wash and dress; beds made
6.30	Knitting and repairing of clothes; learning hymns and other texts; older girls school
8	Family worship and breakfast
9	Housework for the whole school; older girls washing etc till dinner
10	School
12.30 pm	Play in garden
1	Dinner and play
2	Sewing; older girls washing etc
5	Supper and play
6	Knitting; older girls school and family worship
7	Bed

Just as there were reformatory ships anchored offshore, so there were industrial ships where boys were sent to learn the seafaring skills which could qualify them to enter the Royal Navy. Voluntary training ships were for destitute youngsters who had volunteered themselves for such training. In October 1877 the register of those water-based institutions was:

Certified Reformatory or Industrial Ships[22]

Akbar	Birkenhead
Clarence (RC)	Birkenhead
Cornwall	Purfleet, Thames
Cumberland	Helenburgh, Clyde
Formidable	Portishead, Bristol
Gibraltar	Belfast, Lough
Mars	Newport, Dundee
Southampton	Hull
Wellesley	Shields, Tyne

Voluntary Training Ships

Arethusa	Greenhithe
Chichester	Greenhithe
Indefatigable	New Ferry, Cheshire
Warspite	Woolwich

As well as destitute boys, the voluntary training ships also took charge of such boys as those who had been apprenticed but found unsuitable and had their indentures legally cancelled; sons of poor widows unable to cope with large families; workhouse boys and those sent on from charitable institutions and ragged schools. They were recognisably from the perishing and dangerous classes but rescued before they had fallen. When the boys reached a proper age they could be sent to sea having had some experience on the training ship and ship owners expressed a willingness to take them.

The years between 1861 and 1871 saw a substantial rise in the numbers of industrial schools while at the same time the number of reformatories stayed more or less static.

The drop in inmate numbers between 1861 and 1865 may have been due to the fact that the 1861 Act gave power to the Treasury to contribute out of public funds to the maintenance of children sent to industrial schools. The initial expense of this Act was not popular with the

Certified Reformatories[23]

Year	No	Boys	Girls	Total
1861	62	1288	348	1636
1862	65	1069	285	1354
1863	64	976	267	1243
1864	66	1119	264	1383
1865	65	1256	337	1593
1866	64	1327	320	1647
1867	64	1396	310	1706
1868	64	1337	334	1671
1869	65	1357	330	1687
1870	64	1301	327	1628
1871	65	1295	319	1604

Certified Industrial Schools

Year	No	Boys	Girls	Total
1861	41	608	400	1008
1862	45	422	169	589
1863	47	490	159	649
1864	50	466	138	604
1865	50	562	213	775
1866	57	814	241	1055
1867	63	1444	539	1983
1868	77	1859	707	2562
1869	82	2026	554	2580
1870	91	2089	551	2640
1871	95	2157	726	2883

Treasury, with the result that the Secretary of State often refused to certify and therefore control the numbers of schools. He could also discharge children and so limit the number of inmates, so he was able to reduce the rate of allowance and so lessen the burden on the Exchequer. It was also recommended that the minimum age of acceptance be raised from six to eight, as it was discovered that many parishes were sending young pauper children to the schools as an alternative to caring for them in a workhouse. In spite of all this, social pressure must have prevailed, for the numbers detained in these schools increased rapidly, and in 1877 there were still a fair number of six to eight year olds under care:

Ages of Children Admitted to Industrial Schools[24]

	6–8	8–10	10–12	12–14
1871	248	567	1096	873
1877	281	648	1623	1191

The industrial school system which developed in the years between 1857 to 1870 was conducted on a distinctly different track from that of the reformatory schools. Contrary to its name, industrial schools had a much more educational basis and became, from 1870 onwards, the responsibility of the Committee for Education. The other significant difference between the two groups, at least to start with, was that the intervention in the life of a committed juvenile delinquent was based upon his conduct – a matter over which he was assumed to have some responsibility, whereas the intervention in the life of a neglected child was based on his status – a matter over which he was assumed to have no responsibility. This is why the social reformers demanded a clear separation of the delinquent (in reformatories) and the destitute (in industrial schools). Towards the end of the nineteenth century this distinction became less clear, as it was realised that *all* children needed more education, care and protection and less formal punishment.

Despite all the difficulties, it seems likely that many of the children who passed through industrial schools were claimed as successes – and that was no mean achievement, even if much of the acclaim was attributable to the fact that the schools took children from a 'perishing and dangerous' background and allowed them to grow up in a more favourable one.

13

Towards Understanding

'Ignorance is one of the greatest causes of delinquency; generally crime is committed by the uneducated classes and possibly if education could be made compulsory it would have a beneficial effect.'

Gilbert Abbott A'Becket, Metropolitan police magistrate [1]

When juvenile crime is discussed, one of the older generation will sometimes admit that when he was a lad he used to 'scrump' apples but no one would have taken him to court for doing so. But it was a brave child who stole apples in the nineteenth century. Mothers used to watch their children coming home from school along the lanes to make sure they were not tempted to stray into an orchard and pick the fruit. They had good reason to be fearful. Not since Eve yielded to the temptation to pick the forbidden fruit was anyone dealt with so severely for taking apples as was thirteen-year-old Emily Davies when she appeared before the Ross-on-Wye magistrates on 17 September 1875. For 'stealing' a few apples from an orchard Emily was sentenced to fourteen days in prison and four years in a reformatory. Her father was ordered to pay two shillings a week towards her maintenance, for if he were relieved of the expense of keeping her he would have been seen as deriving an advantage from her offence.

The chairman of the magistrates solemnly told Emily and her father that if they did not deal with such cases severely it would be no example to others. 'It is not with any vindictive feeling that we are punishing you, but for the prevention of crime. Others will be deterred from offending through the dread of punishment', the chairman told the weeping Emily. No one can accuse the Victorians of being sentimentalists, or of not believing that a tough childhood strengthened character, but punishment of this severity was more than even they could stomach, especially when they remembered that since 1869 four other children in the region had received prison sentences followed by four years at a reformatory for trifling offences.

Word soon spread and the case was taken up by newspapers in London, Birmingham, Leeds, Manchester and Liverpool which contained editorials complaining about the magistrates. Even *Punch* came to Emily's aid. In her home town she found a champion in Thomas Blake, the Liberal MP for Leominster, who had distinguished himself in his brief term in Parliament by being the only Herefordshire MP to vote in favour of the abolition of the 'cat' in the army and navy. A fortnight after Emily had been sentenced, he wrote to the Home Secretary, Richard Assheton Cross, saying that he had been strongly pressed by the people of Ross to call a public meeting protesting at the severe sentence for stealing a few apples. At the end of October he received a reply from the Home Office stating that the Home Secretary declined to interfere.

Blake now called a public meeting and the hall in the ancient market house in the centre of Ross was packed to capacity on 11 November. One of the magistrates concerned in the case showed that he was at least a man of courage by facing the hostile audience. He spoke at length, but with very little bearing on Emily's fate. After frequent interruptions he sat down and refused to say another word, though entreated by the chairman to continue.

The meeting passed four resolutions. The first said that the chief witness in the case, a ten-year-old boy of dull intellect, himself an accomplice in the theft, ought not to have been allowed to give evidence on oath, the solemn nature of which he could not have understood. The next resolution protested that the sentence was unnecessarily harsh and severe towards Emily, her parents and her friends. It was not for the public good and would neither contribute to the future welfare of the girl or the credit of the justices. The third resolution stated that it appeared that the sentence was not made on evidence given in open court but upon additional one-sided hearsay, information affecting the character and circumstances of her relatives and not made known either to the child, her relatives or the public, and which the justices and Home Secretary refused to make known or substantiate. The final resolution called for copies of the previous resolutions to be printed for general circulation, with a copy to the Home Secretary, and that, should the latter refuse to make known the contents of the secret report he had received from the magistrate, copies of the resolutions should be sent to every Member of the House of Commons and steps taken on the reassembling of Parliament to obtain production of the report and, if possible, the liberation of 'The Little Captive Maid'.

Within a week or two of this meeting there appeared, to quote Thomas Blake's own words, to be a thaw in the Home Office. On 1 December he wrote in the *Ross Gazette* that he had glad tidings for his fellow townsmen – Emily was free. The next day the old market house was again packed, when lengthy speeches were made thanking newspaper editors throughout the kingdom for exerting their powerful influence and tendering the warmest thanks to the Home Secretary for his kindness in reversing the severe sentence.

Richard Assheton Cross's letter to Thomas Blake said that he was of the opinion that it was not desirable that young children should be sent to reformatories on first conviction. Blake respectfully suggested that, if a circular letter containing the Secretary of State's opinion was sent from the Home Office to all county magistrates, it would prevent the infliction of a vast amount of needless suffering of families and contribute much to the public good.[2]

All that fuss, media attention, a threat to reassemble Parliament, an MP's reputation at stake and a Home Office climb-down on behalf of a country girl who had taken a few apples. It would not have happened twenty years previously and illustrates the emergence of a new attitude to young offenders and to children in general.

The 1860s and 1870s were a time of advancing prosperity. Social attitudes changed and opinions towards young offenders were also changing. This enlarged sympathy with children was one of the chief contributions towards civilisation in the latter part of the century. Recognition of childhood as a separate social state played a major part in the structural changes taking place in British society. At the beginning of the nineteenth century child labour was universal and unavoidable; the family was employed as a whole and worked together as a unit, as it had from time immemorial. There was no protection against abuse as the child was regarded as the 'property' of the father and as such was protected from state interference. As the century advanced, reformers like Lord Shaftesbury brought about a feeling of revulsion at the working conditions of children and this, together with the technological advances of the time, created a demand for a controlled, adult workforce. Juvenile institutions became educationally orientated, reflecting the social and economic changes within society. All children, however apparently vicious and degraded, were seen as being capable of being made into useful members of society if placed under the right influences and subjected to judicious control and training. The comparatively few exceptions that might occur did not invalidate this overall principle.

In reformatories and industrial schools children became for the first time wards of state, victims of neglect rather than fully responsible law breakers. New children's rights enforcing parental responsibility were asserted. Parents were now regarded as the guilty parties, rather than the children. Since juvenile delinquency originated in apparent neglect, every parent was chargeable for the maintenance of a child thrown by crime on the care of the state and was held responsible for the maintenance of a child in an institution, or made in some way to suffer for the non-discharge of this duty. Many of the promoters of reform saw punishment of parents and enforcement of parental duties as the chief benefits of the Juvenile Acts. The decline in juvenile crime from the 1850s onwards was frequently attributed to the greater willingness among parents to keep their children off the streets.

Children under the custody of the state were provided with the elements for civilised development which had been missing in their own homes. Substitutes for defective parents were provided by a devoted staff, who often organised the schools on a family system and who believed that a stringent retraining programme based on moral guidance and work would prepare these children for their restoration to society.

This situation did not come about quickly or completely; it was a slow sometimes haphazard process. Staffing and funding problems and the need to safeguard the public tended to outweigh child welfare. The 'rounding up' of street children was an enormous undertaking particularly in the metropolitan areas where the police were already kept busy in dealing with the adult underclass. William Locke, Honorary Secretary of the Ragged School Union suggested:

> That if the police had authority to apprehend all juvenile beggars and street

hawkers and took them before a magistrate it would tend to lessen street begging and thieving very much. Perhaps it could be better accomplished by every parish having a certain number of street guardians to follow and track out young beggars of all kinds and have the deserving relieved and the undeserving punished. If juvenile street hawkers are allowed at all only those who can bring a certificate of good behaviour and regular attendance at some school should be licensed.[3]

The idea of having a street guardian to check on destitute children was tried out in London and Birmingham. The Boys' Beadle was the name given to a new public functionary appointed in 1866 by the Reformatory and Refuge Union as their agent in an important experiment. It was the duty of this special agent to look after the homeless and hapless children on the streets of London, beginning at some prescribed district with those he found wandering, begging or huddled up on doorsteps. He was instructed to approach the children as a friend and to sift through their cases thoroughly, and as their various circumstances required, to take them back to their parents, or to a school or refuge, or to a magistrate or the police. The Boys' Beadle also helped girls. It was soon evident that there was plenty of work for him, especially at first, and it was hoped that magistrates, the police and managers of institutions would help the council of the union in their efforts. In practice, the Boys' Beadle experiment had a slow start – the police had no orders to assist in the work and private people were not interested in helping. Then there was the usual confusion as to whose responsibility the urchins were, the police, the parish or the Poor Law. The union persisted with its scheme and things must have muddled along, for the post was kept going and was still in operation in 1890. A Children's Visitor was appointed in Birmingham, with duties similar to the Boys' Beadle. In 1868 he placed 101 children in schools and refuges during his first year.[4]

One of the biggest problems facing social workers of the time was that of drunkenness. The Church of England Temperance Society appointed agents to work in the metropolitan courts, in a purely private capacity, to assist anyone whom the magistrates might wish to help. It appears that the court officials welcomed these agents and gave them every encouragement, particularly as a large number of those coming before the courts on charges of being drunk and incapable were under

eighteen. Statistics from Liverpool show how necessary these temperance
agents were:

Committed in 1877 for being Drunk and Incapable

Age	Boys	Girls
Under 10	97	18
10–12	217	32
12–14	301	41
14–16	459	56
16–18	668	299

By 1885 there were twenty three temperance agents at work in the police
courts. The society opened homes all over the country to help discharged
prisoners, young and old, and where possible found them employment.
By 1900 the Society employed a hundred men and twelve women agents.[5]

It is not surprising that among the general public old fears remained
strong and large sections continued to regard juvenile offenders as a
nuisance requiring a sharp lesson. Many magistrates chose to ignore
sections of the various Acts appertaining to young criminals, so the
imprisonment of children continued into the 1890s.

The Prison Act of 1877 introduced a new administrative prison service
throughout the whole country.[6] Prisons, which had previously been
under the control of local government, were now transferred to a
department of the national government which soon established a unified
regime all over the country. There was no special provision as to how
best to treat young inmates, boys or girls, who were convicted for the
first time or were recidivists. Children between the ages of twelve to
sixteen were still being committed to prison for every kind of offence.
The prison commissioners also only had their uniform regime as a guide,
which was applicable to all whether forger, professional burglar, petty
pilferer, drunkard or prostitute and thief. The only concession to this
strict formula was that, if a child was charged with an indictable offence
such as larceny or embezzlement, the court could, if thought fit and
having regard to all circumstances of the case, deal summarily with the
offender; whereby magistrates could judge and convict dispensing with
all needless details and formalities. If found guilty, the child could still

be imprisoned with or without hard labour for any term not exceeding three months and, if male, could also be whipped. The system remained pretty well unchanged until 1893 when a further Reformatory Schools Act was passed. This provided that when a youthful offender who, in the opinion of the court, was less than sixteen was convicted of an offence punishable by penal servitude either appeared to be not less than twelve, or was proved to have been previously convicted of a similar offence, the court might in addition to, or in lieu of sentencing him, order him to be sent to a reformatory and there be detained for not less than three or more than five years.[7] This introduced a slight improvement inasmuch as previously a prison sentence before reformatory treatment was a necessity; here the possibility of reformatory treatment without a prison sentence was provided. Six years later in 1899 a further Act said that no offender should be sentenced to both prison and a reformatory.[8]

The reformatories continued their work of educating and training those sent for treatment, benefiting from government aid and the assistance given by the Reformatory and Refuge Union. Most of the young people who received reformatory training were given every opportunity to improve themselves; so the young pickpocket who had preyed on decent citizens could end up as a carpenter and in time run his own business; or be a train driver or even a policeman. Later, reformatories also encouraged inmates to earn some money while they were serving their time and some managed to accumulate a good sum which helped them when they were finally discharged.

One such outward-looking establishment was the Dorset Reformatory at Milborne near Blandford Forum. Here, in 1875, forty boys spent most of their time doing farm labour. Not only did they cultivate their own fourteen acres but their services were also in demand by neighbouring farmers – at harvest time they could earn £5 a day and in 1874 their joint net earnings in this way amounted to £300. In addition, the boys did all their own house duties and cooking and were encouraged in music, singing and learning musical instruments. Each boy had a plot of garden of his own to grow what he liked. Vegetables formed a large part of their diet. The inmates came from all over England as rural Dorset did not have enough young miscreants to fill the institution. Besides their agricultural training, an experienced seaman gave them two to three months drill every year on the 'ship on land'. By this means a large proportion of them acquired an idea of seafaring and many were placed in the merchant services by a friend of the superintendent at Poole. Whatever the boys earned outside the reformatory, while on licence, they kept for themselves, so they had good credit when their detention expired.[9]

At the original reformatory at Hardwicke, Thomas Lloyd Baker retired in 1864 due to failing eyesight and his son, Granville, took over as manager. In 1875 the school report noted:

> The discipline of the school has not been as good as usual. Three boys absconded, one has not yet been recaptured. His mother is believed to have given him money when she visited him and has probably assisted in his flight and concealment.
>
> Admissions are ten this year as against eighteen last. This appears to be the case at most schools. This fact is most satisfactory as proof of the diminution of crime and success of the reformatory movement.
>
> The average number has been forty-one as against 42.5 last year. The number in the school has for some time been too low to enable us to pay our way. As is the case at many other schools it is not likely that we shall be able to increase our numbers. It is also necessary to reduce the staff. Mrs Gee has consented to be schoolmistress at a salary of £20 and we shall be able to dispense with a schoolmaster.
>
> The returns sent to the government of boys discharged in the last three years are as follows – doing well fifty-six, doubtful three, convicted two, none unknown.[10]

The reformatories were victims of their own success. Up to the time of their establishment the old prison system did nothing to deter the young. The odd week or even month in gaol did not impress on them the seriousness of the punishment. However, when boys learnt that their fellows were being sent away for two, three or four years according to their conduct and that they had to work without wages, which they thought a dreadful thing, they started to treat such punishment with respect. Reformatories certainly put an end to the gangs of young criminals as described by Mayhew and to the training of young boys as professional thieves; in fact the establishment of the reformatory school system marked the end of the 'Artful Dodger' era.

By the 1860s people sensed a decline in juvenile crime and began to notice a reduction in the overall population of young vagrants; by the

1870s most agreed that hordes of hardened juveniles were no longer a frightening component of the urban scene; they were no longer viewed as an apocalyptic issue but as a definite social problem which could be tackled along with enclosures, typhus and illiteracy.

It was a fact that young thieves and the multitude of rough children had disappeared from the streets of English towns. In a letter dated 11 December 1886, C. B. Adderley, now Lord Norton, who had chaired the Select Committee on Criminal and Destitute Juveniles in 1852 and 1853, wrote: 'It is almost impossible these days to realise the extent to which juvenile crime prevailed 40 years ago.'[11] And Henry Rogers, Assistant Inspector of Reformatories and Industrial Schools, wrote to the Departmental Committee on Prisons in 1894:

> Boys are not so criminal or so difficult to deal with as they used to be. We do not have the same education in crime that we had. It is useless now to attempt to educate juveniles for a criminal career. It is in my experience that there was not a railway station in London where trained juveniles did not attend when ladies came up with pockets full of money, there were always three or four of these trained boys around. The lads have related to me their experience, they said, 'We have only just to dig our fingers into a lady's pocket and out would come five, six or seven sovereigns'. But we hear little of that kind now, we have broken up the system entirely. You can see from the experience of everyday life that the newspapers do not report cases of pick-pockets now; a few years ago there was nothing heard of in the public courts but 'pocket dipping' as they called it.[12]

The decline in juvenile crime in the second half of the nineteenth century is often attributed to social reformers, reformatories and industrial schools. It is unlikely, however, that such a dramatic decline can be put down to a single element, as over the country as a whole, it is clear that there was no common sentencing policy with regard to juveniles. The number of places available in the schools also varied from one locality to another and the majority of convicted juveniles continued to be sent to ordinary gaols – it was the easy option.

Other elements were involved and one fact that must have had an influence was the improvement in living standards throughout England, as its industry and empire expanded, making it a much wealthier country. As conditions improved, society became more stable as new generations of town dwellers with greater ambitions succeeded those dislocated by the agricultural and industrial revolutions. Whole areas of poverty remained, but they were nothing like the slums and rookeries of earlier years. Another beneficial component must have been the continually strengthening and efficient police force in metropolitan areas, along with the emergence of 'detective' work as a legal criminal investigation method.

The influence of fashion, too, had an impact on street theft. For a long time young pickpockets stole silk handkerchiefs from men's coats, usually from tail pockets, but this became more difficult when short button-up jackets came in. The passing of the crinoline and flouncy petticoats in favour of tighter dresses and coats for ladies also meant less pocket picking. The snuff box had been an easily lifted prize but this habit had disappeared along with the use of large handkerchiefs.

All these factors and numerous others may have contributed to the downward trend in the numbers of young criminals, but the greatest stimulus to this decline was the development, from 1870 onwards, of compulsory education, which proved to be *the* most powerful agent in altering the whole character of juvenile crime. In 1850 W. H. Wills, the assistant editor of *Household Words*, wrote in the journal about the great penal experiments which contrasted the modern conditions at Pentonville, the rigours of Millbank, the squalor of the hulks and the chaos of such London prisons as the Giltspur Street Compter. He ended the article 'A great experiment *never* tried, though immeasurably safer, more humane and incalculably cheaper – is *National Education*.' [13]

Twenty years later the Elementary Education Act of 1870 introduced a new era in the educational history of the country.[14] It proposed to accomplish two objects; first to cover the country with schools and, secondly, to get parents to send their children to them. The Act laid down that adequate provision for elementary education be made in all parts of the country with a School Board elected from the ratepayers which had the authority both to finance schools, partly out of rates, and also to enforce attendance by all children over the age of five who lived in the area. The introduction of a school attendance officer marked another leap forward in the fight against street crime for – compulsory attendance at school for all children removed more juveniles at risk from the streets than the reformatories ever did.

The Reformatory and Industrial Schools Commission of 1884, which enquired into the operation, management, control, inspection, financial arrangements and conditions generally of these schools, came to the conclusion that the removal of children to these institutions had had the effect of preventing large numbers from entering a life of crime. Their conclusions were confirmed by the statistics of juvenile commitments to prison since 1856:

1856	1866	1876	1881
13,981	9356	7138	5483

Many of the commissioners also believed that the diminution in the numbers of hardened adult offenders was also largely the result of the successful reformatory treatment of juvenile offenders.[15]

By the end of the nineteenth century teachers and authorities began, more and more, to recognise that the child and its welfare was the most important single factor in the operation of the reformatory and industrial schools. They also realised that it was not necessary for there to be any substantial difference in the discipline and regime beyond that accounted for by differences in age. By the end of the century the trend of development in the institutional care of the young offender was quite the opposite of what the original schools had found to be effective. Gradually the system moved towards unification. With the abolishment of imprisonment before admission to reformatories in 1899 the external differentiation between the two types of school disappeared.

By 1900 the heyday of the institution as the solution to the problem of juvenile offenders was over. In the view of organisations such as the Howard Association for Penal Reform, the best alternative both to imprisonment of children and committal to reformatories was a properly organised and supervised system of probation. Increasing support of the merits of a probation system for young offenders, and strong criticism of imprisonment for children and reformatory schools, effectively paved the way for the introduction of modern juvenile correctional facilities and the form of probation which is familiar to us today.

Notes

Notes to Chapter 1: Vicious Childhood

1. *Speeches of the Earl of Shaftesbury* (1868), p. 240.
2. Select Committee on the State of Police of the Metropolis, 1834, appendix 9.
3. Select Committee on Criminal and Destitute Juveniles (1853), p. 165.
4. Georgina Battiscombe, *Shaftesbury* (London 1974), p. 192.
5. Kellow Chesney, *The Victorian Underworld* (London 1970), pp. 108–10.
6. Select Committee on Criminal and Destitute Juveniles (1852), p. 237.
7. William B. Neale, *Juvenile Delinquency in Manchester* (1840), pp. 8, 9, 12, 52.
8. Henry Mayhew, *The Criminal Prisons of London* (London 1968), p. 386.
9. Mary Carpenter, *Reformatory Schools* (London 1968), p. 218.
10. Henry Mayhew, *London Labour and the London Poor* (London 1865), iv, p. 87.
11. Mary Carpenter, *Reformatory Schools*, p. 219.
12. Henry Mayhew, *London Labour*, p. 73.
13. Report of the Committee for Investigating Juvenile Delinquency in the Metropolis (1816), pp. 7–9.
14. Select Committee on Police (1828), vi, pp. 39, 152–53.
15. Ibid., p. 12.
16. Select Committee on Gaols and Houses of Correction (1835), fourth report, p. 513.
17. Select Committee on Criminal and Destitute Juveniles (1852), appendix 3, p. 427.
18. Ibid., (11 June 1852), p. 234.
19. Ibid., p. 13.
20. Report of the Inspectors of Prisons, Parkhurst Report (1839), pp. 9–13.
21. James Greenwood, *The Seven Curses of London* (Oxford 1981), p. ix.
22. Henry Mayhew, *Criminal Prisons*, p. 386.
23. Mary Carpenter, *Our Convicts* (London 1864), i, p. 70.
24. Select Committee on Criminal and Destitute Juveniles (21 May 1852), p. 95.

Notes to Chapter 2: Fagin's Academy

1. James Greenwood, *The Seven Curses of London* (Oxford, 1982), p. 3.
2. *Cheltenham Journal*, 4 November 1844.
3. James Greenwood, *The Seven Curses of London*, pp. 84–85.
4. Charles Dickens, *Oliver Twist* (London, 1949), p. 139.
5. Michael Ignatieff, *A Just Measure of Pain* (London, 1978), p. 182.
6. Charles Dickens, *Oliver Twist*, pp. 56–57.
7. Robert Hughes, *The Fatal Shore*, (London, 1988), pp 390–91.
8. Henry Mayhew, *London Labour and the London Poor* (London, 1865), iv, p. 304.
9. Select Committee on Gaols and Houses of Correction (1835), vi, appendix 14, p. 535.
10. Peter Quennell, *Mayhew's London Underworld* (London, 1987), pp. 137–39.
11. Select Committee on Criminal and Destitute Juveniles (1852), appendix 12, pp. 469–71.
12. Ibid., p. 468.
13. Henry Mayhew, *London Labour and the London Poor*, i, p. 459.
14. W. B. Neale, *Juvenile Delinquency in Manchester* (1840), pp. 53–57.
15. Select Committee on Criminal and Destitute Juveniles (1852), vii, pp. 21–22.
16. Henry Mayhew, *Criminal Prisons of London* (London 1968), p. 44.
17. J. J. Tobias, *Crime and Industrial Society* (London 1967), p. 65.
18. Select Committee on Gaols and Houses of Correction (1835), fourth report, iv, p. 513.
19. Peter Quennell, *Mayhew's London Underworld*, pp. 214–15.
20. Select Committee on Transportation (1837), appendix 1, pp. 9–10.
21. J. C. Symons, *Reformation of Young Offenders* (1855), p. 2.

Notes to Chapter 3: Crime and Punishment

1. Suggestions for the Repression of Crime delivered to the Grand Juries of Birmingham 1857.
2. *Daily News*, 28 February 1846.
3. Arthur Koestler, *Hanged by the Neck* (London, 1961), p. 32.
4. *British Journal of Criminality*, v, 1965, pp. 198–207.
5. J. J. Tobias, *Crime and Industrial Society* (London, 1967), p. 17.
6. 10 and 11 Victoria, c 82.
7. Henry Mayhew, *Criminal Prisons of London* (London, 1968), p. 388.
8. *Bedford and Cambridge Journal*, 8 October 1825; *Cambridge and Herts Press*, 5 November 1825.

9. Select Committee on Criminal and Destitute Juveniles (1852), p. 120.
10. Gloucestershire Record Office, Q/G1 1, 16/1–16/8.
11. Charles Dickens, *Bleak House* (London, 1994), p. 243.
12. Dickens, *Great Expectations* (Ware, 1992), p. 410.
13. Select Committee on Criminal and Destitute Juveniles (1852), p. 194.
14. Ibid., p. 53.
15. Gloucestershire Record Office, D3549/25/3/9, Lloyd Baker Papers.
16. Tobias, *Crime and Industrial Society*, p. 80.
17. Report of the Select Committee on Criminal Convictions (1828), vi, p. 12.
18. Mary Carpenter, *Reformatory Schools* (London, 1968), p. 16.
19. Ibid., p. 48.
20. Select Committee on Criminal and Destitute Juveniles (1852), p. 127.
21. Ibid., p. 120.
22. Gloucestershire Record Office, Q/G1 1, 16/8.
23. Luke Owen Pike, *A History of Crime in England* (1876), ii, p. 576.
24. Mary Carpenter, *Reformatory Schools*, p. 89.
25. Joan Rimmer, *Yesterday's Naughty Children* (Liverpool, 1986), p. 118.
26. Select Committee on the City of London (1818), viii, p. 5.
27. Select Committee on Criminal Convictions (1828), vi, pp. 177–93.
28. *Journal of the Statistical Society of London* (1839), i, pp. 235–36.
29. Mary Carpenter, *Reformatory Schools*, p. 304.
30. Henry Mayhew, *Criminal Prisons of London*, p. 380.

Notes to Chapter 4: Prison Life

1. Charles Dickens, *Oliver Twist* (London, 1949), p. 326.
2. Philip Collins, *Dickens and Crime* (London, 1964), p. 38.
3. Ibid., p. 37.
4. *Daily News*, 4 February 1846.
5. Bristol Gaol Delivery Fiats 1741–99, appendix A, pp. 113–16, Bristol Record Society.
6. *Edinburgh Review*, 36, (1822), pp. 353–67, 374.
7. Parliamentary Debates, (1819), xxxix. T. Folwell Buxton – *An Enquiry into Prison Discipline*, (1818), p. 15.
8. Select Committee on Gaols and Houses of Correction (1835), xi, pp. 306–8.
9. Report of the Inspector of Prisons (1836), v, pp. 88–89.
10. Select Committee on Gaols and Houses of Correction (1835), appendix, p. 51.
11. Sydney and Beatrice Webb, *English Prisons under Local Government* (London, 1963), pp. 60–62.

12. 4 George IV, c 64.

13. J. R. S. Whiting, *A House of Correction,* Gloucestershire Record Office Library.

14. Report of the Inspector of Prisons (1843), xxcv, p. 184.

15. Select Committee Report on Prison Discipline, p. 634.

16. Second General Report on Prisons, p. 162.

17. Henry Mayhew, *Criminal Prisons of London* (London, 1968), p. 398.

18. Ibid., p. 580.

19. Prison Inspectors' General Survey (1843), xxv, xxvi, p. 6.

20. Report of the Royal Commissioners Enquiry into Conditions and Treatment of Prisoners in Birmingham Borough Prison (1854), viii, x.

21. Report of the Inspector of Prisons, Millbank Prison (1846), xx, pp. 2–8.

22. Mary Carpenter, *Reformatory Schools* (London, 1968), p. 266.

23. Henry Mayhew, *Criminal Prisons of London,* p. 373.

24. Gloucestershire Record Office, D3549/25/3/9.

25. Philip Priestley, *Victorian Prison Lives* (London, 1985), pp. 151–52.

26. Henry Mayhew, *Criminal Prisons of London,* p. 634.

27. First Report of Poor Law Enquiry Commissioners, appendix A, Chapman's Report, p. 460.

28. Select Committee on Gaols and Houses of Correction (1835), iii, appendix 42, pp. 319–27.

29. *Journal of the Statistical Society of London,* i, (1839).

30. Henry Mayhew, *Criminal Prisons of London,* pp. 411–13.

31. Philip Collins, *Dickens and Crime,* p. 70.

32. J. J. Tobias, *Crime and Industrial Society* (London, 1967), p. 83.

Notes to Chapter 5: The Hulks

1. Sydney and Beatrice Webb, *English Prisons under Local Government* (London, 1922), p. 45.

2. Public Record Office, HO 8/12.

3. William Branch-Johnson, *English Prison Hulks* (London, 1970), p. 147.

4. Ibid., p. 133.

5. Second Report of the Select Committee on the State of Gaols, (1835), xi, pp. 321–24.

6. Ibid., appendix 1, pp. 260–65.

7. *Gloucestershire Historical Studies,* 10, (1979), pp. 53–63.

8. William Branch-Johnson, *English Prison Hulks,* p. 130.

9. Ibid., p. 135.

10. Select Committee on Police of the Metropolis (1828), vi, pp. 103–4.

11. Public Record Office, HO 8/58.
12. Select Committee on Police of the Metropolis (1828), vi, pp. 103–4.
13. Ibid., vi, p. 8.
14. Henry Mayhew, *Criminal Prisons of London* (London, 1968), p. 200.
15. Ibid., p. 379.

Notes to Chapter 6: Parkhurst: The Children's Prison

1. Select Committee on Criminal and Destitute Juveniles (1853), p. 822.
2. Report of Prison Inspectors (1837), xlvi, pp. 11–14.
3. Public Record Office, HO 24/15, Parkhurst Prison Register.
4. Public Record Office, AO 19/75/20.
5. 6 and 7 Victoria, c. 26.
6. Henry Mayhew, *Criminal Prisons of London* (London, 1968), p. 242.
7. Select Committee on Criminal and Destitute Juveniles (1852), pp. 1–2.
8. Ibid., p. 454.
9. Mary Carpenter, *Reformatory Schools*, p. 293.
10. Select Committee on Criminal and Destitute Juveniles (1852), p. 215.
11. Report of Prison Inspectors (1839), Parkhurst, p. 647.
12. Report of Prison Inspectors (1846), xx, p. 20.
13. Select Committee on Criminal and Destitute Juveniles (1852), pp. 259–60.
14. Ibid., p. 279.
15. Report of Prison Inspectors (1841), xviii, pp. 3–40.
16. Select Committee on Criminal and Destitute Juveniles (1853), p. 822.
17. Ibid., p. 272.
18. Public Record Office, HO 45/05, p. 615.
19. Public Record Office, HO 24/15.
20. Select Committee on Criminal and Destitute Juveniles (1852), p. 263.
21. Ibid., p. 279.
22. Public Record Office, HO 45/05, p. 615.
23. Select Committee on Criminal and Destitute Juveniles (1852), pp. 358–59.
24. Ibid., p. 265.
25. Select Committee on Criminal and Destitute Juveniles (1853), p. 825, and *Journal of the Royal Statistical Society* (1853/54).
26. Report of Prison Inspectors (1846), xx, p. 3.
27. Ibid., (1847/8), xxxiv, p. 4.
28. Public Record Office, HO 24/15.
29. Report of Director of Convict Prisons (1854), xxv, appendix 1, p. 58.
30. Public Record Office, P. Com 2/59.

Notes to Chapter 7: Transported Beyond the Seas

1. *Whitehall Evening Post*, 19 December 1786.
2. Public Record Office, Legal Records Information, p. 17.
3. 19 George III, c. 74.
4. William Branch-Johnson, *English Prison Hulks* (London, 1970), p. 146.
5. Report of Prison Visitors (1843), appendix 1, pp. 1–2.
6. Parliamentary Papers (1819), vii, p. 218.
7. Parliamentary Papers (1828), vi, pp. 444–49.
8. Gloucestershire Prison Registers, Epiphany Quarter Sessions, 1840.
9. Redgrave, *Abstract of Criminal Tables*, (1837).
10. Henry Mayhew, *Criminal Prisons of London* (London, 1968), p. 16.
11. Public Record Office, HO 11/1–13.
12. Irene Wyatt, *Transportees from Gloucestershire to Australia*, Bristol and Gloucestershire Archaeological Society Record Series (1988).
13. Charles Dickens, *Great Expectations*, pp. 409–10.
14. David Hopkins, *Transported Beyond the Seas* (Hobart, 1998), p. 8.
15. C. Bateson, *The Convict Ships* (Sydney, 1974), p. 273.
16. Select Committee on Transportation (1837), i, pp. 184–85.
17. Ibid., (1838), iii, appendix B, pp. 38, 216.
18. Ibid., (1837), ii, appendix 12, p. 285.
19. Ibid., (1837), ii, pp. 44–68.
20. Ibid., (1837/8), xxii, pp. 5–16.
21. Parliamentary Papers (1847), xxxviii, pp. 476–573.
22. Mary Carpenter, *Reformatory Schools* (London, 1968), p. 291.
23. *Journal of the Statistical Society of London* (1845), 8, pp. 23–35.
24. Report on Criminal Convictions, (1826), iv, p. 106.
25. David Hopkins, *Transported Beyond the Seas*, p. 18.
26. Select Committee on Transportation (1837/8), appendix B, no. 38, pp. 218–22.
27. Robert Hughes, *The Fatal Shore*, (London, 1987), p. 403.
28. Mary Carpenter, *Reformatory Schools*, p. 293.
29. Select Committee on Criminal Law, second report (1847), xlvii, pp. 279, 291, 293.
30. Select Committee on Criminal and Destitute Juveniles (1853), p. 360.
31. Report of Governor of Parkhurst (1850), pp. 26–30.

Notes to Chapter 8: Missions of Mercy

1. Mary Carpenter, *Reformatory Schools* (London, 1968), preface.
2. G. M. Young, *Early Victorian England* (Oxford, 1951), ii, p. 322.

3. *Cheltenham Journal,* 10 June 1830.
4. Select Committee on Criminal and Destitute Juveniles (1852), pp. 108–9.
5. Select Committee on Police of the Metropolis (1828), vi, p. 39.
6. *Reformatory and Refuge Journal* (November 1874), p. 304.
7. Select Committee on Criminal and Destitute Juveniles (1853), pp. 268–74.
8. Georgina Battiscombe, *Shaftesbury* (London, 1974), p. 205.
9. Henry Mayhew, *London Labour and the London Poor* (London, 1865), iii, pp. 398–410.
10. Select Committee on Criminal and Destitute Juveniles (1852), p. 154.
11. Ibid., pp. 197–201.
12. Ibid., pp. 32–33.
13. Ibid., pp. 42–43.
14. Select Committee on Gaols (1835), fourth report, iv, pp. 521–23.
15. Ibid., pp. 536–37.
16. 1 and 2 Victoria, c. 82 s. 11.
17. Von Holtzendorff, *An English Country Squire* (1878), Gloucestershire Record Office Library, p. 32.
18. Gloucestershire Record Office, 25/3/1–6.
19. Ibid.
20. Select Committee on Gaols (1835), fourth report, iv, p. 398.
21. Ibid., xi, pp. 453, 488.
22. Ibid., xi, pp. 547–50.
23. Select Committee on Gaols (1835), third report, xii, pp. 403–11.
24. Ibid., pp. 412–13.
25. Select Committee on Criminal and Destitute Juveniles (1853), pp. 127–31.
26. *Bristol Mercury,* 12 April 1851.

Notes to Chapter 9: A Leap in the Dark

1. T. B. Ll. Baker, *War with Crime* (London, 1889), p. 57.
2. Select Committee on Criminal and Destitute Juveniles (1852), p. 117.
3. Baker, *War with Crime,* p. 145.
4. Burke, *Landed Gentry* (1937), p. 136.
5. Select Committee on Criminal and Destitute Juveniles (1852), p. 254.
6. Gloucestershire Record Office, D3549/25/3/9, Lloyd Baker Papers.
7. Ibid.
8. 1 and 2 Victoria, c. 82 s. 11.
9. 17 and 18 Victoria, c. 86.
10. Gloucestershire Record Office, D3549/25/3/9
11. Ibid. timetable.

12. Von Holtzendorff, *An English Country Squire* (1878), Gloucestershire Record Office Library, pp. 27–29.

13. Gloucestershire Record Office, D3549/25/3/9.

14. *Gloucestershire Journal,* 15 August 1855.

15. Gloucestershire Record Office, D3549/25/3/9.

16. Ibid.

Notes to Chapter 10: Off to the Reformatory!

1. Gloucestershire Record Office, D3549/25/3/9, School Report (1861).

2. 17 and 18 Victoria, c. 86.

3. 18 and 19 Victoria, c. 87.

4. T. B. Ll. Baker, *War with Crime* (London, 1889), pp. 232–33.

5. 17 and 18 Victoria c. 86; 18 and 19 Victoria c. 87; 19 and 20 Victoria c. 9; 20 and 21 Victoria c. 55.

6. James Greenwood, *The Seven Curses of London* (London, 1981), p. 84.

7. Gordon Rose, *Schools for Young Offenders* (London, 1961), p. 7.

8. *Journal of the Statistical Society of London* (1885), 18, pp. 359/60.

9. *Reformatory and Refuge Journal* (1861), p. 8.

10. Ibid., (November 1876), p. 173.

11. Ibid., (November 1878), p. 340.

12. Ibid., (January 1875), p. 369.

13. Joan Rimmer, *Yesterday's Naughty Children* (Liverpool, 1980), p. 37.

14. Ibid., p. 24.

15. *Reformatory and Refuge Journal* (May 1874), p. 228.

16. Ibid., (January 1876), p. 35.

17. Ibid., (November 1876), p. 174.

18. *Gloucestershire Chronicle,* 17 September 1856.

19. Abstract of Criminal Returns, 1854–1860.

20. *Reformatory and Refuge Journal* (1863), p. 102.

21. I. Pinchbeck and M. Hewitt, *Children in English Society* (London, 1973), p. 478.

22. *Reformatory and Refuge Journal* (March 1873).

23. 20 and 21 Victoria, c. 55.

24. Rimmer, *Yesterday's Naughty Children,* p. 83.

Notes to Chapter 11: Bad Girls

1. Mary Carpenter, *Reformatory Schools* (London, 1968), p. 316.

2. *Reformatory and Refuge Journal* (January 1863), pp. 7–9.

3. Ibid. (August 1883), p. 180.
4. Mary Carpenter, *Our Convicts* (London, 1864), ii, p. 216.
5. Ibid., i, p. 31.
6. Ibid., ii, pp. 272–73.
7. *Journal of the Statistical Society of London*, 20 (1857), pt 1, pp. 33–40.
8. Isabella Beeton, *Household Management* (London, 1861), p. 1001.
9. Select Committee on Police in the Metropolis (1816), v, pp. 261–62.
10. Henry Mayhew, *London Labour and the London Poor* (London, 1865), iii, pp. 395–96.
11. Charles Dickens, *Oliver Twist* (London, 1949), pp. 298–99.
12. David Hayes, *Inverary Jail Guide*, p. 19.
13. *Journal of the Statistical Society of London*, 1(1839), p. 359.
14. Mary Carpenter, *Reformatory Schools*, pp. 265–67.
15. *Journal of the Statistical Society of London*, 2 (1839), p. 102.
16. Henry Mayhew, *Criminal Prisons of London* (London, 1968), p. 478.
17. Ibid., pp. 462–65.
18. Ibid., p. 631.
19. Mary Carpenter, *Our Convicts*, ii, pp. 222–23.
20. *Pall Mall Gazette*, 6 July 1855, pp. 19, 20, 41, 45.
21. *Seeking and Saving*, (April 1886), 15, pp. 94–97.
22. Select Committee on Criminal and Destitute Juveniles (1852), pp. 182–86.
23. Joan Rimmer, *Yesterday's Naughty Children* (Liverpool, 1980), p. 50.
24. *The Red Lodge* (City of Bristol Museum and Art Gallery (1986), pp. 26–27.
25. *Journal of the Royal Statistical Society*, 20 (1857), pp. 35–37.
26. *Reformatory and Refuge Journal* (October 1866), p. 197.
27. Ninth Report of Inspectors of Prisons (1844), iv, Scotland, p. 12.
28. Select Committee on Criminal and Destitute Juveniles (1852), pp. 337, 343.
29. *Seeking and Saving*, 3 and 4, (June 1884), p. 30.
30. *Reformatory and Refuge Journal* (July 1865), p. 68.
31. Philip Collins, *Dickens and Crime* (London, 1964), p. 167.
32. *Reformatory and Refuge Journal* (January 1880), p. 137.
33. Ibid., (January 1887), p. 180.
34. *Seeking and Saving*, 3 and 4, (June 1884), p. 1.

Notes to Chapter 12: Perishing and Dangerous Children

1. Henry Mayhew, *Criminal Prisons of London* (London, 1968), p. 414.
2. Select Committee on Criminal and Destitute Juveniles (1852), p. 225.
3. Ibid., p. 246.
4. Mary Carpenter, *Reformatory Schools*, (London, 1968), pp. 2–3.

5. Ibid., pp. 59–60.
6. Georgina Battiscombe, *Shaftesbury* (London, 1974), p. 195.
7. Select Committee on Criminal and Destitute Juveniles (1852), xii, p. 120.
8. *Morning Chronicle*, 29 March 1850.
9. Select Committee on Criminal and Destitute Juveniles (1852), p. 72.
10. G. M. Trevelyan, *English Social History*, (London, 1945), p. 171.
11. Select Committee on Criminal and Destitute Juveniles, (1852), p. 489.
12. Ibid. (1853), pp. 23–24.
13. 17 and 18 Victoria, c. 74.
14. 20 and 21 Victoria, c. 48.
15. 24 and 25 Victoria, c. 113, s. 9.
16. *Seeking and Saving*, 3 and 4, (February 1884), p. 40.
17. 29 and 30 Victoria, cc. 117 and 118, ss. 14–17.
18. Select Committee on Criminal and Destitute Juveniles (1852), pp. 98–99.
19. 43 and 44 Victoria, c. 5.
20. *Seeking and Saving*, 3 and 4, pp. 5–6.
21. *Reformatory and Refuge Journal*, (June 1864), p. 81.
22. Ibid. (October 1877), p. 427.
23. Ibid. (October 1872), pp. 285–86.
24. Ibid. (October 1878), p. 425.

Notes to Chapter 13: Towards Understanding

1. Select Committee on Criminal and Destitute Juveniles (1852), p. 236.
2. *Hereford County Life* (June 1971), p. 31.
3. Select Committee on Criminal and Destitute Juveniles (1852), appendix 6, p. 443.
4. *Reformatory and Refuge Journal* (October 1866), p. 178 (October 1867), p. 69 (May 1868), p. 139.
5. R. S. E. Hinde, *The British Penal System, 1773–1950* (London, 1951), p. 193.
6. 40 and 41 Victoria, c. 21.
7. 56 and 57 Victoria, c. 48.
8. 62 and 63 Victoria, c. 12.
9. *Reformatory and Refuge Journal* (October 1875), pp. 416–18.
10. Gloucestershire Record Office, 3539 25/3/1–6.
11. *Gloucestershire Chronicle*, 11 December 1886.
12. Report of the Prison Inspectors (1895), lvi, p. 134.
13. *Household Words*, 8 June 1850.
14. 33 and 34 Victoria, c. 75.

15. Report of the Reformatory and Industrial Schools Commission (1884), pp. 45, 10–16.

Bibliography

Baker, T. B. Ll., *War with Crime* (London, 1889).

Bateson, C., *The Convict Ships* (Sydney, 1974).

Battiscombe, G., *Shaftesbury* (London, 1974).

Beeton, I., *Household Management* (London, 1861).

Branch-Johnson, W., *English Prison Hulks* (London, 1970).

Burke, *Landed Gentry* (1937).

Carpenter, M., *Our Convicts* (London, 1864).

Carpenter, M., *Reformatory Schools* (London, 1968).

Chesney, K., *The Victorian Underworld* (London, 1970).

Collins, P., *Dickens and Crime* (London, 1964).

Dickens, C., *Bleak House* (London, 1994).

Dickens, C., *Great Expectations* (Ware, 1992).

Dickens, C., *Oliver Twist* (London, 1949).

Emsley, C., *Crime and Society in England* (London, 1987).

Greenwood, J., *The Seven Curses of London* (Oxford, 1981).

Hinde, R. S. E., *The British Penal System* (London, 1951).

Hooper, F. C., *The Prison Boys of Port Arthur* (Melbourne, 1967).

Hopkins, D., *Transported Beyond the Seas* (Hobart, 1998).

Hughes, R., *The Fatal Shore* (London, 1988).

Koestler, A., *Hanged by the Neck* (London, 1961).

Ignatieff, M., *A Just Measure of Pain* (London, 1978).

Mayhew H. and Binney, J., *The Criminal Prisons of London* (London, 1968).

Mayhew, H., *London Labour and the London Poor*, (5 Vols), (London, 1865).

Neale, W. B., *Juvenile Delinquency in Manchester* (Manchester, 1840).

Pike, L. O., *A History of Crime* (London, 1876).

Pinchbeck, I. and Hewitt, M., *Children in English Society* (London, 1973).

Priestley, P., *Victorian Prison Lives* (London, 1985).

Purves, G. D., *Mudlarks and Ragged Schools* (London, 1968).

Quennell, P., *Mayhew's London Underworld* (London, 1987).

Rimmer, J., *Yesterday's Naughty Children* (Liverpool, 1986).

Robson, L. L., *The Convict Settlers of Australia* (Melbourne, 1965).

Rose, G., *Schools for Young Offenders* (London, 1961).

Symons, J. C., *Reformation of Young Offenders* (London, 1855).

Tobias, J. J., *Crime and Industrial Society* (London, 1961).

Trevelyan, G. M., *English Social History* (London, 1945).

Von Holtzendorff, *An English Country Squire* (1878).

Walvin, J., *Victorian Values* (London, 1987).

Webb, S. and B., *English Prisons under Local Government* (London, 1963).

Wyatt, I., *Transportees from Gloucestershire to Australia* (Bristol, 1988).

Young, G. M., *Early Victorian England* (Oxford, 1951).

Index